CONTEMPORARY TOPICS IN BIOMEDICINE, ETHICS, AND SOCIETY

MEDICAL RESPONSIBILITY: *Paternalism, Informed Consent, and Euthanasia* • Edited by **Wade L. Robison and Michael S. Pritchard** • *1979*

CONTEMPORARY ISSUES IN BIOMEDICAL ETHICS • Edited by **John W. Davis, Barry Hoffmaster, and Sarah Shorten** • *1979*

CONTRIBUTORS

NATALIE ABRAMS • *Philosophy and Medicine Program, New York University Medical Center, New York, New York*

MICHAEL D. BAYLES • *Department of Philosophy, University of Kentucky, Lexington, Kentucky*

TOM L. BEAUCHAMP • *Department of Philosophy and Kennedy Institute, Georgetown University, Washington, D.C.*

MARTIN BENJAMIN • *Medical Humanities Program, Michigan State University, East Lansing, Michigan*

ALISTER BROWNE • *Erindale College, University of Toronto, Toronto, Canada*

JAMES F. CHILDRESS • *Kennedy Institute of Ethics, Georgetown University, Washington, D.C.*

CARL COHEN • *Department of Philosophy, Residential College, University of Michigan, Ann Arbor, Michigan*

CHARLES M. CULVER • *Dartmouth College and Dartmouth Medical School, Hanover, New Hampshire*

BERNARD GERT • *Dartmouth College and Dartmouth Medical School, Hanover, New Hampshire*

LOUIS I. KATZNER • *Department of Philosophy, Bowling Green State University, Bowling Green, Ohio*

DAVID MAYO • *Department of Philosophy, University of Minnesota, Duluth, Minnesota*

JAMES RACHELS • *Department of Philosophy, University of Alabama in Birmingham*

SAMUEL I. SHUMAN • *Law School and Department of Psychiatry, Medical School, Wayne State University, Detroit, Michigan*

STEPHEN TOULMIN • *University of Chicago, Chicago, Illinois*

DANIEL I. WIKLER • *Department of Philosophy, University of Wisconsin, Madison, Wisconsin*

MEDICAL RESPONSIBILITY

Paternalism, Informed Consent, and Euthanasia

Edited by

Wade L. Robison
Kalamazoo College

and

Michael S. Pritchard
Western Michigan University

The HUMANA Press • Clifton, New Jersey

Library of Congress Cataloging in Publication Data
Main entry under title:

Medical responsibility.

(Contemporary topics in biomedicine, ethics, and
society)
    Includes bibliographical references and index.
    1. Medical ethics--Addresses, essays, lectures.
2. Paternalism--Addresses, essays, lectures.
3. Physician and patient--Addresses, essays, lectures.
4. Human experimentation in medicine--Moral and religious aspects--Addresses, essays, lectures.
5. Informed consent (Medical law)--Addresses, essays,
lectures. 6. Euthanasia--Addresses, essays, lectures.
I. Robison, Wade L. II. Pritchard, Michael S.

Library of Congress Cataloging in Publication Data

III. Series.
R724.M298   174'.2   79-87656
ISBN 0-89603-007-5

Preface

In a recent case in New York City, a derelict whom physicians judged needed a leg amputated to prevent gangrene refused to allow the operation. He refused because he "hoped the parts would slough off by themselves as had the tips of four fingers on his hand at an earlier time."[1] The hospital to which he had made his way after sleeping overnight in the cold sued to permit the operation, but the derelict won. He continued to receive treatment at the hospital.

It is troubling to think someone is willing to risk death for such a hope. But, aside from sharing that concern with the rest of us, physicians have special concerns about such a case. We go to physicians to take advantage of the special expertise their long years of training have

---

[1] *N.Y. Law J.,* p. 1, January 11, 1977. See also *N.Y. Law J.,* p. 7, January 13, 1977.

given them, and when we put ourselves in the care of physicians, we create an obligation on their part to use that expertise as best they can to make us healthy. In this case, the derelict made that obligation harder to fulfill by treating the physicians' judgment as advice and rejecting it. The court said the derelict had a right to reject the judgment even though he lacked the requisite medical knowledge and was thus not in a position to evaluate it. Furthermore, the physicians had to continue to treat him—and at public expense.

The court saw the issue as turning on the autonomy of the patient: does a patient have the right to determine what shall be done medically even though his or her decision may not be the best in light of current medical practice? Another issue turns on the conditions for the expenditure of public funds: should someone receiving publicly funded health care have a right to determine that the funds not be spent in a way physicians think best calculated to further the person's health? Though the case is somewhat atypical, the issues it raises are not. They are but a sampling of a large number and variety of issues raised recently in a striking upsurge of interest and concern in moral issues in medical practice.

These issues are the legitimate concern of everyone. Although they arise in medical contexts, decisions and policies concerning them are not merely medical in nature. It may be true that physicians and medical researchers traditionally have borne primary responsibility for decisions about these matters. But this is more the result of public default of responsibility than of any inherent responsibility of the medical world. Medical expertise does not guarantee moral wisdom or qualify one to establish public policy concerning acceptable or unacceptable medical practice. To say this is not to accuse the medical profession of any failing. Rather, it is to emphasize the responsibility we all share in determining how medicine should affect our vital interests.

However, issues in medical ethics arise in such a broad diversity of areas that a systematic and clear presentation of the nature and scope of the problems in medical ethics is difficult to achieve. One possible approach is to present a comprehensive taxonomy of specific topics of concern, such as abortion, euthanasia, human experimentation, behavior control through drugs or psychosurgery, the allocation of scarce medical resources, and the doctor/patient relationship. Or, one might proceed by a case study method as in law, examining a wide variety of actual cases.

Either approach has much to be said for it. But there are dangers in both approaches. In either case, one is examining moral issues within a practice without necessarily asking whether there are underlying principles that need to be brought to light and critically assessed. In the examination of cases, the uncovering of principles is left to the reader, and there is a danger that the reader may have difficulty accomplishing this. And, even if the reader does uncover the principles, there might be a failure to grasp their full generality and scope because of a tendency to think of them in terms of the particular situations in which they are encased. The same problem occurs in the taxonomic approach, for any principles extracted will be confined within the subject matter examined —abortion, health services for the aged, and so on. Thus, if there are some moral concerns that permeate (and, therefore, unify) medical practice, neither approach is calculated to bring them to light.

This volume is intended as an introduction to medical ethics that displays common moral concerns underlying the apparently diverse problems in medical ethics. The approach of this volume is in some respects less ambitious than either of the above approaches. It makes no attempt to provide the reader with a comprehensive picture of the variety of specific problems of medical ethics. Instead, by focusing more intensely on a smaller range of specific problems, the volume permits a fuller development of underlying philosophical concerns. The concern of the essays is to clarify crucial concepts, to examine fundamental philosophical assumptions and values, and to come to grips with the normative concerns surrounding the problems to which they are addressed. As a result, it can be seen that there are common philosophical threads which tie together seemingly diverse problems in medical ethics.

The volume begins with a pervasive feature of medical practice, the paternalistic attitude physicians, experimenters, and other medical practitioners often have toward their patients and subjects. It has been claimed, in fact, that such paternalism is the hallmark of medical practice: the specialized knowledge of physicians and other medical practitioners guarantees that they must make decisions for those who come to them for care.[2] But, for whatever reasons, medical practitioners have typically assumed a paternalistic attitude toward their patients and subjects.

The general nature of paternalism is examined in the first three essays, and then, as one moves through the volume, it is examined in various contexts—in regard to whether paternalism is appropriate when considering whether prisoners should be allowed to be experimental subjects, whether it is appropriate when the competence of the

[2]Kenneth J. Arrow, *The Limits of Organization,* W. W. Norton, New York. 1974, pp. 36–37.

patients or subjects is in question (for example, children, fetuses, the comatose, and animals), and whether it is appropriate for purposes of genetic screening. So, one advantage of the taxonomic approach is saved: a number of different specific topics are considered.

A second advantage is that the cases present natural moral questions about some aspects of paternalism. For example, one's concern with whether voluntary consent is possible in a prison setting naturally gives rise to the question of whether prisoners ought to be permitted to take part in experimentation. The essays thus avoid imposing moral principles upon cases.

At the same time, as one moves from case to case and expands one's understanding of paternalism, there is a growing moral complexity. One comes to see that the paternalistic attitude of physician/patient relationships is tied with other moral concerns in complex ways. By the time the last set of essays is reached, the reader will come to see that the principles evoked by paternalism must sometimes be understood in a context of competing moral principles that deserve to be considered in their own right. The examination of these principles will reveal the common philosophical threads tying together seemingly diverse problems in medical ethics.

To begin to bring those threads to light, we need to consider two idealized models of the relationship between the physician and the patient. The first is one in which the physician gives the patient medical information, and the patient is expected to make up his or her mind about what it would be best to do. This model has perhaps its clearest application in a situation in which a plastic surgeon advises a patient about what is involved in a face lift and what results can be expected. The patient then has to consider this information and weigh the desire for a more attractive appearance against such factors as the cost and bother of undergoing surgery. The decision called for here is not a medical one, even though medical information is obviously relevant. Nor is it a decision that the surgeon has a right to make for the patient. The decision is the patient's, and it involves weighing some values (such as physical attractiveness) against others (such as economy and temporary discomfort).

The second model is one in which the doctor is regarded as a medical expert, and the patient, in going to see a doctor, puts himself or herself in the doctor's hands. It is not the patient, therefore, who makes the decision about what ought to be done, but the doctor who, being the expert in such matters, decides for the patient. This model might seem to be a gross distortion of what actually happens. However, the extent to which the realities approximate this model is a function of two factors: *(a)* the extent to which the patient is well-informed about the likely consequences of the prescribed treatment and alternatives to that treatment; and *(b)* the willingness of the patient to defer judgment to the doctor. Of course, these two factors are interrelated. Because of our ignorance of medical matters, we may find it very difficult to raise intelligent questions about a doctor's prescription of drugs or treatment. One might expect those who are least well-informed typically to be the most willing to defer judgment to someone more knowledgeable.

When the decisions called for are not simply medical ones, serious problems can arise. There is no guarantee that the doctor's decision about what is in the patient's best interest in regard to physical health will be in agreement with the patient's informed judgment about what is in his or her best interests in regard to not only physical health but economic well-being, spiritual concerns, or other fundamental values. Such a conflict occurred in the case of the derelict.

Furthermore, the closer the approximation to this second model, the greater the responsibility the doctor must bear if something unexpectedly goes wrong (say, in surgery). The immense increase in the number of malpractice suits and in the costs of their settlement is a clear indication of the consequences of approximations of this model. There are a number of possible responses that can be made to the problem of malpractice suits. The recent counter-suits initiated against lawyers for bringing malpractice suits without due care is one attempt to stop the growing trend. But what is really required is a thorough re-examination of what ought to be the relationship between doctors and patients.

Such a re-examination is presently taking place in the medical world. Questions such as the following are being asked: Can patients be informed about a medical problem if they do not have medical training? What is the nature of the information they must have? Can patients be said to consent to an operation, for example, when they are ill and thus not in a good position to make decisions at all, let alone decisions about the reliability of a physician's judgment or the effects of the proposed treatment? What fundamental values are at stake in determining in what respect, and to what extent, informed consent should be obtained and paternalism avoided?

One serious practical problem is that, in the absence of knowledge on the part of the patient, the physician's knowledge of medicine tends to result in a paternalistic relationship that precludes the patient from having any serious say in the matter. This exclusive power creates more responsibility than doctors may wish to have and, many would say, more than they should have. Such power, in effect, denies patients the right to make informed decisions concerning their vital interests. Yet, unless a principle of informed consent can be meaningfully articulated and applied in medical contexts, objections to paternalistic practices will be seriously weakened.

The first essay in this volume, "The Justification of Paternalism," by Bernard Gert and Charles Culver, is a clear illustration of the relevance of philosophical inquiry for dealing with questions like those just raised. Gert and Culver are concerned with questions about the justification of paternalism. They undertake four important philosophical tasks in dealing with those questions: *(1)* the attempt to provide a clear, acceptable analysis of the concept of paternalism; *(2)* the attempt to provide an acceptable general theory of moral justification; *(3)* the combination of their conceptual analysis and theory of justification in order to arrive at an acceptable view concerning the justification of paternalism; and *(4)* the attempt to show how their view of the justification of paternalism can be applied to particular kinds of situations.

The second essay, James Childress' "Paternalism and Health Care," focuses on the tension between liberty and paternalism in health care. It tries to clarify the nature of paternalism, the conditions for its justification, and the relations between consent and paternalism. Childress argues that paternalism bears a special burden of justification because of the challenge it poses to letting people decide matters for themselves.

The recent emphasis on obtaining the informed consent of patients and experimental subjects in medical contexts is evidence of the importance attached to letting people decide matters for themselves. However, the question of what constitutes informed consent needs to be answered. Louis Katzner's "The Ethics of Human Experimentation: The Information Condition" attempts to clarify what is involved in consenting in an informed way to medical experimentation. Katzner also discusses the question of to what extent such consent is morally required.

In "Medical Experimentation on Prisoners," Carl Cohen discusses problems in obtaining fully informed, voluntary consent from prisoners to be subjects in medical experiments. And, in "Catch-22 Paternalism and Mandatory Genetic Screening," Michael Bayles addresses the question of whether paternalistic justifications for compulsory genetic screening are possible. Both Cohen and Bayles are concerned with protecting the value of fully informed, voluntary consent. Bayles concentrates on problems concerning the value and possibility of being fully informed, whereas Cohen concentrates on the question of whether the prison setting makes voluntary consent impossible.

In "Informed Consent and the 'Victims' of Colonialism," Samuel Shuman raises a question about competency. The previously mentioned essays concentrate on the importance of obtaining informed consent from those who are competent to decide matters for themselves. But who can be said to have this competence? Shuman argues that children as well as adults might have the requisite competency. So, he concludes, the requirement of informed consent should not be withheld from them.

The essays by Browne, Toulmin and Abrams move into areas in which the relevance of informed consent is even more problematic. What if informed consent is not obtainable from the subjects in medical experimentation? Alister Browne's "Morality and Medical Experimentation" poses this question in the context of experimentation on nonhuman animals. In addition to exploring the general moral questions about fetal experimentation, Stephen Toulmin's "The Moral Admissibility or Inadmissibility of Nontherapeutic Fetal Experimentation" considers the relevance of obtaining consent (and from whom) to perform such experimentation. Natalie Abrams' "Justice in Fetal Experimentation" also touches on problems of informed consent. However, both Abrams and Browne focus primarily on another philosophical issue, one raised earlier in Gert and Culver's discussion of the nature of moral justification.

Gert and Culver insist that the justification for violating a moral rule (such as paternalistic interference with an individual's autonomy) requires that what is justified be a *kind* of violation rather than simply the particular act under consideration. Underlying this insistence is that relevantly similar situations be judged similarly. Browne is concerned with whether there is any relevant difference between human suffering and nonhuman suffering that can justify drawing a fundamental distinction between experimentation on humans and nonhumans. Abrams is concerned with the question of whether there is, for purposes of medical experimentation, a morally relevant difference between fetuses that will be aborted and those that will not be aborted. By insisting that relevant differences be presented before different treatment can be justified, Browne and Abrams raise serious moral questions about the justification of practices that seem to have utilitarian consequences.

This concern for determining morally relevant similarities and dissimilarities is also present in the essays on euthanasia. James Rachels' "Euthanasia, Killing, and Letting Die" addresses itself to the question of whether there is any morally relevant difference between killing a patient and letting the patient die. This is further pursued by Martin Benjamin, who tries to show that adherents to this distinction have an inadequate conception of moral agency. Since this distinction is taken with great seriousness both by physicians and by the general public, Rachels' and Benjamin's essays raise issues of profound practical importance. Their essays are followed by a rejoinder by Tom Beauchamp, who attempts to show that there may be reasons for distinguishing morally between killing and letting die.

The essay "Euthanasia and the Transition from Life to Death" by David Mayo and Daniel Wikler joins issues concerning euthanasia with those of paternalism and informed consent, and it suggests new lines of philosophical inquiry as well. Mayo and Wikler address themselves to the potential conflict of three fundamental moral principles when individuals are in various transitional states from life toward death. These principles are concerned with respect for life, beneficent regard for the well-being of others, and respect for individual autonomy. In certain types of situations, any two of these principles might come into conflict, and Mayo and Wikler discuss how these conflicts should be resolved. A fundamental aspect of their discussion pivots around the distinction between the concept of human life and the concept of human life having value. They argue that, if these concepts are kept distinct, we can keep more clearly in mind the necessity of making moral decisions about whether human life should be prolonged.

This collection is not presented as an attempt to provide definitive answers to the problems posed. Perhaps some readers will be satisfied with various answers offered by the authors. Others may reject the answers offered. The importance of these essays does not require affirmation or denial. It is hoped that the essays in this volume will stimulate further philosophical thinking about problems in medical ethics.

May, 1979
Wade L. Robison
Michael S. Pritchard

ACKNOWLEDGMENTS

This volume had its inception at a Conference in Philosophy, Law and Medicine jointly sponsored by the Departments of Philosophy of Kalamazoo College and Western Michigan University in the fall of 1976. We wish to thank the Michigan Council for the Humanities and the Franklin J. Machette Foundation for their financial support. We also wish to thank those many persons who submitted papers for the Conference, attended the Conference, and in various ways helped make it successful enough to encourage us to put together this volume. We particularly wish to thank Gwen West for her invaluable assistance in making arrangements for the Conference and in typing parts of the manuscript.

Our volume is not a publication of the proceedings of the Conference. Only some of the papers presented at the Conference are included, and each of these has been substantially revised for this volume. Also, several of the papers included were not presented at the Conference. They were selected because of their special relevance to the themes of the volume.

Some of the papers in this volume that were originally presented at the Conference have since been published elsewhere. Bernard Gert and Charles Culver's "The Justification of Paternalism" appeared in *Ethics,* Vol. 89, No. 2, January 1979. It is reprinted with permission of The University of Chicago Press. Carl Cohen's "Medical Experimentation on Prisoners" appeared in *Perspectives in Biology and Medicine,* Vol. 21, No. 3, Spring 1978. It is reprinted with permission of The University of Chicago Press. Natalie Abrams' "Justice in Fetal Experimentation" appeared in *The Journal of Value Inquiry,* Vol. XIII,

No. 2, Summer 1979. It is reprinted with permission of Martinus Nij-
hoff B. V. Publishers.

A shorter version of James Rachels' "Euthanasia, Killing and
Letting Die," appeared in *The New England Journal of Medicine,* Vol.
292, No. 2, January 9, 1975. Portions of his paper that appeared in the
shorter version are reprinted with permission of *The New England
Journal of Medicine.* The present version of Rachels' paper appeared
in John Ladd, ed., *Ethical Issues Relating to Life and Death*, Oxford
University Press, 1979. It is reprinted with permission by Oxford University Press. "A Reply to Rachels on Active and Passive Euthanasia"
is printed with permission of the author, Tom Beauchamp, who has
retained copyright.

Stephen Toulmin's "Fetal Experimentation: Moral Issues and Institutional Controls" is reprinted from National Commission for the
Protection of Human Subjects of Biomedical and Behavioral Research,
Research on the Fetus: Appendix, Washington, D.C., U. S. Department
of Health, Education and Welfare, 1975. The Introduction and Appendix of Toulmin's article were omitted.

The remaining papers are published for the first time in this volume.

CONTENTS

1

The Justification of Paternalism[1]

Bernard Gert and Charles M. Culver

*Dartmouth College and Dartmouth Medical School,
Hanover, New Hampshire*

I. THE FEATURES OF PATERNALISM

In discussing the justification of paternalism, two features are essential:
one is a clear account of paternalistic behavior, the other is a general
theory about moral justification.[2] It is important to relate particular
cases to a general theory of justification and to a general account of
paternalistic behavior; otherwise, one does not get the full benefit of
agreement on clear cases for application to cases that are not so clear.

The following is our definition of paternalistic behavior[3]:

---

[1]An earlier version of this paper was read on October 17, 1976, at the Conference
in Philosophy, Law and Medicine, sponsored by Kalamazoo College and Western
Michigan University, in Kalamazoo, Michigan. The material in this paper is the
product of a faculty seminar at Dartmouth which included the following members of
the Departments of Philosophy, Psychiatry and Religion: Bernard Bergen, Ph.D.; K.
Danner Clouser, Ph.D. (Department of Humanities, Hershey Medical School); Ronald
Green, Ph.D.; James Moor, Ph.D.; Joel Rudinow, Ph.D.; Gary Tucker, M.D.; and
Peter Whybrow, M.D.

[2]In this paper, we intend to apply the general theory of moral justification con-
tained in *The Moral Rules* by Bernard Gert, New York, Harper Torchbooks, 2nd
paperback edition, 1975.

[3]See Bernard Gert and Charles M. Culver, "Paternalistic Behavior," *Phil. and
Public Affairs,* Fall, 1976, for a fuller account.

A is acting paternalistically toward S if and only if A's behavior (correctly) indicates that *A believes that:*

(1) his action is for S's good;

(2) he is qualified to act on S's behalf;

(3) his action involves violating a moral rule (or will require him to do so) with regard to S;

(4) S's good justifies him in acting on S's behalf independently of S's past, present, or immediately forthcoming (free, informed) consent[4];

(5) S believes (perhaps falsely) that he (S) generally knows what is for his own good.

From this account, it becomes clear that paternalistic behavior needs justification because it involves doing that which requires one to violate a moral rule; indeed, in almost all cases, it involves an actual violation of a rule.[5] The definition also indicates that one feature used in justifying a violation of a moral rule is not open to A when acting paternalistically—namely, the consent of S toward whom A is violating the rule. For if A has S's consent, A's behavior is no longer paternalistic. Thus standard medical practice where one causes pain, and so on, is not usually paternalistic, because the physician almost always has the consent of the patient to do so.

Since in paternalistic behavior we do not have the consent of the person toward whom the moral rule is violated, the only way in which the violation can be justified is if we are thereby preventing significantly more evil to S by the violation than we are causing.[6] For if A believes that A's violation of the moral rule with regard to S is justified only because of benefits that accrue to others, then A's behavior is not paternalistic. This is not to say that paternalistic behavior cannot benefit anyone other than S, but to be justified paternalism, it must be justifiable solely by reference to S's good. Here we may run into a

---

[4]This feature has been slightly reworded from that presented in "Paternalistic Behavior." Also, James Rachels has pointed out that our earlier discussion of feature 2 suggested that being qualified required superior knowledge and that this is misleading. He correctly noted that one could believe oneself qualified not because of superior knowledge, but because of superior ability to act, for example, when the subject of paternalism is suffering from a phobia.

[5]It is not necessary that one explicitly hold some theory about what counts as a violation of a moral rule. All that is required is that one believes A is doing one of the following: killing, causing pain (physical or mental), disabling, depriving of freedom, opportunity or pleasure, deceiving, breaking a promise or cheating. All of these are universally regarded as requiring moral justification and, hence, are regarded by us as violations of moral rules.

[6]See Gert, *The Moral Rules,* pp. xx–xxi, 98–100, 119, 126.

linguistic difficulty: though we have talked of "S's good" and of "benefiting S," what is intended is the prevention or relief of S's suffering some evil, such as death, pain, disability, loss of freedom, opportunity or pleasure. Unless we can accurately describe the benefit to S, or S's good, in terms of avoiding or relieving one of these evils, we are not justified in paternalistically violating the moral rule with regard to S. And even if we can describe S's good in these terms, this does not provide a sufficient condition for justifying our paternalistic behavior, only a necessary condition. It must also be true that the evils that would be prevented to S are so much greater than the evils, if any, that would be caused by the violation of the rule, that it would be irrational for S not to want to have the rule violated with regard to him- or herself. But even this is not sufficient; to make it sufficient, one must also be able to universally allow the violation of this rule in these circumstances or, in somewhat more technical terminology, to be able to publicly advocate this kind of violation.

The following example illustrates many of the above points:

> Mr. K. is pacing back and forth on the roof of his five story tenement and several times appears about to jump off. When questioned by the police, he sounds confused. When interviewed by Dr. T. in the emergency room, Mr. K. admits being afraid he might jump off the roof and says that he fears he might be losing his mind. He speaks of the depression he has been experiencing the past several months and begins weeping uncontrollably. He claims not to know the source of his despair, but says he can stand it no longer. He adamantly refuses hospitalization, but will not say why. Dr. T. decides that he must commit Mr. K. to the hospital for a 48-hour period for Mr. K's own protection.

According to our definition, this is a clear case of paternalistic behavior. Dr. T. commits Mr. K. to the hospital for what he believes is Mr. K.'s own good; Dr. T. believes he is qualified to carry out such an act on Mr. K.'s behalf; he knows he is violating a moral rule with regard to Mr. K. by depriving him of his freedom; he believes Mr. K.'s good justifies his acting without Mr. K.'s consent; and, further, he views Mr. K. as being someone who believes he generally knows what is for his own good.

Since this is an instance of paternalism, it requires justification as noted above. Dr. T. could attempt to justify depriving Mr. K. of his freedom without his consent by claiming that there was a very great likelihood that by so doing he was preventing the occurrence of a much greater evil: Mr. K.'s death (or serious injury through attempted self-destruction). Dr. T. could further claim that in his professional experience the overwhelming majority of persons in Mr. K.'s condition who were in fact hospitalized did subsequently recover from their depression and acknowledged the irrational character of their suicidal desires.

Note that it need not be Dr. T.'s claim that self-inflicted death is an evil of such magnitude that paternalistic intervention to prevent it is *always* justified. Rather, he could claim that it is justified in Mr. K.'s case on several counts. First, Mr. K. seems to have no reason for killing himself and so his action seems irrational. Second, there is evidence that he suffers from a condition that is well known to be transient. Third, the violation of a moral rule (deprivation of freedom) which Dr. T. has carried out results in Mr. K.'s suffering a much lesser evil than the evil (death) which Mr. K. may perpetrate on himself.

But it is not sufficient justification for Dr. T. merely to show that the evils prevented for Mr. K. by his paternalistic action outweigh the evils caused to Mr. K. He must also be willing to publicly advocate the deprivation of Mr. K.'s freedom in these circumstances. That is, he must be willing to claim that all rational persons could agree with his judgment that, in these circumstances, Mr. K. should be deprived of his freedom for a limited period of time. We believe that, accepting the case as described, not only could all rational persons agree, but that all rational persons would agree with Dr. T.'s judgment completely and that Dr. T.'s paternalistic behavior is therefore strongly justified.

By contrast, consider the following case:

Mrs. R., a 29-year-old mother, is hospitalized with symptoms of abdominal pain, weight loss, weakness, and swelling of the ankles. An extensive medical work-up is inconclusive. Exploratory abdominal surgery is carried out which reveals a primary ovarian cancer with extensive spread to other abdominal organs. Her condition is judged to be too far advanced for surgical relief and her life expectancy is estimated to be at most a few months. Despite her oft-repeated request to be told "exactly where I stand and what I face," Dr. T. tells both the patient and her husband that the diagnosis is still unclear, but that he will see her weekly as an out-patient. At the time of discharge, she is feeling somewhat better than at admission and Dr. T. hopes that the family will have a few happy days together before her condition worsens and they must be told the truth.

Dr. T.'s behavior is clearly paternalistic: he has deceived Mrs. R. for what he believes to be her own good; he believes he is qualified to do so on her behalf; he believes the benefit to her justifies his violating the moral rule against deception, without her consent; and he views her as someone who believes she generally knows what is for her own good.

Dr. T. could attempt to justify his paternalistic act by claiming that the evil, psychological suffering he hoped to prevent by his deception is significantly greater than the evil, if any, he caused by lying. While this might be true in this particular case, it is by no means certain. By his deception, Dr. T. is depriving Mrs. R. and her family of the opportunity to make those plans that would enable her family to deal more adequately with her death. In the circumstances of this case as described, Mrs. R.'s desire to know the truth is a rational desire; in fact, there is no evidence of any irrational behavior or desires on the part of Mrs. R. This contrasts very sharply with Mr. K.'s desire to kill himself which is clearly irrational. Furthermore, though we regard Mr. K.'s desire not to be deprived of freedom, considered in isolation, as a rational one, we would not consider it rational for one to choose a very high probability of death over a few days of freedom.

II. THE NATURE OF JUSTIFICATION

We have already noted that in order to justify one's paternalistic behavior, it is necessary (not sufficient) that the evil prevented for S by the violation be so much greater than the evil, if any, caused to S by it, that it would be irrational for S not to choose having the rule violated with regard to him- or herself. When this is not the case, as in Dr. T.'s deception of Mrs. R., then the paternalistic behavior cannot be justified. If it would not be irrational for S to choose suffering the evil rather than have the moral rule violated with regard to him- or herself, then no rational person could universally allow the violation of the rule in these circumstances. This becomes clear when we specify what counts as "these circumstances." For us, specifying the circumstances is the same as specifying the kind of violation that one could publicly advocate. We hold that the *only* factors that are relevant in specifying a given kind of violation are:

(a) the moral rule(s) which is (are) violated;
(b) the probable amounts of evil caused, avoided, or prevented (relieved) by the violation (probable amount includes both the kind and severity of the evil and the probably length of time it will be suffered);
(c) the rational desires of the person(s) affected by the violation.

Thus these factors alone determine the circumstances we must take into account when we determine the *kind of violation*. What is then needed is to determine whether to publicly advocate this *kind of violation*. This is done by deciding whether the evil prevented (relieved) or avoided by universally allowing this *kind of violation* outweighs the evil that would be caused by universally allowing it. If all rational persons would agree that the evil prevented by universally allowing the violation would be greater than the evil caused by universally allowing it, the violation is strongly justified; if none would, it is unjustified. If there is disagreement, we call it a weakly justified violation, and whether it should be allowed or not is a matter for decision.[7]

In order to make this point clearer, let us use the case of Mrs. R. to clarify some of the technical terminology we have used. Dr. T. is deceiving Mrs. R. This requires moral justification. For us (as for almost all philosophers after Kant), morally justifying a violation of a moral rule requires that one be able to hold that everyone be allowed to violate the rule in the given circumstances. If one is violating a moral rule in circumstances where one would not allow others to violate it, one is not acting impartially. And it is universally agreed that morality requires impartiality. We believe that one should determine whether he or she would allow everyone to violate the moral rule in the given circumstances by seeing if he or she would publicly advocate this *kind of violation.* We regard determining the *kind of violation* as determining what counts as the relevant circumstances in which one is violating the rule. In the case under discussion, Dr. T. is violating the rule against deception in circumstances where there is a high probability that he is preventing mental suffering for several weeks or months. There is an even higher probability that he is depriving a person of the opportunity to make the most appropriate plans for her future; and the person affected by the deception has a rational desire not to be deceived.[8]

Given this description of the kind of violation, determining whether one would publicly advocate it or not is the same as determining whether one would allow everyone to deceive in circumstances so described. The following may make the point even clearer: suppose someone ranks unpleasant feelings for several weeks as a greater evil than the evil involved in the loss of some opportunity to plan for the future. Should this person be allowed to deceive those who may have a different rational ranking, if this deception will result in their suffering what the deceiver regards as the lesser evil? Would any rational person

---

[7]We think that following the procedure outlined in this essay will reduce the number of cases in which there is disagreement. In those cases of disagreement that remain, we believe that some type of decision making body should be consulted whenever possible. This is an important practical matter that we do not discuss further here.

[8]We realize the lack of precision in this description, but we believe that, often, no greater precision is possible. This is one factor that makes coming to decisions sometimes difficult. See Aristotle, *Nicomachean Ethics,* Book I.3, 1094[b].

hold that everyone be allowed to deceive in these circumstances—that is, would any rational person publicly advocate this kind of violation? We think that once the case is made clear enough, no rational person would publicly advocate such a violation. For, it amounts to allowing deception in order to impose one's own ranking of evils on others who have an alternative rational ranking. Allowing deception in such circumstances would clearly have the most disastrous consequences on the trust one could put in the words of others, and thus allowing this *kind of violation* would have far worse consequences, on any rational ranking, than not allowing it. Thus, no rational person would publicly advocate such a violation. On this analysis, Dr. T.'s deception was an unjustified paternalistic act.

We are not maintaining that all lying to patients is unjustified. But we think it is justified only when, if a person, acting rationally, were presented with the alternatives, he or she would always choose being lied to. The following is such a case:

> Mrs. E. is in extremely critical condition after an automobile accident which has taken the life of one of her four children and severely injured another. Dr. P. believes that her very tenuous hold on life might be weakened by the shock of hearing of her children's conditions, so he decides to deceive her for a short period of time.

Anyone acting rationally who was presented with the option of being deceived for a short period of time or of greatly increasing his or her chance of dying, would choose the former. Thus, if Mrs. E. said that she wanted to know, knowing that the truth might kill her, we would not regard such a desire as a rational one. (We are excluding any other considerations such as religious beliefs or her desire to die because of such a loss.) In these circumstances, we have deception which significantly decreases the chance of death, and which causes no significant evil. Would a rational person publicly advocate this kind of violation? What would be the effect of universally allowing this kind of violation? As far as we can see, there would be no significant loss of trust, and whatever loss there might be would seem to be more than balanced by the number of lives that would be saved. Thus, we hold that all rational persons would publicly advocate this kind of violation.

In discussing the justification of paternalism, it is very easy to fall into the error of supposing that all that we need do is to compare evils prevented with evils caused, and always decide in favor of the lesser evil. It is this kind of view, a relatively straightforward negative utilitarianism, which seems to be held by many doctors, and which may account for much of their paternalistic behavior. If A holds this view, then A thinks that if A is preventing more evil for S than A is causing S, A is justified in violating a moral rule with regard to S.[9] Taking this kind of straightforward negative utilitarian view, one can easily understand why paternalistic acts of deception done in order to prevent or postpone mental suffering, as in the case of Mrs. R. described above, are so common. Little if any evil seems to be caused, and mental suffering is prevented, at least for a time; thus, it seems as if such acts are morally justified. Paternalistic acts where someone is deprived of freedom, as in commitment, are recognized to be more difficult to justify, for then we have a significant evil, the loss of freedom, which is certain and which has to be balanced against the evil we *hope* to prevent.

But negative utilitarianism is not an adequate ethical theory. We do not regard the forseeable consequences of a *particular act* as the only morally relevant considerations; they are, of course, very significant, as they help determine the kind of act involved. But, if an act is a violation of a moral rule, we must then consider the hypothetical consequences of universally allowing this *kind of violation.* In a great many individual cases, balancing the evil that would be caused against the evils that would be prevented in universally allowing this *kind of moral rule violation* leads to just the same moral judgment as if only the consequences of the *particular act* had been weighed. It is probably for this reason that some writers have taken the simpler balancing to be sufficient.

However, part of the standard philosophical literature against utilitarianism is comprised of examples where it is inadequate to consider only the foreseeable consequences of a particular act. For example, consider a well-trained and very competent law student, Miss K., who did not study during the weeks preceding the state bar examinations she is now taking. She therefore cheats on the exams in order to decrease her chance of failing to qualify for the practice of law and thereby prevent the unpleasant feelings to herself and her parents which would accompany failure. Her cheating has not caused harm to anyone (assume the exam is not graded on a curve) and on a simple negative utilitarian view would therefore be morally justified. But we may hypothesize that if we allow cheating for the purpose of decreasing unpleasant feelings, then some individuals, who may believe themselves qualified when in fact they are not, will cheat and thereby pass. Thus

---

[9]Since it is only the evils caused and prevented with regard to S that are relevant, we are not involved in the kinds of interpersonal comparisons of utility that seem to present so many problems to utilitarian theorists.

we will destroy the value of these tests on which we partly rely to determine who is qualified for legal practice. The effect of less qualified people becoming lawyers is an increased risk of the population's suffering greater evils such as the deprivation of freedom, and this outweighs the suffering caused to those who fail to qualify.[10] Thus, by using this more complex balancing, we conclude that such acts of cheating are not morally justified.

The procedure used in the earlier examples may be applied to the cheating example as follows: there is no evil directly caused by this particular act of cheating; the evil avoided or prevented is unpleasant feelings for Miss K. and her parents. There are supposedly no persons directly affected by this violation of the moral rule against cheating, so the rational desires of others need not enter the calculation. But, imagine if anyone who thought that no harm would come of her cheating, and that, by cheating, she could prevent a few people from having unpleasant feelings, were allowed to cheat. We believe that the hypothetical long-range evils associated with universally allowing this kind of violation so far outweigh the unpleasant feelings that would be prevented, that it would be irrational to universally allow this kind of violation. Thus, it could not be publicly advocated.

III. FURTHER EXAMPLES OF THE JUSTIFICATION PROCEDURE

Paternalistic acts committed by physicians may involve the violation of any of a number of moral rules, but the three most common violations seem to be: deprivation of freedom, deception, and causing pain or suffering. We believe that in the case of all three violations there are both justified and unjustified paternalistic acts. We have given examples above of deprivation of freedom (Mr. K.) and of deception (Mrs. E.), which we have argued are justified, and an example of deception (Mrs. R.), which we have argued is not. Let us consider two more cases of medical paternalism in order to review the various components of our account of moral justification and to

---

[10]It is this fallibility of persons, their inability to know all the consequences of their actions, which explains not only why no rational person would publicly advocate cheating simply on the grounds that no one would be hurt by it, but also explains why moral rules are needed at all. We cannot consider the nature of a violation after we see how things actually turn out but must do so when the violation is being contemplated; then the fallibility of persons will play its proper role. See Gert, *The Moral Rules,* p. 126.

show how certain changes in these components can effect the final moral judgment reached:

> Mr. C. is a 26-year-old single patient with a history of intense participation in physical activities and sports, who has suffered severe third-degree burns over two-thirds of his body. Both of his eyes are blinded due to corneal damage. His body is badly disfigured and he is almost completely unable to move. For the past nine months he has undergone multiple surgical procedures (skin grafting, removal of his right eyeball, and amputation of the distal parts of the fingers on both hands). He has also required very painful daily bathings and bandage changings in order to prevent skin infections from developing over the burned areas of his body. The future he now looks forward to includes months or years of further painful treatment, many additional operations and a final existence as at least a moderately crippled and a mostly (or totally) blind person. From the day of his accident onward, he has persistently stated that he does not want to live. He has been interviewed by a medical center psychiatrist and found to be bright, articulate, logical and coherent. He is firm in his insistence that treatment be discontinued and that he be allowed to die. Nonetheless, his physicians are continuing to treat him.[11]

According to our definition Mr. C.'s doctors are acting paternalistically: they believe that saving Mr. C.'s life justifies causing him great physical and psychological pain without his consent; they believe that they are qualified to act for Mr. C.'s good and they further believe that Mr. C. believes he generally knows what is for his own good.

Mr. C.'s physicians could claim that they are acting as they are because they believe that the pain they are causing him by continuing treatment is a lesser evil than the death that would occur should they stop. This is certainly a rational ranking on their part. If Mr. C. agreed, then the physicians would still be violating a moral rule, but with Mr. C.'s consent and no moral dilemma would exist. But Mr. C. ranks the evils differently: he prefers death to months of daily pain, months or years of multiple surgical procedures, and a final existence as a deformed and crippled person. His ranking, like that of his physicians, is a rational one.

We would then say that the kind of violation being engaged in by the physicians involved their causing a great amount of pain by imposing their (rational) ranking of evils on a person whose own (rational) ranking is different. No rational person would publicly advocate this

---

[11]This case is adapted from Case No. 228, "A Demand to Die" in *Hastings Center Report,* June, 1975, and is used with the permission of Robert M. Veatch.

kind of violation because of the terrible consequences of living in a world where great pain could be inflicted on persons against their rational desires whenever some other person could do so by appealing to some different rational ranking of evils of his or her own. Thus, when we universalize the kind of violation in which the physicians are engaged, we conclude that their paternalistic act is unjustified. (Note that the form and conclusion to this analysis are similar to those in the case of deceiving the cancer patient.)

We have mentioned above that if Mr. C. agreed with his physicians, then no moral dilemma would exist. The case could also be varied in another way which would change our moral judgment. Suppose Mr. C. had to undergo only one week of painful treatment and then had a high likelihood of resuming an essentially normal life. If he claimed to prefer death over one week of treatment, we would say that his ranking of evils was not rational. While we would sympathize with his loathing his daily painful treatments, we would also expect that if forced to undergo them, he would at some future time acknowledge that his previous desires had been irrational. We would now describe the kind of violation being engaged in by the physicians as involving their causing a great amount of pain for a short time by imposing their rational ranking of evils on a person whose own ranking of evils is irrational.[12] A rational person would publicly advocate this kind of violation. Thus, universalizing this kind of violation, we conclude that the paternalistic intervention of the physicians would be justified.

All of the above cases have involved the balancing of great evils such as dying, deception about terminal illness, and the infliction of severe pain. The paternalistic interventions described have been obvious and often dramatic: commitment to a mental hospital or lying about whether a person's child was alive. The health care professionals making the decisions have all been physicians and in most of the cases (though we have not mentioned this feature) the possibility of legal intervention has been present, in the form of suits for negligence or battery, or injunctions to stop treatment. However, we believe that the vast majority of paternalistic interventions in medicine take place on a smaller scale. The following case illustrates what we consider to be a much more common kind of paternalism:

> Mrs. W. is a 50 year old patient in a rehabilitation ward who is recovering from the effects of a stroke. A major part of her treatment

---

[12]We realize that there will not be universal agreement on the rationality of all examples of the ranking of evils, but we think there will be on many and that, thereby, a portion of the initially unclear cases will become much clearer. See footnote 7.

consists of daily visits to the Physical Therapy unit where she is given repetitive exercises to increase the strength and mobility of her partially paralyzed left arm and leg. She is initially cooperative with Mr. S., her physical therapist, but soon becomes bored with the monotony of the daily sessions and frustrated both by her failure to adequately move her partially paralyzed limbs and by her very slow progress. She tells Mr. S. she does not wish to attend the remaining three weeks of daily sessions. It is Mr. S.'s experience that if patients like Mrs. W. stop the sessions early, they do not receive the full therapeutic benefit possible and may suffer for the remainder of their lives from a significantly more disabled arm and leg than would be the case if they exercised now in this critical early post-stroke period. Accordingly, he first tries to persuade her to continue exercising. When that is not effective he becomes rather stern and scolds and chastises her for two days. She then relents and begins exercising again, but it is necessary for Mr. S. to chastise her almost daily to obtain her continued participation over the ensuing three weeks.

Mr. S.'s scolding and chastising is paternalistic behavior by our account: he is causing Mrs. W. psychological pain without her consent for what he believes is her own good. He further believes he is qualified to do so and also believes that Mrs. W. believes she generally knows what is for her own good.

Mr. S. could attempt to justify his action by claiming that the relatively minor amount of evil he is inflicting through chastising her into exercising is much less than the relatively greater evil Mrs. W. might experience by being significantly more disabled than need be over the ensuing years of her life. Mr. S. could thus claim that Mrs. W.'s ranking of the relevant evils is irrational. We would describe the kind of violation being engaged in by Mr. S. as his inflicting a mild degree of suffering on Mrs. W. (through his chastising and her resumed exercising) by imposing his rational ranking of evils on Mrs. W. whose ranking is not rational. A rational person could publicly advocate this kind of violation and we conclude that Mr. S.'s paternalistic behavior is justified.

Note that this case involves the balancing of evils which, while significant, are not of the intensity of our earlier cases. The amount of evil associated with the possibility of Mrs. W.'s needlessly greater life-long disability seems just significant enough (and her balancing of the evils of three weeks of exercising versus life-long disability seems just irrational enough) to justify causing her some mild to moderate degree of transient suffering without her consent.

However there are some kinds of violations we would think not justified in Mrs. W.'s case. We would think it unjustified to inflict great physical pain on her to force her to exercise: the amount of evil associated with the possibility of her increased disability is simply not great enough so that one could publicly advocate that kind of violation.

Philosophically, the most interesting alternative to consider is the possibility of lying to her. Suppose Mr. S. told her that unless she continued to exercise for three more weeks she would regress and never be able to walk again. Suppose, further, that he knew that in her case this was untrue, that in fact she was almost certainly going to be able to walk in any event, but that, as described above, physical therapy would very likely decrease her ultimate level of disability. If Mr. S. did lie in this way, it might prove quite effective in quickly remotivating Mrs. W. to exercise daily without the need for Mr. S. to chastise her at all. In fact such a deception might cause Mrs. W. less total suffering than daily chastising if she now perceived the exercising as something she wanted to do because through doing it she was staving off the possibility of a certain inability to walk. Thus, using a simple negative utilitarian method of calculation, it might seem that if chastisement were justifiable paternalism, lying would be even more strongly justifiable. But, when we describe the kind of violation that Mr. S. would commit by lying, we see that this is not the case. It is true that Mrs. W.'s desire to discontinue physical therapy is, in the circumstances, one that we would regard as irrational. Thus, we do not have lying in order to impose one person's rational ranking of the evils on another person's different rational ranking, but rather lying in order to substitute a rational ranking for an irrational one. Thus, we must describe the act as deception in order to prevent the possibility of a permanent (up to 20 or 30 years) though moderate amount of disability, and thereby causing a temporary (three weeks) mild physical discomfort (of physical therapy). Would a rational person allow lying in these circumstances; would a rational person publicly advocate this kind of violation of the rule against deception? We find this a difficult question to answer. Allowing lying in a situation where trust is extremely important (such as between a doctor, nurse, or therapist and a patient) in order to prevent evil significant enough that it is irrational not to avoid it (such as the possibility of permanent moderate disability) is an issue on which we think rational persons could disagree. The erosion of trust that would follow from universally allowing this kind of violation may have such significant evil consequences (for example, legitimate warnings may come to be disregarded) that it is not clear that even preventing a significant number of persons from suffering permanent moderate disability is enough to counterbalance these consequences. Our conclusion in this circumstance is that rational persons would disagree; some would publicly advocate violation, some would not.

The conclusion of the previous paragraph rests upon the assumption that lying is the only method whereby one can get Mrs. W. to continue her treatment. However, if we have an alternative to lying, namely, the method of chastising and scolding, then we hold that all rational persons would publicly advocate using this method rather than lying. We have found, in informal testing, that when presented with these alternative methods of getting Mrs. W. to continue treatment, everyone regarded chastising and scolding as morally preferable to lying, and that some regarded lying as completely morally unacceptable. If one uses a simple negative utilitarian theory, this result cannot be accounted for since in this particular case lying results in no more and almost certainly less overall suffering than chastising and scolding. However, if one applies the method of justification that we have been presenting, these moral intuitions are accounted for quite easily. For, using *only* the relevant facts of the particular case: *(a)* the moral rules violated—causing pain (the unpleasantness caused by the scolding) versus deception (lying about consequences of stopping treatment) and *(b)* the evil probably prevented—unpleasantness of treatment in both cases plus unpleasantness of scolding in the former case as determining the *kind of violation* and then seeing whether one could publicly advocate this kind of violation, one will end up with the result that accords with the moral intuitions that one actually finds.

We believe the above case is typical of a multitude of everyday situations in medicine where doctors, nurses and other health-care workers act or are tempted to act paternalistically toward patients. Consider the problems presented by the patient with emphysema who continues to smoke, by the alcoholic with liver damage who refuses to enter any treatment program, or by the diabetic or hypertensive patient who exacerbates his or her disease by paying little heed to dietary precautions. Each of these patients is apt to stimulate paternalistic acts on the part of a variety of health-care professionals (as well as the patient's own family members). We think it is an important task to determine, whenever possible, which kinds of paternalistic acts are justifiable and which are not.

2

Paternalism and Health Care[1]

James F. Childress

*Kennedy Institute of Ethics, Georgetown
University, Washington, D.C.*

My intention in this essay is to identify some major issues raised by
paternalism in health care. The tensions between liberty and paternalism pervade public policy and medicine, for instance, in the debates
about saccharin and laetrile, suicide and suicide intervention, and compliance with treatment. I shall present several cases in order to raise
three questions. First, what is paternalism? Second, under what conditions can paternalism be justified? Third, what is the relation of past,
present, and future consent to paternalism? Although I shall state what
I take to be a defensible position at several points, I shall concentrate
on analyzing some major issues rather than developing a position.

Case #1

"Mr. N, a member of a religious sect that does not believe in blood
transfusions, is involved in a serious automobile accident and loses a

[1]This essay is a revised version of my essay "Liberty, Paternalism, and Health
Care" in *Social Responsibility: Journalism, Law, Medicine,* Vol. 4, Louis W. Hodges,
ed., Lexington, Va., Washington and Lee University, 1978. It was originally delivered
as a lecture at Washington and Lee University and at the College of Physicians and
Surgeons of Columbia University. Persons at both institutions made several helpful
suggestions for which I am grateful.

large amount of blood. On arriving at the hospital, he is still conscious and informs the doctor of his views on blood transfusion. Immediately thereafter he faints from loss of blood. The doctor believes that if Mr. N is not given a transfusion he will die. Thereupon, while Mr. N is still unconscious, the doctor arranges for and carries out the blood transfusion."[2]

Case #2

As a result of a chronic brain syndrome with arteriosclerosis, Mrs. Catherine Lake had periods of confusion and mild loss of memory, interspersed with times of mental alertness and rationality. Because she often wandered away from her home, she was involuntarily hospitalized in order to reduce the risk of harm. Mrs. Lake indicated that she understood her condition and the risks involved in living outside the hospital, but that she preferred to accept these risks rather than endure continued hospitalization. The District Court denied her petition for release on the grounds that she is "a danger to herself in that she has a tendency to wander about the streets, and is not competent to care for herself."[3]

Case #3

A 65-year-old retired army officer who had had several abdominal operations for gallstones, postoperative adhesions, and bowel obstructions, was admitted to a psychiatric ward because of chronic abdominal pain, loss of weight, and social withdrawal. Although he had had a productive military, teaching and research career, he was now somewhat depressed and unkempt, and had poor hygiene. Furthermore, he and his wife had curtailed their social activities because he could not control his pain without assuming awkward and embarrassing postures. Each day, he relied on six self-administered injections of Talwin (Pentazocine) which he believed to be essential to control his pain. Having used this non-addictive medication for more than two years, he had so much tissue and muscle damage that he had difficulty finding injection sites. His goal for therapy was to "get more out of life in spite of my pain."

In this psychiatric ward, which included individual behavior therapy programs, daily group therapy, ward government, social ac-

---

[2]B. Gert and C. Culver, *Phil. and Public Affairs* 6 (1), p. 46, 1976. I shall assume that Mr. N is a Jehovah's Witness.

[3]This case is based on material in J. Katz, J. Goldstein and A. M. Dershowitz, *Psychoanalysis, Psychiatry, and Law,* New York, Free Press, 1967, pp. 552–54.

tivities, and so on, the staff ignored pain behaviors in order to avoid reinforcing them. Their positive procedures included relaxation techniques, covert imagery, and cognitive relabeling. Although the patient had voluntarily admitted himself to this ward, where adjustment in medication was a clear expectation, he refused to allow direct modification of his Talwin dosage levels on the grounds that his experience showed that the level of medication was indispensable to control his pain. After considerable discussion with colleagues, the therapists decided to withdraw the Talwin over time, without the patient's knowledge, by diluting it with increasing proportions of normal saline. Although the patient experienced nausea, diarrhea, and cramps, he thought that these withdrawal symptoms were actually the result of Elavil (Amitriptyline), which the therapists had introduced to relieve the withdrawal symptoms. While the therapists did not use Elavil to deceive the patient, it served that purpose because he blamed it for his discomfort. The staff had informed the patient that his medication regime would be modified, but had not given him the details.

After three weeks of saline injections, the therapists explained what had been done. At first the patient was incredulous and angry, but he asked that the saline be discontinued and the self-control techniques continued. When he was discharged three weeks later, he reported that he experienced some abdominal pain, but that he could control it more effectively with the self-control techniques than previously with the Talwin. A follow-up six months later showed that he was still using the relaxation techniques and had resumed social activities and part-time teaching.

The therapists justified this deceptive use of a placebo on the grounds of its effectiveness:

> We felt ethically obliged to use a treatment that had a high probability of success. To withhold the procedure may have protected some standard of openness, but may not have been in his [the patient's] best interests. We saw no option without ethical problems. Although it is precarious to justify the means by the end, we felt most obliged to use a procedure designed to help the patient achieve a personally and medically desirable goal.[4]

---

[4]This case is based on an actual case described by P. Levendusky and Loren Pankratz, *J. of Abnormal Psychol.* 84 (2), pp. 165–168, 1975.

I. WHAT IS PATERNALISM?

Because the term "paternalism" is sex-linked, it is not wholly felicitous. It is drawn from the role of the paternal figure, the father, in the family. While it might be desirable to use another term such as "parentalism," "paternalism" is hallowed by usage and philosophical discussion. Actually, what William James said of "pragmatism" also applies to "paternalism": it is a new name for a very old way of thinking. Although the Oxford English Dictionary dates the term "paternalism" from the 1880's, the idea is much older and, indeed, appears very early in human thought. Its meaning, according to the OED, is "the principle and practice of paternal administration; government as by a father; the claim or attempt to supply the needs or to regulate the life of a nation or community in the same way as a father does those of his children."

While it is sometimes held that paternalism involves the use of a "biological model of the caring parent,"[5] fatherhood is a social role and not merely a biological role. In discussions of paternalism in health care, one social role is used as an analogue for another social role: the social role of father is used as an analogue for the social role of health care professional or government. The analogy need not be perfect. It may hold only at some points. But, as in any analogical reasoning, it is important to ask just how much light it sheds.

When this paternal analogy is used to illuminate the role of the professional or the state in health care, two features are emphasized: *(1)* the father's motives and intentions are directed at his children's welfare, and *(2)* he makes all or at least some of the decisions regarding his children's welfare rather than allowing them to make these decisions. These two features of paternalism involve a distinction between acting *on someone's behalf* and acting *at someone's behest.* Paternalism is morally interesting and important in part because the paternalist claims to act on a person's behalf but not at that person's behest; indeed, the "beneficiary" of the paternalist's actions may even explicitly repudiate those actions on his behalf.

The first feature of paternalism, then, is benevolence or beneficence —that is, the motivation and intention to prevent harm to or to benefit another person. Paternalism thus rests on important principles in our moral and religious traditions—for example, the principles of agape and concern for the neighbor. It characteristically focuses on the patient's *needs* rather than his or her *rights,* and it holds that the agent

---

[5]David J. Rothman, in W. Gaylin, I. Glasser, S. Marcus, and D. Rothman, *Doing Good: The Limits of Benevolence,* New York, Pantheon, 1978, p. 69.

can determine and meet those needs better than the patient. Such a perspective has been emphasized at various points in our history, for example, by the Progressives, but it has come under a cloud of suspicion since the 1960's. David Rothman[6] thinks that this suspicion is based on the belief that the claim to be doing good for others masks the agent's real motives, such as self-interest. In fact, the suspicion probably stems from the absence of shared beliefs about what is good for persons and what they really need.

If benevolence or beneficence were the only feature of paternalism, there would be little concern about its justification. Despite its motivation and intention, paternalism stands in need of justification, as our cases indicate, because of a second feature: it involves a refusal to accept or to acquiesce in an individual's choices, wishes, and actions. It thus interferes with autonomy, self-determination, and liberty. While it claims to be benevolent and beneficent, it does not allow the recipient to determine his or her own good or interests. It usurps a right of decision-making on the grounds that someone else can make better decisions. As a result, paternalism is prima facie wrong and requires justification.

Many discussions and examples of paternalism identify "coercion" as the second feature of paternalism. For example, in an important essay, Gerald Dworkin[7] defines paternalism as "roughly the interference with a person's liberty of action justified by reasons referring exclusively to the welfare, good, happiness, needs, interests or values of the person being coerced." Such a definition is too narrow, for positive services may also be paternalistic—for example, providing food stamps rather than money which might be spent in different ways. Such positive services express concern for the recipient's welfare and also refuse to accept the recipient's choices, wishes, and actions. Hence, they are paternalistic.

Another major recent discussion of paternalism identifies this second feature as the violation of moral rules. In their discussion of Case #1 above, Gert and Culver[8] hold that the physician's provision of a blood transfusion for the unconscious Mr. N, a Jehovah's Witness, who has already refused such transfusions, will require the physician either to deceive the patient or to cause the patient painful feelings by disclosure of the transfusion. They argue that the physician's action is pater-

[6]*Ibid*, p. 82.

[7]G. Dworkin, in R. A. Wasserstrom, ed., *Morality and the Law,* Belmont, Calif., Wadsworth, 1971, p. 108.

[8]Gert and Culver, *op. cit.,* p. 51.

nalistic and requires justification *because* it will lead him to violate either the moral rule against deception or the moral rule against causing pain. The Gert-Culver argument is needlessly circuitous and even misleading. They rightly hold that the physician's action in this case does not interfere with liberty of action or attempt to control the patient's behavior, much less coerce him. But the physician's action is paternalistic because his benevolent motives and intentions involve a refusal to accept the individual's own choices and wishes, not because it would lead to a violation of the moral rules against deception or causing pain. And the physician's action requires justification precisely because of its refusal to acquiesce in the patient's own choices and wishes. Of course, deception and causing pain also make the action prima facie wrong, but the action would be paternalistic and would require justification even if these features were absent.

What distinguishes paternalism from other refusals to acquiesce in an individual's choices, wishes, or actions is the *target* of its benevolent motivation and intention. Another reason for non-acquiescence is to prevent harm to or to benefit another party. This reason is concerned with X's choices, wishes, or actions only insofar as they harm or diminish the benefits to Y, another party.[9] Yet another reason is the principle of justice or fairness, which sometimes, but not always, can be restated in terms of the first reason. For example, X's actions might create or impose unfair burdens on others by requiring too much of the common resources to which the members of the community have contributed. A third reason might be that X's choices, wishes, or actions violate some moral principles. For example, some arguments for the legal prohibition of some sexual acts between consenting adults hold that these acts are wrong even if they do not harm others or violate principles of justice or fairness.

Paternalism, in contrast to these other reasons, appeals to the welfare of the party whose choices, wishes, or actions are not accepted. Obviously, many important debates in health care and public policy involve several of these reasons. For example, in the debates about legislation requiring motorcycle helmets, some arguments are clearly paternalistic: helmets are required to protect the motorcyclists them-

---

[9]It is important to distinguish the prevention of harm from the promotion of good. The duty to prevent harm is more stringent than the duty to promote good. In this discussion, I concentrate on the prevention of harm to others and, particularly, to the one whose wishes, choices, and actions are not accepted. If it is possible to make a case for justified paternalism, it will probably appear in the prevention of harm. Nevertheless, it is often difficult to distinguish between prevention of harm and promotion of good.

selves. Other arguments strain to show harm to others (for example, hazards to passing vehicles) and unfair burdens for ambulance drivers, nurses, neurosurgeons, as well as the public. Still other arguments appear to be based on the conviction that the lifestyle of motorcyclists is immoral or at least unpatriotic.[10]

Various reasons are given for holding that paternalism is at least prima facie wrong and requires justification. First, individuals know their own interests better than others. Second, paternalism will increase the power of health care professionals and the state. Third, paternalists will intervene wrongly and in the wrong places. The first reason is probably false, the second is true, and the third is true at least some of the time. The main reason for opposing paternalism, however, is the evil of not letting alone, of not letting people decide matters for themselves. Justice Louis Brandeis defended this right to be let alone in his dissent in Olmstead v. U.S.:

> The makers of our Constitution . . . sought to protect Americans in their beliefs, their thoughts, their emotions and their sensations. They conferred, as against the government, the right to be let alone—the most comprehensive of rights and the right most valued by civilized men. . . . Experience should teach us to be most on our guard to protect liberty when the government's purposes are beneficent. Men born to freedom are naturally alert to repel invasions of their liberty by evil-minded rulers. The greatest dangers to liberty lurk in insidious encroachment by men of zeal, well-meaning but without understanding.[11]

This right to be let alone was graphically expressed by Robert Frost, who said that the first inalienable right of any man is to go to hell in his own way. But at most, there is only a prima facie case against paternalistic interventions; they can sometimes be justified.

II. WHEN IS PATERNALISM JUSTIFIED?

The conditions for justifying paternalistic interventions can be analyzed in relation to risk-taking. Each person has what Charles Fried[12] calls a life plan consisting of aims, ends, and values. This life plan includes a *risk budget,* for we are willing to run certain risks to our health and

---

[10]L. H. Tribe, *American Constitutional Law,* Mineola, New York, Foundation Press, 1978, pp. 938–41.

[11]Olmstead v. United States, 277 U.S. 438 Dissenting opinion, 1928.

[12]Charles Fried, *An Anatomy of Values,* Cambridge, Mass., Harvard University Press, 1970.

life in order to realize some aims, ends, and values. We do not sacrifice all other goods merely in order to survive or to be healthy. Our willingness to run risks of death and ill health for success, friendship, religious convictions, and so on, discloses the value of those ends for us and gives our lives their style. When is it justified to interfere with a person's wishes, choices, and actions in order to prevent or reduce risk-taking?

Two sorts of justifications are often given, sometimes singly, sometimes jointly, for paternalistic interferences with risk-taking: *(1)* The decision-maker's defects, encumbrances, or limitations, and *(2)* the magnitude and probability of harm. It is important to see how these justifications function, how much weight they might have, and how they are related.[13]

(1) The decision-maker's defects, encumbrances, and limitations. First, the decision-maker's competence might be limited or impaired, as was claimed in Case #2. For example, the person might be so severely retarded as to be unable to understand the risks of certain situations or actions. If a person is incompetent, he or she is unable to make informed and voluntary choices. Competence is a precondition of or a capacity for making such choices. It is sometimes construed less as a presupposition for understanding and for voluntary choices and more as a summary term for understanding and voluntariness.

Second, because of ignorance or false beliefs, a person might be unable to predict consequences and evaluate them properly. Such risk-taking cannot be said to be voluntary. Mill gave one example in *On Liberty:*

> If either a public officer or anyone else saw a person attempting to cross a bridge which had been ascertained to be unsafe, and there were not time to warn him of this danger, they might seize him and turn him back, without any real infringement of his liberty; for liberty consists in doing what one desires, and he does not desire to fall into the river.[14]

If the person crossing the bridge were to continue to believe falsely that the bridge was safe after being informed that it was unsafe, the question of false belief would arise.

Third, a person's choices or actions may be informed but non-voluntary because of compulsion, drug addiction, and so on.

Is it necessary to identify one or more of these defects, encumbrances, or limitations before paternalistic interventions can be jus-

---

[13]For important discussions of some of these issues, see T. L. Beauchamp, *Monist* 60 (1), pp. 62–80, 1977; J. D. Hodson, *Amer. Phil. Quart.* 14 (1), pp. 61–69, 1977; and J. G. Murphy, *Archiv für Rechts und Sozialphilosophie* 60 (4), pp. 465–486, 1974.

[14]J. S. Mill, *On Liberty,* Gertrude Himmelfarb, ed., Harmodsworth, England, Penguin, 1976, p. 166.

tified? Is it sufficient to identify them? Before I indicate whether these conditions are necessary and/or sufficient, I shall consider other conditions that are sometimes offered.

(2) Probability and magnitude of harm. Some definitions of "harm" are so broad as to include injuries to reputation, property, and liberty. For example, if the object of harm is always an interest, as Feinberg suggests,[15] it is possible to have various interests that could be violated or damaged (such as health, property, and domestic relations). Then, it would be possible to distinguish trivial and serious harms by the order and magnitude of the interests involved. Some philosophers use a narrow definition of harm, distinguishing physical (and mental) harms from injuries to other interests such as property and liberty. I am concentrating on physical and mental harms without denying the importance of damage to property, and so on. In addition, several commentators hold that *irreversible* harms are more likely to justify paternalistic interventions than *reversible* harms.

It is necessary to determine both the probability and the magnitude of harm. The former involves prediction, while the latter involves evaluation, but even the former is not value-free. Furthermore, the agent contemplating paternalistic intervention on grounds of the serious harm that is likely to befall a person must also consider the benefits that person seeks in his or her risk-taking. In short, the agent should engage in a risk-benefit analysis. The terms "risk" and "benefit" are somewhat misleading since "risk" is a probabilistic term while "benefit" is not. It would be more accurate, but excessively cumbersome, to compare "probability and magnitude of harm" with "probability and magnitude of benefit." In general, physicians and the courts should not substitute their own risk-benefit analyses for a competent patient's risk-benefit analysis based on adequate information and voluntarily chosen even if the patient's value system is alien to the physicians and the courts. For example, in Case #1, a Jehovah's Witness refused a blood transfusion on the grounds that his salvation depended on obedience to God's will in the Scriptures, and that God prohibited the consumption of blood. He was willing to risk his life in order to gain the great benefit of salvation. Even if, in such cases, a competent patient should be permitted to choose a course of action consistent with his or her own risk-benefit calculation, it does not follow that he or she should be permitted to make such a choice for an incompetent patient (such as a child).

---

[15]J. Feinberg, *Social Philosophy,* Englewood Cliffs, New Jersey, Prentice-Hall, 1973, p. 26.

What is the relation between these two sets of conditions for paternalistic interventions—the decision-maker's defects, encumbrances, and limitations and the probability and magnitude of harm? If we accept the first set of conditions as necessary, we have what is called *weak paternalism,* for we would intervene only where wishes, choices, or actions are nonvoluntary. If we accept the second set of conditions as sufficient, we have what is called *strong paternalism,* for we could justifiably intervene even where the patient's wishes, choices, or actions are informed and voluntary because his or her risk-benefit analysis is found to be unreasonable.[16]

One plausible interpretation of the two sets of conditions is that, in general, both are necessary. Even if there is incompetence, lack of information, or involuntariness, we may justifiably intervene, in the absence of harm to or unfair burdens on others, *only* when the intervention is necessary to prevent harm (trivial as well as major) to the one whose wishes, choices, or actions are not accepted. In cases of competent persons, who are making informed and voluntary choices, we generally should not intervene even to prevent major and irreversible harm (for example, in the Jehovah's Witness cases). There may be exceptional cases, but they are very rare. Where there is a high risk of major and irreversible harm (such as death), health care professionals and others tend to construe a patient's assumption of such a risk as evidence of incompetence. A Catch-22 situation can result: only competent persons are allowed to take certain risks, but the assumption of those risks is itself a sign of incompetence. Procedural safeguards are needed in order to prevent violations of patients' rights to have their voluntary and informed choices, wishes, and actions accepted.

III. CONSENT

Earlier, I distinguished between acting on someone's behalf and acting at someone's behest. Since paternalism usually involves acting on a person's behalf, but without that person's request or permission, it might appear that his or her consent would make the intervention nonpaternalistic. But this matter needs to be carefully explored. Consent may be given prior to, at the time of, or subsequent to the intervention, and its impact on description (is the intervention paternalistic?) and evaluation (is the intervention justified?) may vary according to the time of the consent.

[16]*Ibid.,* pp. 45–52.

Let us start with consent at the time of the intervention. If a patient validly consents to an intervention on his or her behalf, the intervention is not paternalistic, for it is consistent with the patient's expressed wishes and choices.

Odysseus provides an example of prior consent. Before Odysseus and his men sailed by the Island of the enchanting Sirens, who used beautiful music to draw sailors to their death, he had his companions bind him to the mast and swear not to release him. Hearing the music of the Sirens, Odysseus demanded his release and threatened his companions with death if they did not comply. They obeyed his earlier orders. Their actions were paternalistic in that they refused to accept Odysseus' expressions of his wishes at the time they forcibly constrained him. Their actions could be justified because Odysseus' wishes at the moment were not voluntary, but also because he had given prior consent to this constraint.

Even where there is explicit prior consent to intervention in medical care, difficulties remain. Often, it is not easy to determine when a person has revoked prior consent. It is necessary, then, to continue to assess the person's competence and the level of understanding and voluntariness of his choices (such as Odysseus' compulsion). In other cases, where explicit consent is absent, it may be possible to argue that the patient has *implicitly* consented to an intervention. For example, in Case #3, it could be argued that the paternalistic substitution of a placebo for medication in the control of pain was justified not only because of its results but also because the patient had implicitly consented to such a practice. After all, he had voluntarily admitted himself to a ward where adjustment in medication was a clear expectation, and he sought the goals of the program.

Several theories of justified paternalism emphasize the importance of the patient's consent after the intervention. Some theories (for example, Gert and Culver[17]) draw a distinction between consent that is immediately forthcoming and consent that is given later. They hold that if an intervention evokes consent from the patient immediately after its performance, the intervention is non-paternalistic. It is not clear, however, that such an intervention is not paternalistic. When the agent has to decide whether to acquiesce in a patient's choices, wishes, or actions, his or her decision *not* to acquiesce is paternalistic even though he or she expects the patient to consent when he or she is subsequently informed. However, the patient's anticipated consent,

[17]Gert and Culver, *op. cit.,* pp. 52–53.

whether immediate or later, does figure prominently in the justification of the intervention.

John Rawls[18] contends that for justified paternalism, "we must be able to argue that with the development or the recovery of his rational powers the individual in question will accept our decision on his behalf and agree with us that we did the best thing for him." For such a view, which I call a "ratification theory"—since the patient ratifies the action on his or her behalf—future consent is a necessary though not a sufficient condition for the justification of paternalism. Thus, in Case #3, the patient who was subjected to deceptive techniques in pain control later ratified his therapists' decisions and actions. At first, he was incredulous and angry, but he asked that the self-control techniques be continued. His ratification was necessary for the justification, but not sufficient. Ratification cannot be sufficient because some interventions, such as brain-washing, may create the conditions of their own ratification.

For the ratification theory, then, a necessary condition for justified paternalism is the patient's future consent.[19] The agent's assessment of the risks, the probability and magnitude of harm, is taken as evidence that the patient will probably ratify the intervention in the future, when he or she regains rational powers. For those who emphasize the probability and magnitude of harm, rather than the probability of the patient's future consent, probable future consent is not irrelevant. It is taken as evidence of the rightness of the intervention which is based primarily on the prevention of harm for the patient.

IV. CONCLUSION

I have tried to indicate some of the issues in the debates about paternalism in health care by clarifying the nature of paternalism, the conditions for its justification, and the relations between consent and paternalism. There should be a presumption against paternalism which can, nevertheless, sometimes be justified. In trying to limit and control paternalism, we need to be aware of symbolic expression and communi-

---

[18]John Rawls, *A Theory of Justice,* Cambridge, Mass., Harvard University Press, 1971, p. 249.

[19]Since many individuals who are subject to paternalistic interventions in health care will never regain rational powers, the ratification theory often takes a hypothetical form: what individuals *would* consent to if they *could* consent. This version of the ratification theory, of course, appeals to some vision of what rational individuals do and should desire.

cation through acts and policies. Anti-paternalistic acts and policies may have symbolic significance that we sometimes overlook; for example, if we do not intervene because of anti-paternalism to prevent suicides, our nonintervention may be construed as an expression of a conviction that the deaths do not matter. A policy that affirms "you should care for yourself" may be read as "we don't care for you." Autonomous individualism may have tragic costs, and "benign neglect" may not be so benign. In short, we need to seek ways to gesture care and concern—the attitude of benevolence that undergirds paternalism—even while being suspicious of and trying to limit the second feature of paternalism—the refusal to accept or to acquiesce in an individual's wishes, choices, and actions regarding his own welfare.

3

Catch-22 Paternalism and Mandatory Genetic Screening

Michael D. Bayles

*Department of Philosophy, University of Kentucky,
Lexington, Kentucky*

This essay attempts to provide the outlines of defensible paternalism in one area of preventive medicine.[1] The paternalist basis of preventive medicine is especially important when the state adopts legislation compelling paternalist measures. In such cases, there is mutual reinforcement between those who are authorities and those who are in authority. Rarely can legislation be clearly classified as paternalistic, because such descriptions are based upon the reasons for the legislation and various reasons may often be given for it.

However, if mandatory genetic screening is to be justified, paternalist reasons are apt to be important. The usual private harm rationale for liberty–limiting laws—to prevent people injuring other individuals —does not support mandatory genetic screening. One might expect that rationale to apply to a screening program for carriers of defective genes who risk having children with a disease. Elsewhere,[2] I have

---

[1] I wish to thank Holly Goldman, Ruth Macklin, and members of the original University of Kentucky Metaphysical Club for useful comments and criticisms of earlier versions of this essay.
[2] M. D. Bayles, *Phil. Public Affairs* 5, 292, 1976.

argued that the private harm principle does not apply to such cases. Moreover, it is usually completely irrelevant to screening for a disease or defect or susceptibility to diseases.

The other major nonpaternalist rationale would be the public good —for example, avoiding high costs in caring for those with genetic defects and diseases and eugenic considerations.[3] The public good is a strong justification for limiting peoples' liberty—for example, by quarantine or compulsory immunization, when they have contagious diseases. It is less strong with respect to genetic defects and diseases, since they are not communicable to others in society. The possible effects on the public good are then chiefly burdens on medical and financial resources[4] and on the gene pool. If mandatory genetic screening is not justifiable by public good considerations alone, it may be if there are both paternalist and public good reasons for it. This essay attempts to provide a paternalist rationale for mandatory genetic screening.

Many discussions of paternalism have been confused due to a failure to carefully define it. Elsewhere,[5] I have presented a more detailed analysis of paternalist principles for legislation which is generally followed here. The major defining feature of paternalist principles or reasons is that they support doing something to or for a person for his or her own good or well-being without his or her assent, even over his or her objections. Hence, paternalist considerations pertain only to "benefits" to persons resulting from their own screening.

Paternalist principles may be classified in two ways. First, they may be preservative or promotive. The aim of preservative principles is to maintain an individual's level of well-being as it is at the moment of intervention, to avoid harm or a diminution of the individual's well-being. The goal of promotive principles is to increase a person's well-being. Second, paternalist principles may be weak or strong. Strong principles support interventions even if an individual is capable of a fully informed and voluntary choice or action. Weak principles use a voluntariness criterion of application and do not support interventions if individuals are capable of fully informed and voluntary choices or actions. For a choice or action to be fully informed and voluntary, it must be taken with knowledge of all relevant, readily obtainable facts, without coercion or compulsion, and without psychological distur-

---

[3]M. D. Bayles, *J. Value Inquiry* 11, 186, pp. 191–196, 1977.

[4]P. Reilly, *Genetics, Law, and Social Policy,* Cambridge, Mass., Harvard University Press, 1977, pp. 18–19.

[5]M. D. Bayles, *Principles of Legislation,* Detroit, Mich., Wayne State University Press, 1978, pp. 119–125.

bance.[6] This criterion thus includes the two elements of informed consent—information and voluntariness.

There are four paternalist principles. Strong promotive paternalism is the claim that there is a good (but not conclusive) reason for doing something to or for a person to increase that person's well-being regardless of whether the person is capable of a fully informed and voluntary choice or action about the matter. Weak promotive paternalism is the claim that there is a good (but not conclusive) reason for doing something to or for a person to increase that person's well-being only if the person is incapable of a fully informed and voluntary choice or action about the matter. Strong preservative paternalism is the claim that there is a good (but not conclusive) reason for doing something to or for a person to prevent a decrease in that person's well-being (harm) regardless of whether the person is capable of a fully informed and voluntary choice or action about the matter. Weak preservative paternalism is the claim that there is a good (but not conclusive) reason for doing something to or for a person to prevent a decrease in that person's well-being (harm) only if the person is incapable of a fully informed and voluntary choice or action about the matter.

It is not possible herein to present in detail the method by which such principles may be justified or the arguments for accepting specific principles. Essentially, principles can be justified by showing that they are acceptable to reasonable persons contemplating their use by others in formulating policies and rules to which the persons will be subject.[7] Reasonable persons are people who, whatever their particular values may be, are not mentally ill or unintelligent and who are open to evidence and persuasion by argument. Reasonable persons make decisions on the basis of all relevant, readily obtainable information. Moreover, they can be persuaded by arguments pro and con. While not every psychological abnormality—for example, a mild neurosis—prevents persons from being reasonable, severe ones involving reality distortion do so. Finally, reasonable persons are intelligent in the sense of being able to understand principles and the types of choices and actions they support in various circumstances. Reasonable persons are thus capable of fully informed and voluntary choices and actions unless others intervene by coercion or duress.

Reasonable persons would not accept either of the strong paternalist principles.[8] Even though their judgments might be mistaken, they

---

[6]J. Feinberg, *Can. J. Phil.* 1, 105, pp. 110–111, 1971.
[7]Bayles, 1978, *op. cit.,* pp. 51–58.
[8]*Ibid.,* pp. 125–133.

would not be willing to have their fully informed and voluntary judgments as to their well-being overridden by those of others. While being fully informed and voluntary does not guarantee that choices and actions will be correct (one may make mistakes or have weakness of will), they are more likely to be so than those which are not. Furthermore, people value autonomy, making their own decisions affecting their lives. However, reasonable persons would accept the weak paternalist principles, for when they are incapable of fully informed and voluntary choices, they have a basis for relying on those of others. While the grounds for these assertions have not been presented, the following discussion assumes that only weak paternalist principles are acceptable.

Before applying paternalist considerations to genetic screening, it is useful to have a rough outline of the different types of genetic screening. Essentially, there are three types of screening—for carrier status, for disease or abnormal genes, and for disease susceptibility. *(1)* Carrier screening is to determine whether one has abnormal genes which may be transmitted to offspring—for example, those for sickle cell anemia or Tay Sachs. If one has a recessive gene and procreates with another carrier, one risks having a child with the disease or defect. *(2)* Disease screening is to determine whether an individual has a disease or defect. It may be subdivided into two types. *(a)* In one type, the person screened may have the disease. Examples are screening children for phenylketonuria (PKU) and adults for diabetes. *(b)* The other type of disease screening is prenatal, in which a pregnant woman undergoes a test to determine whether the fetus has a disease or defect such as Tay Sachs or Down's syndrome. Usually, this type of screening is used to determine the desirability of an abortion. *(3)* Disease susceptibility screening is to determine whether one has genetic factors making one more susceptible to diseases such as cancer. The justifications for various types of screening programs may vary depending upon the type of screening involved. Before turning to factors relevant to determining the justifiability of different types of screening programs, a general paternalist argument for mandatory genetic screening is given.

Since the weak paternalist principles use the voluntariness criterion of application, it may appear that they cannot support mandatory screening. If a person withholds informed consent to screening, then does one not need strong principles to require it? However, as infants and children are incapable of the relevant, fully informed and voluntary choices, only weak paternalist principles are needed to support screening them.[9] Legally, parental consent is often substituted for the consent

---

[9]Fetuses are not included here. Women are the relevant patients in prenatal screening as far as paternalism is concerned.

of children. However, parental consent is not that of the children and may not even be based on considerations of their well-being. Paternalism with respect to children can be avoided only by completely ignoring their well-being. Consequently, the only practically significant issue with respect to infants and children is who is to exercise paternalism —parents, the medical profession, or the state. With respect to adults, however, the objection has more force.

An essential step in applying the weak paternalist principles is to distinguish different actions or choices which a patient may make. In particular, one must distinguish choosing to be screened from later choices and actions which may be based upon information gained from the screening. For example, screening for carrier status may provide information relevant to reproductive decisions, and screening for disease susceptibility may provide information relevant to decisions about whether to quit smoking due to risk of cancer. If one refuses screening in the appropriate circumstances, then one may render oneself incapable of fully informed and voluntary choices and actions in the future due to ignorance of readily obtainable relevant information. Screening is thus primarily information gathering so that future choices or actions may be fully informed and voluntary.

Suppose a person in the appropriate circumstances makes a fully informed and voluntary choice not to be screened. Since that choice is fully informed and voluntary, weak paternalist principles do not support intervention with respect to it. However, having made that choice, the person is incapable of fully informed and voluntary choices and actions concerning other matters, such as reproduction and smoking. Weak promotive paternalism supports intervention to increase a person's well-being. When a person is incapable of fully informed and voluntary choices and actions, the chief aim of weak promotive paternalism is to remove the incapacity, if possible, and thereby render the person capable of fully informed and voluntary choices and actions.[10] In the present context, since the inability to make fully informed and voluntary choices and actions is due to lack of information, weak promotive paternalism supports providing it. Providing the information involves genetic screening. Hence, in appropriate circumstances, weak promotive paternalism supports genetic screening of those who refuse it.

This argument has the appearance of being a Catch-22.[11] A person appears to be capable of making a fully informed and volun-

---

[10]Bayles, 1978, *op. cit.,* pp. 131–132.
[11]J. Heller, *Catch-22,* New York, Dell, 1961, pp. 46–47.

tary choice with respect to being screened. If the person decides not to be screened, then that person was not capable of a fully informed and voluntary choice and may be compelled to do the opposite. However, the defect in Catch-22 arguments is that the decision itself is taken as conclusive evidence *it* was not fully informed and voluntary. In the argument for mandatory screening, the choice to refuse screening is not considered not fully informed and voluntary, but *other choices* the person might make are. Hence, while the effect of the argument is similar—namely, one may be compelled to do the opposite of what one chooses to do—it is not because the original choice was not fully informed and voluntary, but because subsequent choices cannot be so.

Two points should be noted about this argument. First, it does not rest upon persons being rendered generally incapable of fully informed and voluntary choices and actions, but upon their being rendered incapable of fully informed and voluntary choices and actions in specific areas. Weak paternalism is sometimes mistakenly thought to require persons being incapable of any fully informed and voluntary choices and actions. But even persons with severe psychoses are capable of fully informed and voluntary choices and actions with respect to some affairs. Most mentally ill persons are competent to decide what to eat, when to go to the bathroom, what clothes to wear, and so on. Almost all conscious adults are capable of some fully informed and voluntary choices and actions.

Second, the argument is not that mandatory screening is justifiable because a person will make an objectively wrong decision. A decision which is not fully informed and voluntary may be correct, and one which is fully informed and voluntary may be incorrect. The argument is not that those who refuse screening will do the wrong thing, but that their subsequent choices, whether right or wrong, will not be fully informed and voluntary. No substantive criterion of subsequent decision-making is imposed or assumed. A person may make a fully informed and voluntary choice on the basis of avoiding the worst possible outcome (maximin), average utility, or other principle.

The issue is whether reasonable persons would accept the weak promotive paternalist principle for this type of situation. They could so qualify the weak promotive paternalist principle that it would not apply to situations of this sort. In order to determine whether they would want to do so, one needs to formulate a sub-principle for these types of situations. That sub-principle is as follows:

If a person would make a fully informed and voluntary choice which would prevent some of that person's subsequent choices from being fully informed and voluntary due to lack of readily obtainable relevant information, then there is a good reason to intervene to prevent that person from making the first choice.

As previously noted, unless others intervene by duress or coercion, reasonable persons are capable of fully informed and voluntary choices and actions. Moreover, they have reasons of "correctness" and autonomy for remaining capable of them. Autonomy is not very significant with respect to this sub-principle, because even if uninformed, choices are still autonomous in the sense of being voluntary, although they are not in the sense of expressing what a person actually desires. Hence, reasonable persons would want to continue to be capable of fully informed and voluntary choices and actions unless other values outweigh the value of greater likelihood of correct choices and actions.

There are two ways in which other values may outweigh the value of information. First, they may render the method of obtaining it objectionable. For example, a reasonable person might hold certain religious beliefs by which even a simple blood test is objectionable and, thus, find the disvalue of screening greater than the value of the information. Physically, the information would be readily obtainable, but from a value perspective the costs would be too high. Second, other values may be such that the information would not affect subsequent choices and actions. For example, if a woman is morally opposed to all abortions except to save a pregnant woman's life, then prenatal screening to determine whether a fetus has a defect would not affect her choice to have an abortion. Because of her values, the information is not relevant to future choices and actions.

Paternalist justifications depend upon the potential benefits outweighing the potential harms. For interventions to be for a person's good, they must increase more than they decrease that person's ability to satisfy wants. Consequently, for the argument for screening to apply, judgments must be made about the relative importance of the values involved in the screening itself and in the future choices and actions for which it provides information.

Policies are based upon the judgments and values of most people in society. Persons with different values might not concur in these judgments. Clearly definable classes of these persons may be excused from required genetic screening. However, paternalist principles also use the sacrifice criterion of application.[12] According to this criterion,

---

[12]Bayles, 1978, *op. cit.,* pp. 130–131.

the fully informed and voluntary choices and actions of some persons may be limited to prevent choices or actions of others which are not fully informed and voluntary. For example, some people might knowingly and voluntarily contract into slavery, but to protect those who would not, but might mistakenly be thought to have done so, the state may refuse to enforce any contracts for slavery.[13] Similarly, while the decisions of some people not to be screened might be fully informed and voluntary, those of many others might not be; to protect them, the liberty of those whose decisions would be fully informed and voluntary may have to be sacrificed. In short, the freedom of some people with different values may have to be sacrificed.

The remainder of this essay considers those general factors which most people would consider relevant in determining whether the potential benefits of screening (including avoidance of harms) outweigh the potential harms. Hence, they indicate when weak paternalist principles support mandatory screening. By implication, they also indicate when it would be reasonable for most persons to forgo genetic screening.

The possible harms from screening may be divided into physical, psychological, and social factors. The physical harms, usually those of drawing blood, are quite minor—bruises and perhaps fainting. With adults, however, screening may also involve amniocentesis which carries a higher risk to the patient. In such cases, as the risk of harm in screening is greater, it requires a proportionately larger potential benefit to be supported by paternalist considerations. Since, for paternalism, the patient is the pregnant woman, potential risks to the fetus are relevant only insofar as they may affect the woman.

The usual psychological harm is anxiety about the development of a disease, having a defective child, or transmission of a trait. The amount of anxiety involved varies. Moreover, some situations may involve much greater psychological harm than mere anxiety, such as the psychological effects on a "woman" who discovers "she" is genetically a male suffering from testicular feminization. While children are very young, they cannot understand what has occurred and should not suffer any psychological harm. However, if they have been determined to have a defect or be carriers, when older they may suffer much anxiety. Of course, anxiety is produced only if the results of tests are communicated to screenees. But, if the justification of screening is to provide information so that future decisions may be fully informed and voluntary, paternalist considerations cannot support generally withholding the results. To minimize anxiety, results may be withheld from

---

[13]Feinberg, *op. cit.,* pp. 119–121.

children until they are of such an age as to be able to receive and understand the information. Of course, the information gained should always be presented so as to minimize misunderstanding and anxiety.

Finally, social harm is that which results from discrimination or the adverse reactions of others. For example, if a male child is determined to have XYY chromosomes, then his treatment by parents, teachers, and others, may cause harm. To prevent the possible appearance of criminal tendencies, parents may be excessively restrictive. Another example of social harm would be rejection of a child by a putative father when screening reveals he could not be the father. Whether or not there is social harm depends upon whether the results are made available to others. If the information is kept confidential, paternalist support is stronger as social harm is decreased. Conversely, paternalism supports keeping the information confidential.

The paternalist and privacy grounds for confidentiality may conflict with other considerations. For example, suppose a person is identified as a carrier of sickle cell anemia. The person's siblings have an interest in this knowledge, for it indicates that they too may be carriers. Or, if a person has Huntington's chorea, life insurance companies have an interest in knowing the results. Providing the information to others weakens the paternalist support for the screening. It may well be in one's interest not to know that one has Huntington's chorea rather than be unable to obtain life insurance. Here, nonpaternalist considerations (public good) may weaken the paternalist support for mandatory screening while providing alternative support for it.

Some major factors in determining the benefits of screening are the number of people at risk in the population to be screened, the reliability of the test, the severity of the defect, and whether the information can be acted upon. The factors of risk and reliability are of major importance, for they provide probabilities which must be considered in evaluating the other conditions. For example, if only one in 100,000 persons to be screened is at risk of a severe disease, the screening may not be justified; however, if one in 1,000 is at risk of a moderately debilitating disease, screening may be justified. The expectable utility is greater in the latter than the former situation. However, reliability of the test is also very important. For example, if, as with the PKU screening,[14] 10 per cent of the tests provide false negatives, then the situation is the same as if fewer persons were at risk with a completely reliable test, because the chances of detecting the defect are similar.

The severity of the defect requires little explanation. Obviously,

[14]Reilly, *op. cit.*, p. 28.

the more severe the defect, the greater the harm that may be avoided. However, while the general principle is clear, its application is not easy. There are two major problems. First, it is not clear how one evaluates the severity of a defect except that physical and mental incapacity are the basic categories. There are no clear and generally accepted criteria for judging the comparative disvalue of different incapacities. Second, the likelihood of incapacity may vary greatly. While all persons with Down's syndrome have some mental retardation, its degree varies enormously.

As the purpose of genetic screening is to obtain information in order to render subsequent choices and actions fully informed and voluntary, the information obtained must be relevant to some choices and actions; that is, it must be capable of being acted upon. Either new options are made possible or the reasons for previously available ones are altered. Consequently, if one is testing for the presence of a disease or defect, an important consideration is its treatability. "Treatability" here must cover a wide range of measures from eyeglasses for myopia to complicated surgery for spina bifida. Also, one must consider the possible harm in treating a person who does not have the disease. For example, many states quickly adopted mandatory screening for PKU. However, the special diets which are beneficial to those with the disease are harmful to those who do not have it. As the test was not highly reliable and had a high rate of false positives, many normal children were placed on restrictive diets with the possible result of reduced mental development and other harms.[15] If an abnormality is not treatable—for example, Huntington's chorea—then it is questionable whether there is any basis for screening. At most, the benefits can only be those of knowing that one does or does not have a defect or disease. The knowledge may avoid the harm of unexpected onset of the disease; however, it only removes the unexpectedness, and it adds the anxiety of waiting for the onset. Yet, advance warning may enable one to make plans and preparations—for example, to save money to pay for the later care and do things which one might otherwise have postponed. Nonetheless, in the absence of any treatment, the paternalist reason for screening for a disease is much weaker. Since the chief point of carrier screening is to provide information relevant to reproductive decisions, there is no paternalist reason for screening persons too young to reproduce[16] unless other medical problems may accompany carrier status.

In the future, one of the major uses of genetic screening will

---

[15] A. M. Capron, in *The New Genetics and the Future of Man,* M. P. Hamilton, ed., Grand Rapids, Mich., Eerdmans, 1972, p. 144.

[16] Reilly, *op. cit.,* pp. 70–72.

probably be to determine genetic combinations making people more susceptible to certain diseases such as lung cancer from smoking cigarettes.[17] In such cases, even if the genetic condition is itself untreatable, knowledge of it makes possible informed choices between alternative life styles which are more or less risky to health. It would be unduly stretching the concept of treatability to cover this type of situation. However, such screening clearly fulfills the condition of providing relevant information for fully informed and voluntary choices and actions.

One of the major harms to be avoided by genetic screening for adult carriers is the birth of children with defects or diseases. However, paternalist considerations apply only when the harm avoided would occur to the screenee. Consequently, paternalist considerations do not directly take into account the suffering of children with defects whose births could have been avoided. They apply only to avoidable harm to the screened parents, such as the mental anguish and economic costs of having a child with a severe defect. In order to avoid such harm, prospective parents must take steps to see that any children they have are free of the defect. With different diseases, different actions are possible. For example, a person at risk of having a child with Tay Sachs disease may have a test for the disease by amniocentesis during each pregnancy and abort any fetus with it. However, a person at risk of having a child with a disease for which prenatal diagnosis is unavailable can avoid having an affected child only by not procreating with another carrier.

Screening adults for carrier status raises two major issues. First, it is unclear whether the knowledge that one is a carrier is a harm or benefit (factor enabling one to avoid the harm of a defective child). Such knowledge may produce anxiety about reproducing with another carrier and having a child with the disease or defect, which would appear to be a psychological harm. While one may avoid having a defective child by not reproducing with another carrier, the anxiety still exists. Moreover, one may contend that the knowledge is a harm, because it restricts freedom of marriage and reproduction. Available partners are limited to noncarriers.

This last contention is misleading. Freedom is the absence of limits to actions. One is actually free if there are no limits preventing one from doing what one wants to do. One is dispositionally free if there are no limits preventing one from doing something if one wants to.[18] Lack of desire cannot be a limit to one's freedom of either sort. Obviously, lack

[17]B. Childs, *J. Pediatrics* 87, 1125, 1975.
[18]J. Feinberg, *Social Philosophy,* Englewood Cliffs, New Jersey, Prentice-Hall, 1973, pp. 5–6.

of desire cannot be a limit to actual freedom, for this concept applies only when a person desires to do something. Nor can lack of desire be a limit to dispositional freedom. One is dispositionally free to do something provided there are no limits preventing one's doing it *if one wants to.* Thus, one may be free to do it even if one does not want to. Limits must, therefore, exist independent of one's desire to perform an action. Moreover, the absence of information can be a limit to freedom; it may prevent one from doing what one wants, such as avoid having a defective child.

Consequently, the knowledge that one is a carrier of a defective gene does not limit one's freedom. One's options as to reproductive partners are restricted only by one's desire to avoid defective offspring. The information that one is a carrier enables one to choose between partners with whom there is or is not a chance of defective children. One's available options are thus increased rather than decreased. Hence, screening for carrier status provides benefits to both those who are determined to be or not to be carriers. They remove any anxiety the latter may have and provide an opportunity for the former to avoid a cause for anxiety.

One final issue may be considered. For the knowledge gained from genetic screening to be of value in avoiding harm, one must be able to act upon it. The issue arises as to whether paternalism requires that screenees would or only could act upon the information gained. Must the harm be that which the screenee would avoid or only that which the screenee could avoid? Concretely, to use paternalist reasons to support screening adults for the sickle cell trait, is it enough that they could make reproductive decisions to avoid having children with the disease or trait, or need one be assured that they will so make their reproductive decisions? If the latter is required and one has reason to believe many people will not act upon the information gained, paternalism will not support mandatory screening.

The requirement that people act upon the information gained has been a component of some programs screening by amniocentesis. Physicians claimed that the risks of the procedure were not justified unless the patient were prepared to abort a fetus which had a disease. Unless the patient would act upon the information, the harm of a defective child would not be avoided and the patient would have been put at risk for no possible benefit.

At this point, it becomes crucial how one characterizes the benefit of genetic screening. If one characterizes it as the avoidance of the anxiety and burdens of having a child with a defect, then the screening itself does not produce the benefit. Hence, to justify mandatory screening on paternalist grounds, one must also require any appropriate further conduct to avoid harm. Since requiring such further conduct limits people's freedom of fully informed and voluntary choices and actions, the unacceptable strong paternalist principles would have to be used.

If one characterizes the benefit as avoiding not fully informed and voluntary decisions, then the screening itself produces it and weak paternalist principles support mandatory screening. However, the weak paternalist principles do require that the information be relevant to choices and actions. Thus, if a couple would not consider the risk of defect relevant to whether or not to procreate, the weak paternalist principles do not support mandatory screening. If they would seriously consider not procreating with one another, then, even though they may eventually decide to have a child, weak paternalist principles support mandatory screening. Similarly, in amniocentesis, if a woman would not have an abortion unless her life was threatened, then the weak paternalist principles do not support the screening. But if she would seriously consider aborting a defective fetus, then whether or not she would ultimately do so the weak paternalist principles support mandatory screening. In short, the weak paternalist principles do not support requiring that patients actually choose to avoid reproduction (at risk) of defective children, but they only apply when people would seriously consider so doing. In order to require that people actually choose to avoid having defective children, some other principles must be employed, such as limiting conduct to avoid bringing into existence persons who would be less happy than others who might have been brought into existence.[19]

One can perhaps see the rationale of the weak paternalist principles by comparing their application to that of the harm principle. The private harm principle supports limiting the conduct of persons which might harm other individual persons without their fully informed and voluntary acceptance of the risk.[20] A person who smokes cigarettes while unaware of the risk of cancer does not make a fully informed and voluntary choice to do so. Hence, cigarette manufacturers injure them. However, if manufacturers are required to place warnings on cigarette packages, then smokers may be presumed to be aware of the risks of cancer and their acceptance is fully informed and voluntary.[21] Although

---

[19]Bayles, 1976, *op. cit.,* pp. 300–302.

[20]Bayles, 1978, *op. cit.,* pp. 104–110.

[21]This example is further explained by M. D. Bayles in *The Limits of Law: Nomos XV,* J. R. Pennock and J. W. Chapman, eds., New York, Lieber-Atherton, 1972, pp. 176–177. J. S. Mill (*On Liberty.* C. V. Shields, ed., Indianapolis, Bobbs-Merrill, 1956, p. 117), for example, maintains that it is justifiable to prevent persons from crossing

it differs with respect to whom is coerced, the informational aspect of genetic screening is analogous to requiring the warnings on cigarette packages. People are required to undergo screening so that their decisions are fully informed. If persons who have been screened and found to be highly susceptible to lung cancer from cigarette smoking continue to smoke, then acceptance of the risk is fully informed and voluntary. Similarly, if, aware of the risk of a defective child, a couple still chooses to reproduce, then as far as the weak paternalist principles are concerned, a defective child is not a harm *to them* which they may be compelled to avoid.

In conclusion, weak paternalist principles may support mandatory genetic screening provided the screening of adults is viewed as providing information necessary for making fully informed and voluntary decisions or the screenees are children and treatment for a defect may be initiated at the time of screening. While the weak paternalist principles do not support generally requiring adults to act on the basis of the information so gained, they do require that there be a possibility of acting to avoid harms, that screenees consider the information relevant to their decisions, and that the harms which may be avoided be worse than those inflicted by the screening procedures. Whether or not these principles support screening for particular defects depends, among other things, upon the current status of knowledge about the diseases and defects, their severity, the availability of treatment, and the reliability of the tests. Each specific disease or defect must be examined to determine whether the weak paternalist principles support mandatory screening and the type of program indicated. Finally, one must remember that paternalist reasons for screening are only one of several different kinds of considerations. Their failing to support screening is not conclusive of its unjustifiability. Similarly, while their supporting screening is not conclusive of its justifiability, they may justify it or combine with other good reasons (such as the public good) to do so when none of the reasons alone would suffice.

---

an unsafe bridge and warn them of the risk. If they then choose to risk crossing it, they ought not be prevented from doing so.

4

The Ethics of Human Experimentation: The Information Condition[1]

Louis I. Katzner

Department of Philosophy, Bowling Green State University, Bowling Green, Ohio

To discuss thoroughly the issue of the ethics of human experimentation is a complex task indeed. This is because a complete account of when such experimentation is and is not justified must deal with a very wide range of issues. For one thing, it must consider the question of experimental design. Will the experiment actually accomplish what it is designed to do? Has it been designed to minimize the potential risks to the subjects? Will the experiment further knowledge or merely replicate something that has already been done? These are all empirical questions which can best be answered by those who are most familiar with experimental techniques and results. But, there are normative questions as well: Are the potential benefits of the experiment worth the financial cost? Are they worth the risks to the participants? And so on.

A second set of issues that must be addressed are those surrounding the nature of the experiment. Are there some experiments that

---

[1]My special thanks to Tom Beauchamp for his helpful comments on an earlier draft of this essay.

should not be done: such as those involving DNA, the creation of life *in vitro,* the dissection of living beings, and so on? In other words, are there certain things that it is inappropriate for human beings to do (to each other) or develop the ability to do? To address this range of issues, one must determine whether or not there are any limitations upon what may legitimately be done by and to human beings.

Finally, there are the issues which surround the notion of informed consent. These require an explanation of what it means to consent in an informed way. They also require an explanation of what counts for (or replaces) informed consent for those human beings (for example, children, the mentally retarded, and so on) who are incapable of giving such consent. And finally, they require an answer to the question, Is informed consent morally necessary in all or only some cases?

Most problematic are those cases in which there is no discomfort or risk created by the experiment for the subject. For example, can my medical records be used in an experiment without my consent? Or, can my appendix, removed because of the threat it poses to my life, be used for experimental purposes?

A complete theory of the ethics of human experimentation must treat all of these issues. It must provide guidelines for the adequacy of experimental design, indicate the limits (if any) upon the kinds of experiments that may be done, and present an account of informed consent. To accomplish all of this is a formidable task indeed, requiring far more time and space than that allotted here. We shall thus focus upon only one aspect of the problem of the ethics of human experimentation: informed consent.

All discussions of the justification of experimentation on human beings center upon this notion. However, in a society in which the social good is the only concern, this would not be so. In such a society, the only question would be: Is the potential good to society worth the social cost? But, in a society such as ours, in which individual autonomy is also an important concern, the central question becomes: Will an experiment violate the rights of the individuals who participate in it? And, the requirement that the participants must consent to an experiment in an informed way is viewed as insuring that individual rights are protected.

Thus, there is general agreement that informed consent is a necessary condition of legitimate therapeutic and nontherapeutic human experimentation. But what constitutes informed consent? It is not enough that the individual agree to the experiment, for there are all sorts of ways to extract agreement illegitimately. The consent must be legitimate—that is, it must be voluntary. Moreover, voluntariness requires that an act (choice) be informed (a person who acts upon misinformation is not acting in a fully voluntary manner) and not "loaded" or biased ("Your money or your life" is not a fully voluntary choice).

Accordingly, analyses of the concept of informed consent are divided into two parts: they first seek to identify the conditions which must be met in order for consent to be informed, and then turn their attention to identifying the other conditions of genuine (uncoerced) consent. Moreover, without exception, these discussions gloss over the information condition while treating the other conditions of consent with considerable rigor. This is something I shall not do. Instead, I shall focus entirely upon the information condition, leaving the other conditions of consent for discussion at another time. My goal is to present a rigorous analysis of the information condition which will *(1)* clarify what is involved in the idea of "being informed" and *(2)* show that the information condition of voluntariness is far more complicated and problematic than is generally acknowledged.

The discussion will be limited in two other ways as well. First, I shall be concerned primarily with those individuals capable of giving consent. The perplexing issue of how to deal with those deemed incapable of giving informed consent is interesting and important, but its consideration would take me too far afield from my central task. Secondly, I shall focus upon those experiments which pose a significant risk and discomfort to the participants. This is because the clearest set of cases are those in which there is risk and discomfort. Where there is neither—for example, using someone's medical history in an experiment—what is at stake in the issue of human experimentation becomes much more elusive and problematic.

The accounts that have been given of the information condition cover a very broad spectrum. At one end lies the view that this condition requires *full information.* Those who interpret this literally in effect present a *reductio ad absurdum* argument against human experimentation. That argument is: Legitimate human experimentation requires complete information. It is impossible for the patient/participant (hereinafter simply referred to as the subject) to be told everything that is going to be done and all of the possible effects of these things. Therefore, human experimentation is never justified. At the other extreme lie those who insist that all subjects need to be told is what the physician/experimenter (hereinafter simply referred to as the investigator) thinks he or she wants to know. In other words, investigators' only responsibility is to tell their subjects as much as their questions indicate they want to know. This view obviously raises the spectre of subject manipulation by the investigator.

Neither of these analyses of what counts as "being informed" is adequate. On one hand, the requirement of full information seems to be much too strong. Indeed, I cannot think of a single context in which this is what "being informed" means. Lawyers do not fail to inform their clients because they do not tell them everything that will be said, and every move that will be made, in their behalf; the general outline and salient features are sufficient. Similarly, suspected criminals, when being read their rights, do not have to be told how what they say may be used against them, nor what specific things would be usable against them. They simply have to be told that whatever they say may be used against them.

The same is true, it seems to me, with regard to experimentation. The subjects need not be told everything, but do have to be told the *important things*. Of course, there is much room for disagreement as to what information is important and what is not. But, the point to see is that this is where the issue lies. The question is *not*, Have the subjects been told everything? Rather the question is, Have the subjects been told the *important* things?

On the other hand, the suggestion that all the subjects should be told is what the investigator believes they want to know is much too weak. The problem is not merely that leaving it up to the investigator to determine what the subjects should be told leaves the latter entirely at the mercy of the former, and hence opens the door to a wide range of abuses of the subjects' rights. The problem is also that there may well be some things which subjects give no indication of wanting to know that they should be informed of before participating in an experiment. If they choose to ignore these things once they have been informed of them—that is, should they choose not to take them into account in reaching their decisions—that may be up to them. But, there are some things—the important things—which subjects should be told whether they request such information or not.

This requirement obviously precludes experiments in which individuals cannot even be told that they are being used as the subjects of an experiment. It also precludes lying or withholding information out of fear that individuals will refuse to participate in an experiment. But, what about those situations in which, because of the nature and design of the experiment, individuals can be told no more than that they will be the subject of an experiment? In such cases, as long as the individuals are informed of the kinds of things that are done in the name of experimentation and the kinds of risks that are involved in such things, I see no reason why they must be informed of any of the specifics of the experiment in which they are being asked to participate. If they agree to cooperate on the basis of this very limited information, that is their decision. And, if they later regret that decision, the one thing they should not claim is that they were not informed. Of course, there is a sense in which this is true. But, in the relevant sense, they were informed. They were told that they would be the subject of an experiment and that they could not be told anything about the nature of it. People who agree to participate under such conditions may be fools, but I see no reason to say they were not adequately informed.

The same would seem to be true of individuals who say the following to the investigator: "I am placing myself entirely in your hands. I do not want to be told anything about what you are going to do to me. I know that if you tell me I will lose my nerve and back out, and I do not want to do this. So go ahead and use your judgment." However foolish we may judge such a statement to be, such people cannot legitimately complain that the investigator failed to inform them of what was involved in the experiment. This is because their lack of information results from an explicit request on their part not to be told what is going to be done.

These two limiting cases suggest that the information condition is merely a presumptive requirement of legitimate experimentation. Although standard operating procedure should be for investigators to inform their subjects of the important things about the experiment, such information is not a necessary condition of legitimate human experimentation. Subjects may waive this requirement either on their own initiative or in response to a request dictated by the experimental design. But, there is a presumption that the important information will be given. And this must be done unless the information condition is *explicitly* waived by the subject (assuming the individual can make this decision in a rational way—see the discussion of rationality which follows).

Notice how well this interpretation of the information condition conforms to our usage in other contexts. Imagine a swimmer who wants to compete in the Olympics. Knowing it will be a long and arduous grind, the swimmer says the following: "Coach, I know there will be times in my training when I will want to quit. But when I reach those points, please don't let me. Make me stay in the water and work, even if you must lie to me or use physical force!"

What would we say at that critical moment when the only way the coach can carry out the swimmer's wishes is by lying or using physical force? Has the swimmer consented to this action or not? The answer seems to be both yes and no. Consent has been given, even though it is not being given at that particular moment. Moreover, it would seem that the consent given at the outset is the controlling notion here, for it was in anticipation of precisely this kind of situation that the consent to use deceit or coercion was given.

The point is not that it is never possible to withdraw one's consent to harsh and deceitful training methods or to being the subject in an experiment. It is rather that depending upon the purpose of the consent, there seem to be situations in which attempts to withdraw it should not be binding. And these are precisely those situations which were the reason for the consent to be given in the form it was in the first place.

In other words, in our cool, reflective, rational moments, we may recognize that in the heat of a moment we may want to do things which would frustrate our considered goals. In such cases, it is perfectly reasonable to voluntarily give other people the right to force us to follow our coolly chosen path. And, although there must be some provision for withdrawing this right when our goals really change, such change must be the result of a cool, reflective decision rather than a heated impulse.

Given, then, that there is a presumption that potential subjects be told the important things about the experiments they are being solicited for, what are the important things? I suggest they are the following: *(1)* the general features of what is going to be done, *(2)* the kind and extent of discomfort that may accompany it, *(3)* the potential benefit, *(4)* the chances for success, *(5)* any risk to life and overall health, and *(6)* any uncertainty on the part of the investigator concerning *(1)–(5)*. Notice that these criteria are stated in general terms and have been left somewhat vague. The subject should be told "the general features of what is going to be done" rather than every detail; "the kind and extent of discomfort," not necessarily the particulars; and "any uncertainty on the part of the investigator concerning *(1)–(5)*," but not the degree of uncertainty of each specific aspect of each of these items.

Despite the fact that it leaves room for abuse by overzealous investigators, this vagueness is both intentional and necessary. To require "complete disclosure"—that is, to require the investigator to tell all, even just about the important things—would in effect prohibit experimentation on human beings by making *informed* consent impossible. It would simply take too long for investigators to explain every little nuance and possibility. Moreover, the longer the investigator's narrative, the greater the chance that its real meaning would be lost on the potential subject. The average person simply could not sift through the voluminous information and focus in on the elements that should be in the forefront in making the decision. There is no choice but to have the investigator sift through the information with an eye to bringing into focus for the potential subject the important elements.

This analysis of the important things about an experiment is clearly what I shall call "rationalistic"—it is based upon the things a cool, reflective, rational person would be expected to take into account in deciding whether or not to participate in an experiment. As such, it differs from another more "realistic" account—namely that the important things are those an individual is likely to take into account in reaching a decision. These may include all or some of the "rationalistic" features outlined above. But, they may also include such things as the individual's feelings towards the investigator (Does the subject like the investigator? Does he or she want to please the investigator?) and feelings toward himself or herself (Is the subject looking for an escape from marital problems? Is the subject feeling guilty about his or her parents' death?).

In order to illustrate the difference between these two interpretations of the "important things," let me sketch a hypothetical case which in some ways resembles the well-known Jewish Chronic Disease Hospital case.[2] Suppose an investigator wants to determine the consequences of injecting live cancer cells into human beings. The concern may either be therapeutic—for example, to see if such injections would bring about cancer remission in the subjects—or nontherapeutic—for example, to test the body's ability to reject such cells. In either case, the potential subjects who are approached may either agree or decline to participate on rational grounds. In the therapeutic situation, this would involve basing the decision upon an assessment of the potential benefit to oneself (and others) versus the risks and discomfort to oneself. In the nontherapeutic situation, it would involve basing the decision upon an assessment of the potential benefit to others versus the risks and discomfort to oneself. But, the potential subjects may also reach their decision in nonrational ways. Refusal to participate may result from fear of the term "cancer," while agreement to participate may come from a compulsion to please the investigator. And, this might occur in spite of the fact that the important things about the experiment have already been stated. In other words, a deep seated fear or compulsion may be the determining factor in one's decision even though the investigator has supplied all of the information a rational person would take into account in reaching a decision.

If we are concerned with having potential subjects decide as rational persons would, the investigator would have to present the information to these persons in a way which is designed to circumvent their

[2]See Jay Katz, *Experimentation With Human Beings,* New York, Russell Sage Foundation, 1972, pp. 7–66.

fears or compulsions (for instance, either by not telling them that they will be injected with *live cancer cells* or by making it unclear which course of action—agreeing or declining to participate—would please him or her). If, on the other hand, we are concerned with informing the potential subjects of anything which might affect their decisions, then the investigator must tell them that the injection contains live cancer cells or what decision—agreeing or declining to participate— would please him or her.

The fact that both therapeutic and nontherapeutic experiments can be either participated in or not for rational or nonrational reasons produces eight permutations:

(1) A therapeutic experiment agreed to on rational grounds;

(2) A therapeutic experiment agreed to on nonrational grounds;

(3) A therapeutic experiment rejected on rational grounds;

(4) A therapeutic experiment rejected on nonrational grounds;

(5) A nontherapeutic experiment agreed to on rational grounds;

(6) A nontherapeutic experiment agreed to on nonrational grounds;

(7) A nontherapeutic experiment rejected on rational grounds;

(8) A nontherapeutic experiment rejected on nonrational grounds.

Spelling out the different possibilities in this way clearly indicates that the information condition involves more than the mere capacity to understand the experimental procedure and the potential risks and benefits associated with it. The reason for requiring that potential subjects be informed of the important things is so they will base their decisions upon this information. And, doing this involves assessing the potential benefits and risks in terms of one's values. In other words, the information condition presupposes a certain kind of decision-making capacity as well as the more obvious intellectual capacity necessary for understanding the information.

Spelling out the permutations in this way also puts us in a position to consider the problems created by the information condition in a systematic way. First the therapeutic situation.

Whenever an ill person would decide to undergo experimental therapy on rational grounds *(1),* the physician is surely obligated to explain the important things prior to soliciting consent. But, what if the patient would not make a decision in this way? What if the person would refuse the treatment on nonrational grounds *(4)?* Is it permissible (or perhaps obligatory) for the physician to present the information in a way which would hide the nonrational factors which would determine the patient's decision (for example, not say that the injections contain live cancer cells)?

The answer to this question is not obvious. It depends upon one's views about the appropriateness of intervention in an individual's decision-making process. If one believes that such intervention is never warranted, then the physician should present the important information without regard to the role this information will play in the individual's decision. If, on the other hand, one believes that intervention is justified when it is necessary to insure that an individual will make a decision in a rational way, then it would be appropriate for the physician to present the information in a "doctored" way. Without resolving this issue, the least that can be said is that a case can be made for the physician presenting information in a way that will circumvent irrational fears and result in what is best for the patient—that is, undergoing the treatment. If it really is the best thing to do, then perhaps the information given should be "doctored" in such a way that this will not be obscured because of some hangup the patient has.

At the same time, however, the realization that there are rational grounds for *refusing* to undergo experimental therapy *(3)* must give one pause. We must not assume that a patient is not rational just because that individual does not want to undergo the experimental therapy his or her physician recommends. It may simply be a matter of the patient and the physician weighing the potential risks and benefits of such treatment in different but equally reasonable ways. In such a case, it would surely be wrong for the patient to be fed "doctored" information which would result in the decision the physician thinks is the correct one, but the patient thinks is the wrong one (for example, it would be wrong for the physician to play down the risks and play up the benefits of the therapy).

The realization that a patient can *agree* to experimental treatment nonrationally *(2)* should also give us reason for pause. We normally overlook this possibility because we tend to assume that therapy is good, and, hence, we only examine a person's thinking when a decision is made which rejects this good. As we have seen, however, experimental therapy is not an unqualified good. Indeed, there are cases in which it simply may not be worth the price. This means that when a person agrees to undergo experimental treatment nonrationally, that person might very well be doing something which, if intervention is justified, we should prevent him or her from doing. Moreover, it is not at all clear how this could be determined. Reasonable people may well disagree in the weight they assign to potential risks and benefits. It would seem that the goal should be to assess the experimental therapy in terms of the patient's view of how risks and benefits should be weighed, yet the problems of doing this are both legion and obvious. For our purposes, it is sufficient to point out that when it comes to therapeutic experiments, a case can be made for presenting "doctored" information to patients who would make the decision whether or not to undergo experimental treatment nonrationally. And, this is just as true for those who would decide to undergo the treatment as it is for those who would reject it.

When it comes to nontherapeutic experiments, on the other hand, the situation is even more complicated. That a person may either agree or refuse to participate in a nontherapeutic experiment on rational grounds (5 and 7) should not surprise anyone. And, people who would make the decision on rational grounds should certainly be given the information a rational person would use in making this decision—that is, they should be informed of *(1)* the general features of what is going to be done, *(2)* the kind and extent of discomfort that may accompany it, *(3)* the potential benefit, *(4)* the chances for success, *(5)* any risk to life and overall health, and *(6)* any uncertainty on the part of the experimenter concerning *(1)–(5)*.

But what about the person who would decide not to participate in an experiment on nonrational grounds *(8)?* Notice that if we allow the "doctoring" of the information that is given for the purpose of filtering out those elements which might lead to a decision being made on nonrational grounds, the justification for doing this must be that we want to encourage the subject to act in the socially useful way (as opposed to the way which is best for that individual). In other words, in this case, "doctored" information would be presented not for the subject's own good, but for the good of society (or others).

We saw in the case of therapeutic experiments that the "doctoring" of information on the grounds that it is for the patient's own good can be justified. It should be clear that it is much harder to justify similar action for the good of society. This is not to deny that there may be situations in which the well-being of others takes precedence over the well-being of oneself. But, these would all be situations in which participation in experiments is obligatory, not merely desirable. And, if it is obligatory, then if the information condition is operative at all, it is not as a presumptive condition of consent (since consent is no longer an issue), but rather as something that we owe to people once we conscript them as subjects for experiments.

But, as long as being the subject in a (nontherapeutic) experiment is an act of charity rather than an obligation, intervention in the subject's decision-making process to insure that he or she will decide to participate in an experiment when it is the rational thing to do is an unwarranted intrusion. If the decision is made on rational grounds, fine. But, if it is made nonrationally, sobeit. The mere fact that a person is acting nonrationally surely does not justify interferring with that individual's behavior.

On the other hand, the case of a person *agreeing* to participate in an experiment on nonrational grounds *(6)* is somewhat more problematic. To say that such a person should be told those things a rational person would consider in reaching the decision is to allow that person to put him or herself at risk nonrationally (for example, the decision will be determined by a compulsion rather than the individual's values informed by the facts). This is not to deny that there may be perfectly rational grounds for participating in the experiment. But these are not this subject's grounds. Under such circumstances, is the investigator either warranted or under an obligation to "doctor" the information given to the potential subject to eliminate, as far as possible, the nonrational elements from his or her decisions?

The most obvious variable operative here seems to be the element of risk. People put themselves at risk every day of their lives, yet we do not insist that they have rational grounds for doing this. On the other hand, a case can be made for intervening to protect people from risk, and the greater the risk involved, the easier it would be to make this case. The least that can be said is that there is a real problem here, and that it is one that is often overlooked. Because the goal of investigators is to have people participate in their experiments, there is a real incentive for them to examine why individuals refuse to participate. But there is no similar incentive for them to examine why subjects agree to participate. Once agreement is secured, it is time to get on with the experiment!

It follows that in order to operationalize the idea of informed consent in a way that does justice to the information condition, *(1)* it must be possible to determine whether or not an individual will make a decision about participating in an experiment on rational grounds; *(2)* if he or she will, it must be possible to provide information about the experiment in a way which excludes the values of those conducting the experiment, thereby resulting in a decision informed by the important information and the subject's values; and (3) if the individual will not make the decision in a rational way, there are at least some cases in which it must be possible to identify the nonrational elements which will determine the decision and then "doctor" the information provided to eliminate these factors from the decision. This is a formidable task indeed. And, one should be under no illusion about the difficulties involved in determining these things.

To begin with, it is not enough to determine that someone is the kind of person who normally makes decisions in a rational way; rather it is *this particular kind of decision* that must be made in a rational way. This presupposes not only that we have a sufficiently precise way of distinguishing rational from nonrational grounds, but also, because seemingly few decisions are made on *purely* rational grounds, that we come to some conclusion concerning how much in the way of nonrational factors can be involved in a rational decision. It also presupposes that we have a test which indicates which individuals satisfy these criteria and which do not.

It is equally difficult to insure that the information upon which an individual bases a decision is value neutral. And this is true both conceptually and procedurally. Conceptually, we must find a way of formulating the benefits and risks of an experiment which does not have built into it the investigator's values concerning the desirability of risk, the good of the subject, or the good of society. Procedurally, we must find a way of guaranteeing that the information will be presented in this way. The biggest obstacle to this is the fact that investigators not only have their own views concerning the value of such things, they also have a vested interest in the potential subject's participation. Perhaps the only way to protect the potential subject against this is to require that the information about the experiment be given by someone other than the investigator, or at least that a third and neutral party be present when this information is presented by the investigator to insure the minimizing of the role the investigator's values and interests play in the presentation.

Finally, and most difficult of all, is the need to identify the nonrational factors which will determine some subjects' decisions, and "doctor" the information they are given to eliminate these factors from their decisions. The problem is not merely that the number of nonrational factors that may determine someone's decision is open-ended. Nor is it merely that all we may do in eliminating some nonrational factors is open the door to others. The problem is also that allowing "doctoring" of information obviously opens the door to a whole range of abuses. Moreover, it presupposes that we can tell what individuals should be told, and how they should be told it, in order for them to make the decision whether or not to participate in a rational way.

The situation is indeed this complicated! But there is an important asymmetry in the consequences of this complexity for therapeutic and nontherapeutic experimentation respectively. In cases of therapeutic experimentation, the individual involved is already at risk. The person's life or health is threatened, and we are searching for ways to meet that threat. It may be best to do nothing. Or, it may be preferable to run the risks involved in experimental treatment in an attempt to effect a cure. As we have seen, this assessment depends upon each individual's attitude toward risk and the kind of life he or she values. The important point is that in the therapeutic situation, we are faced with a forced option because the patient is at risk no matter what is done. And, because the option is forced, it would be capricious to insist that all experimental treatment be stopped until the issues are resolved. Acting wisely in the face of the uncertainties and complexities we have catalogued is a herculean task, yet it is something which of necessity physicians and their patients must do on a regular basis.

The nontherapeutic situation is different. The potential subjects are not at risk or, if they are, the experiment will not reduce that risk. They are being asked to put themselves at risk (or greater risk) for the betterment of others. In such a situation, a more conservative attitude is in order. Stopping all high-risk human experimentation which requires informed consent would seem preferable to violating individual rights by putting people at risk illegitimately; hence, there is a presumption against nontherapeutic experimentation. The burden of proof is upon those who favor such experimentation to show that their subjects are being recruited in an acceptable way. And, if it is not clear that this is so, either because we are not sure what the acceptable way is, or because we know what it is, but are not able to tell if it is being followed, such experimentation should be suspended until it can be made clear.

In light of this, one might conclude that we should simply prohibit all high-risk nontherapeutic experiments which require informed consent. But this would preclude even those high-risk nontherapeutic experiments in which the subject clearly satisfies the information condition. It would also preclude our reaping the benefits which come from such experiments.

Fortunately, this conclusion is needlessly strong. Although the limits of legitimate intervention are unclear, what is clear is that a person who is acting rationally, is not harming others, and is doing something that is socially useful should not be interferred with. It is also clear that the epistemological problems which are unsolved are those which arise when we try to determine how we must "doctor" the information we give to those persons who would make a decision on nonrational grounds so that they will make it rationally. Thus, if we limit the pool of potential subjects for nontherapeutic experiments to those who will make the decision to participate on rational grounds, neither the unclear limits of justified intervention nor the unsolved epistemological issues are a problem.

In other words, we should require that all potential subjects for nontherapeutic experiments take a test (administered by an independent testing agency) to determine *(1)* their capacity for understanding the kind of information they will be given by the investigators and *(2)* their ability and propensity to base decisions (especially the decision to be the subject of an experiment) upon the assessment of the information at their disposal informed by their values. This would eliminate from the pool of potential subjects both those who cannot understand the information they are given about the experiment and those who, although they can understand it, are unlikely to base their decision upon it. In other words, it would eliminate from contention those who, if they are going to make the decision rationally, would have to be given "doctored" information. And, it is in precisely these cases that the problem of intervention and the epistemological issues we have raised are crucial.

I am under no illusion about the difficulties involved in constructing this kind of test (the first part would be hard enough to develop, the second even harder). But the intentional putting of people at risk must be done with the greatest of care (people do a fine job of putting themselves at risk when left to their own devices, but this does not justify others doing it at will). When individuals choose to put themselves at risk in a rational way, that should be their right. But when they choose in a way which, in order to be rational, requires that they be given "doctored" information, that is something else. To allow that they be given such information opens the door to their manipulation by the investigator. It also presupposes answers to both epistemological and normative issues which are not resolved.

Thus, in addition to developing guidelines (such as those developed in the earlier part of this paper) which define what things potential subjects must be told about the experiments they are being solicited for, there is also the need for a way of determining that an individual is capable of understanding this information and basing his or her decision on it. And, if such a test can be developed, and administered by an independent testing agency, there is no need to suspend high-risk human experimentation which requires consent until such a time as the other issues are worked out.

5

Medical Experimentation on Prisoners

Carl Cohen

Department of Philosophy, Residential College,
University of Michigan, Ann Arbor, Michigan

I. PROLOGUE

Ought we permit medical experimentation on prisoners? The issue is both practically important and morally complex. Some argue as follows: No human subject may be used in a medical experiment without that person's informed and freely given consent. But prisoners, by virtue of their total custody, cannot give free and uncoerced consent. Hence prisoners—no matter how valuable experimentation with their cooperation may prove—must be excluded from all populations of subjects in medical experimentation.

This argument, when expanded and reinforced, is very persuasive, as I shall show. I aim also to show that its key premise is simply mistaken, and the argument unsound.

Government agencies (HEW, NIH, the National Commission for the Protection of Human Subjects) and human subject review committees all provide assorted rules and guidelines for prison experimentation. It is not my aim to report these. My question is this: *Should* we adopt the rule, now proposed by some, excluding all or almost all experimentation involving prison volunteers?[1]

Some clarifications first. The principle that informed consent must be got from every human subject in a medical experiment is well established. It was eloquently formulated in the Nuremberg Code, and by the World Health Organization in the Declaration of Helsinki. It grounds a set of detailed regulations governing the operation of all institutions for medical research in this country funded in whole or in part by any federal agency. It is the focus of concern for untold numbers of committees, medical practitioners and researchers, lawyers, and laymen who deal, day-to-day, with a heavy, valuable, and sometimes threatening stream of research protocols. But "informed consent" involves more than information. Better thought of as "full consent," what is demanded in fact entails three elements: information, competency, and voluntariness. Where the consent received is defective in any one of these respects, we will rightly think the subject to have been improperly used.

Problematic defects of information arise when experiments are proposed in which the subjects cannot be told the truth, or the whole truth, about the investigation of which they are part—because their knowing what the investigator is after will have the effect of his not getting it. Deception is not uncommon in behavioral research, but I bypass the problem here. Problematic defects of competency arise when

---

[1] The report and recommendations of the National Commission for the Protection of Human Subjects of Biomedical and Behavioral Research (*Research Involving Prisoners,* Washington, D. C., 1976) is an important example. The Commission recommends that "research involving prisoners should not be conducted or supported" unless a lengthy set of detailed conditions in the prison are fully realized. Voluntariness of consent is held to presuppose grievance procedures with elected prisoner representatives and prison advocates, and living conditions which, in turn, are specified to include such items as single-occupancy cells for all who desire them; arrangements for frequent, private visits; high standards for education, vocational training, health care, and recreation facilities, and so on. Since virtually no prisons are able to meet or approach the standards imposed, the recommendation (if adopted) would have the effect of forbidding almost all experimentation in prisons. It would appear that the Commission seeks to use permission to experiment in prisons as a social lever for what it views as needed prison reforms. Leaving aside the question of the necessity of the reforms demanded, it is unfortunate that the serious question of whether the consent of prisoners can be truly voluntary is there dealt with as an instrument to influence policy in other spheres rather than on its own merits. Regrettably, the Department of Health, Education and Welfare has acted favorably upon the Commission's report, sharply restricting research involving prisoners (where Federal support is given) on the mistaken conviction that it is generally not possible for a prisoner to give voluntary consent to participation as a subject in a medical experiment.

experiments call for subjects who are not (in fact or in law) competent to give their consent—infant children, the mentally disabled, the comatose, and so on. Some experiments with persons in these categories is essential, obviously, if care for them is to be improved; hence principles must be devised for determining who may give third-party consent ("proxy consent") for the incompetent, and under what restrictions it may be given. These issues of competency are sorely vexed, but here I bypass them also. Problematic defects of voluntariness arise when potential subjects, although fully informed and competent, are coerced into giving their consent by threat or excessive inducement, or other inappropriate manipulation. This is the more likely where the potential subjects are more vulnerable, more precariously placed. Among these precariously placed potential subjects, prisoners are critical because, on the one hand, their incarceration renders them specially vulnerable, while on the other hand that same incarceration renders them peculiarly well suited for some very valuable long-term experiments. Some resolution of this matter is essential.

II. CAN A PRISONER GIVE VOLUNTARY CONSENT?

Voluntariness, the third element of full consent, is most difficult to specify. We insist that a subject's consent be freely given and uncoerced. What does that entail? Clear cases of "volunteers" who did not give their consent freely are not hard to recall or imagine. The archetype—which reality often approximates—is the army platoon, lined up before the first sergeant who asks sternly for volunteers, and orders those who do not volunteer to take two steps forward. At the other extreme, cases of honest volunteering, genuinely autonomous, are legion. But very many cases fall between the extremes, and that of the prison volunteer is one of these.

It may well seem that, by virtue of the complete custody of their persons, prisoners lack the capacity to act with the kind of uncoerced voluntariness required. If they do lack it, they ought not be subjects. So I want now to put, more carefully than I have found it put anywhere, what precisely it is about the prisoner's condition that might render him or her unfit to be a consenting subject in a medical experiment.

The argument goes like this: The prison environment, both in fact and in principle, is such that consent without coercion is not possible there. This is not because of any defect in prisoners; it flows from the deeply intrusive, literally totalitarian character of prisons. One may take this as a condemnation of prisons, or simply as an unpleasant but

unavoidable fact about them. Attitudes about prisons are not in contention here. Prisons being what they are, their inmates are in a state of
constant coercion, from which there is no escape within the walls. No
matter what the prisoners say, or we say to them, coercion is the essence
of their condition. In that condition no consent to put oneself at risk
should be accepted as full consent. Hence medical experimentation on
prisoners should be forbidden, flatly.

That is the general thrust. Now, more concretely and specifically,
see how this coercive spirit permeates the prison environment.

First. The body of the prisoner is simply not under his own control.
Orders committing persons to prison are very blunt about this, generally containing the phrase: "the body of the defendant shall be delivered" to the custodial institution appropriately identified. No system of
criminal punishment that relies upon prisons, however humane its
intent, can evade this fact. The U.S. solicitor general (in a brief filed
with the U.S. Supreme Court, in a 1974 case dealing with the transfer
of prisoners from one institution to another) puts the matter brutally
but truthfully.

> . . . The very fact of his conviction for a crime, and the legitimate
> placement of his person into the hands of a custodian who will be respon-
> sible for his safekeeping and the supervision of the most intimate details
> of his life removes from the prisoner any legitimate expectation that he
> will be able to control the conditions of his confinement.[2]

Second. Not only is the prisoner's person unfree, but the control
of that person, and the secure incarceration of his body, are his keepers'
chief and overriding concerns. Prisons are closed, tightly guarded
places. Anyone who has not visited a medium or maximum security
prison can hardly imagine the impact of omnipresent locks, bars, and
armed guards. Supervision of hour-by-hour conduct is close; inspection
is constant; privacy is nil; coercion is the flavor of every moment.

Third. Most prisoners are very poor, and have tightly limited
opportunity to earn the most puny wages. Some states pay no wages
for prison labor; most states pay less than one dollar per day; only six
states pay more than that. And even where wages are paid, not all
prisoners have the chance to earn them. From this poverty any decent
payment for service is partial rescue.

Fourth. Boredom, killing monotony, is that feature which, next to
control, most pervades prison life. The state tells every prisoner when

---

[2]Brief for the United States, as *Amicus Curiae,* Preiser v. Newkirk, O. T. 1974,
no. 74–107, p. 15.

to sleep, when to rise, when to eat and what, when to work and when to play, what to do and how to do it—all with maddening sameness. From this barrenness, any change is relief.

Fifth, and finally. The dominant concern in every prisoner's life is release and the eventual date of it. In this country prison sentences of indeterminate length are very common. That single most important date is therefore subject to the judgment, even to the whim, of administrators whom the prisoner can rarely reach or even address. His behavior in prison—in ways he cannot be sure of—must affect, perhaps determine, his date of release. Even for those with determinate sentences, that date remains indeterminate if there is, as usually, a parole board to be pleased. The felt need to please officials—doing what (at least in their own minds) prisoners think might please those who might be in a position to effect a somewhat earlier release—is an unavoidable pressure upon the behavior of prisoners.

It is in this environment that voluntariness of consent to subjection to medical experimentation must be assessed. However freely it appears that he consents, the prisoner is coerced so fully by his circumstances that even asking him must be unfair. His service as subject must be seen by him as a precious opportunity to escape, if only for short or infrequent periods, from the drabness and routine of prison life. He will see new faces, talk to interesting people who are neither inmates nor guards, leave his normal, grim surroundings on occasion for a setting that is lit by freedom and interest. And he is further coerced by the monetary rewards—dollars at a crack, even scores of dollars in a long experiment—promising opportunity for riches not possible otherwise. The risks run are overshadowed by the partial escape from state-imposed penury. Fifty dollars a month, say, for prison subjects in a malaria test—why, that is coercion turned green! And above all, what an opportunity to prove one's good will, one's eagerness to pay his debt to society, one's sincere intention to make up for past evils and be good! Surely they who have power in this sphere will note this evidence of good character. Surely it will not work against the prisoner when parole or release is being considered—and it may, it just *may* do some good. How can the rational prisoner not be coerced by such a concatenation of pressures? He cannot. It is not right (this argument concludes) even to ask the prisoner whether he wishes to put himself at risk when doing so is encouraged by his circumstances so strongly and so perniciously. No matter the circumspection and honest care of the investigator. If, as we have seen, full and uncoerced consent simply cannot be given by prisoners, the request for volunteers must not, in fairness, be made to them.

The argument has two addenda.

(1) Everything above applies to prison experiments even when delicately and justly supervised. But the de facto circumstances in real prisons are such as to make delicacy rare, and justice less than universal. There is enormous potential for abuse in prisons; there *is* a great deal of abuse in prisons. Knowing that, we cannot in good conscience undertake medical experiments that may, in fact, be tainted by that abuse in various ways, but above all in the selection of subjects.

(2.) Those who support medical experimentation in prisons quickly point to the great benefits they have yielded for mankind—experiments on polio virus strains, for example, which led directly to the selection of strains now used worldwide in the preparation of polio virus vaccine administered by mouth. Then there is the work on malaria, and dengue fever, and so on. All that is very fine—but if such experiments rely upon the wrongful use of human subjects, they simply should not be done. The critical issues here concern what is right, what is just—not the balancing of benefits. Until the justice of such experimenting on prisoners has been shown, the calculation of benefits simply cannot be reached.

III. A CLOSER LOOK AT COERCION

There is the case, and it is a strong one. But it is not strong enough. The argument is rightly cautionary. Its several considerations show, I submit, that medical experiments using prisoners as subjects must go forward, if at all, under rules more constraining, and supervision more strict, than such experimentation in more ordinary contexts. It has not been shown, I contend, that a prisoner cannot give full consent in the sense that being a voluntary subject requires full consent.

I begin by granting much of the factual description of the prison environment presented above—although that account was deliberately put in rather purple language. But it is so; prison life is controlled, barren, poor, monotonous. Coercion is the spirit of the prison. Regrettably, however, those who accept the argument above, or some variant of it, are led by their detestation of prisons to equivocate upon the word "coercion." When careful with it we find, reasonably enough, that there are respects in which prisoners are coerced and respects in which they are not—and, indeed, that the same is true of everyone. We need to identify carefully that sense of coercion employed when we say that coercion vitiates an apparently free consent. Then we must decide whether, when given an opportunity to volunteer as subject, the prisoner is coerced in that sense. We will find upon reflection, I think, that another sense of coercion—looser and more suggestive, characterizing the flavor of prison activity—has been drawn upon. To make the argument work a transition is made, perhaps inadvertently, from that broad sense of coercion to a tighter, narrower sense that bears directly upon freedom in making choices.

By "coercion" our common meaning is compulsion by physical or moral pressures. Thus A coerces B when B is compelled or constrained to act as A wishes him to, as a result of measures taken by A to effect just that result. The bandit coerces me, with his revolver, into handing over my wallet. The threat of criminal prosecution if I do not file an income tax return is a coercive instrument designed to constrain my behavior. We are tempted—and too many yield—to leap from this to calling coercive whatever restrains or limits or influences behavior. I may be coerced into giving to the United Fund, say, by the threat of discharge or defamation; but I am not coerced into charitable giving by my strong desire to be admired as a public benefactor. Again, if my wealth were unlimited I should sail the seas in splendor; my means being what they are, I cast an admiring glance at every ocean racing yacht, and go on splashing about in my little sailing dinghy. It is an elastic use of English to say I am coerced into doing so. There are, too, desires of the utmost intensity which influence my conduct and with which I must come to terms. But these desires are not imposed (unless one holds a satanic view of the human condition) in order to bend my volition; they are the normal matrix of my life. It is facile or confused to suppose that I am coerced by my own wants. Even my most passionate wants, my sexual desires, cannot be said to coerce me into seduction.

We sometimes think powerful inducements, as well as threats, to be coercive. Sometimes they may be, but only when the subject in question is caused, by an extraordinary and deliberate temptation, to do what should not ever be done. If a poor person is tempted by a huge sum to accept a risk we think it not proper to urge upon anyone, the offer is there coercive. But if the reward be for conduct that is itself reasonable, the fact that one's condition renders that reward exceptionally attractive does not show that coercion has been applied. Professional football players are not coerced by huge salaries into risking their necks, nor are workers coerced into work by their need for earnings.

A definitive account of coercion I do not seek to provide here. No doubt any account, however refined, will leave some rough edges. But moderately thoughtful reflection will show, I believe, that the coercion that full consent precludes is the coercion flowing from the deliberate effort on the part of one who offers the choice (or his agent) to pressure the offeree into a particular decision. The pressure must be such that the offerer could have refrained from exerting it, but deliberately did not refrain.

If I seek admission to a research hospital specializing, say, in eye disease, desperate about my failing sight, and I am admitted upon the condition that I put myself at serious risk in an experiment having nothing to do with my condition, I have indeed been coerced improperly. Even in matters involving minor risks, if I am subjected to a moral barrage regarding the social value of medical research and the importance of the experiment at hand to all mankind, when asked for my consent to serve as subject, I am coerced, if mildly, by the deliberate pressures of the investigator. We do not permit such distortions of potential subjects' volitions, rightly. But if I suffer from a serious disease for which cure is unknown, it is quite reasonable that I should find serving as subject, in an experiment aimed at enlarging knowledge about that disease, attractive in a way that one who does not suffer from that disease does not find attractive. My diseased condition does not coerce me. Or if one insists upon the lingo in which such sickness inevitably renders me "coerced," then certainly that so-called coercion could not begin to establish that my freely expressed consent was really involuntary.

Our lives are led, and our decisions made, within a network of needs and wants, some natural, some arising from the acts of others, some aggravated by the acts of the state. We are all bored, or threatened, or tantalized in differing degrees by a perilous world, some hostile people, and a not very sensitive government. Sometimes, within that framework, we are coerced by the design of persons or institutions into choosing X rather than Y. Such design, introduced in order to manipulate our choosing, is the coercion here chiefly of concern to us. The Nuremberg Code, in defining voluntary consent, puts the matter well. It insists that the person involved must in his situation be able to exercise free power of choice "without the intervention of any element of force, fraud, deceit, duress, over-reaching, or other ulterior form of constraint or coercion. . . ."

Let us now apply this view of coercion to the case of the prisoner giving informed consent to serve as medical subject. The opportunity is given him, let us suppose, to respond by letter to a notice on a bulletin board, after which, if he proves a suitable subject, he is given full information about procedures, risks, pay, and the rest by a research investigator. Is he coerced into giving consent by the fact of his imprisonment? On reflection I think we will see that he is not.

The question is not, "Are prisoners coerced?"—for we agree that, in general, theirs is a condition in which many more choices are fore-closed, and decisions compelled, than in conditions of ordinary life. But the pervasive presence of restraints in the prison leaves open the question of whether, with respect to a particular option put before him, he is coerced. He has a chance, say, to participate as subject in a set of drug tests, requiring intermittent hospital visits, small to moderate risks, occasional days of complete bed rest, and paying $20 per month for the 6 months of the tests. Most experiments using human subjects involve less time, less money, and less risk. Some involve more. Take this one as a realistic illustration.

It is true that his participation may promise occasional release from boredom. Boredom, however, is not a condition over which the investigator has any control, or in which he has any interest. It is simply the condition that the potential prisoner-subjects (as well as a good many nonprisoner-subjects) were in when the choice of participating or not was encountered by them. They are no more coerced into consenting by their boredom than I am coerced into seducing by my lust. The conditions in which we find ourselves powerfully affect our responses to choices put before us. If the standard of noncoercion be that potential subjects be free of all conditions that may significantly influence their willingness to consent, we will have no subjects and no experiments.

"But," the critic may reply, "although we are, indeed, all in conditions that constrain us in some respects, there remain enormous differences of degree. The prisoner's conditions are unusually severe, and that severity is what we underscore. When, for example, he supposes that giving his consent may help him, somehow, achieve an earlier release, he is in the special condition of desperately wanting release, and blindly hoping that someone up there will be more moved to help him because he did consent. That is what is unusual about his condition."

This reply will not work; it does not serve to distinguish the prisoner's case from the case of others whom we do not regard as improperly coerced. It is not only prisoners who have desperate desires that they hope may come nearer to fulfillment because of participation in experiment. Indeed, while the prisoner's hopes along that line may be tenuous and largely the result of his own wishful thinking, many nonprisoners are faced with the opportunity to participate in experiments involving considerable risk, which offer more serious hope of fulfilling desperate wants. Consider the person with psoriasis covering much of his body, given the opportunity to participate in an experiment using a new and very powerful ultraviolet light that may increase the likelihood of his developing cancer and may injure his eyes. No pressure whatever is brought to bear on him by the researcher. But he or she must feel very great pressures from the intense longing to be rid of that disfiguring affliction. Is that potential subject coerced by virtue of the desperation of his desire? Not in any sense that precludes his consent, surely; and if we thought he and others like him were truly coerced, we should have to forbid the experiment. Again, it is not rare for persons suffering from what appear to be terminal cancers to be offered the opportunity to participate in a controlled experiment with a new, highly toxic, chemical therapy that offers only slight hope of remission. All else has failed. Will the patient give consent to be experimental subject? Very probably; he reaches for every chance to live. Is he coerced into being a guinea pig by the intensity of his desire? Not if the facts are presented to him truly and fairly. Indeed, we are likely to think that, though the new chemotherapy may have dreadful side effects, he is entitled, after being fully informed of the facts, to make up his own mind and, if given his circumstances he thinks it worth the risks, to consent to the desperate try.

If the researcher in this latter case had portrayed the patient's condition more grimly than the facts warranted, in order to get him to consent, we would think the patient to have been coerced, not by the intensity of his desire to live, but by that deceptive account. If the researcher had refrained deliberately from telling the patient of some alternative therapy offering equal hopes, in order to woo his participation, the patient would have been coerced, not by his needs or their grip on him, but by the manipulation of the investigator. Analogously, it is not the degree of boredom, or the passion of the desire for release, or the level of any condition that the prisoner is in, that can coerce him. It is only deliberate conduct, conduct designed to deceive, to pressure, to constrain, that would coerce in the sense required. Therefore the boredom, the desire for early release, the being under constant guard —these cannot in themselves constitute coercion of a potential subject.

The critic may take another tack. "I see now [he may say] that it is not the intensity of desire that marks off the prisoner's case, or renders him coerced. Yet the precariousness of his condition is the key to the immorality I've been driving at. It is the deliberate choosing of prison populations to do experiments we would not do with others, taking advantage of their desperation, that is coercive. This, I now see, is the root of my complaint. By using prisoners the researcher gets away with an exploitation of subjects that would be impossible elsewhere— and that calculated exploitation must not be allowed."

Here the critic gives a caution that deserves to be taken seriously; but its scope must not be overblown. If we do on prisoners experiments we would not do on others, believing that for ordinary persons the risks clearly outweigh the potential benefits, the calculated choice of a precariously placed population enabling us to get away with that would, indeed, be wrongful. What troubles so about it, however, is that experiments would then be done which ought not be done at all. In the same way, where great risk far outweighs potential benefit we would not tolerate huge sums used to inveigle the participation of indigent welfare recipients. To do with some, because we can get away with it, what we ought to do with no one is surely unconscionable. Some experiments in prisons, in the past, have been like that.

But this argument does not have the general force its advocates may suppose. When, for example, subject populations are enlisted both in and out of prisons on the same terms—as is often done—this objection has no place. When the judgment of experimental justifiability is made independently of the special circumstances of possible subject pools, an improper reliance upon those special circumstances cannot be complained of.

Moreover, the special circumstances of subjects may rightly enter when the experiment is of a kind that requires just that kind of subject for scientific reasons. Persons suffering from a given disease are reasonably chosen for experiments dealing with that disease, obviously, and any inclination they have to serve as subjects arising from that circumstance is neither avoidable nor pernicious. Again, some experiments have special requirements for long-term regularity and control, calling for subjects in unusually restricted circumstances. Seeking out those who fit the requirements of the investigation—an investigation whose worthiness is independently established—is equally reasonable, and no less so if those subjects be prisoners. It is a fact that for some scientific purposes prisoners are irreplaceable as subjects. Prisoners constitute extraordinarily stable populations, under constant and detailed observation. Diet, activity, whereabouts, and other factors possibly critical to the experiment are thoroughly known and dependable. And all of this is the case not as an imposed demand of the investigator, but as a consequence of the incarceration with which he had nothing to do. For experiments requiring repeated trials, over long periods, rigorously free of perturbing variables, there are no populations like these. One can imagine the sequestering of a nonprison subject pool for months or years, but there is no practical likelihood of it. Very few other persons, identifiable and accessible, are so situated that the time they must devote as subjects to lengthy experiments does not impose heavy burdens in removing them from what would be their alternate activities. The short of it is that, for reasons having nothing to do with manipulative intent but everything to do with scientific reliability, prison populations serve medicine as no other populations can. The critic rightly insists that prisoners should not be preyed upon, that we must not do in prisons what should not be done. This is a long way from showing that no experiments ought be conducted in prisons, or that prisoners ought not be allowed to volunteer as subjects.

What shall we say of payment to prisoners? That, after all, clearly is a factor under the researcher's full control. Moderate remuneration, of course, is widely given to subjects, in and out of prison. Insofar as those sums are deliberately offered to allure and tempt they are, in every case, manipulative. And of course their manipulative force is the greater as the potential subject is the poorer. This argues against payment to subjects in any context, and I think that is an alternative worthy of serious consideration. On the other hand, the prospect of a small money reward (which does serve as a major motivating force in prisons)[3] neither threatens nor pressures nor tempts to do what should not be done. The very moderate sums involved—$20 or $40 or so—are also viewed by many not so much as lures as compensation for inconvenience. Some who would be pleased to volunteer cannot otherwise afford the time. In that spirit the sums involved do not coerce anyone. We ought no more permit large sums to tempt prisoners into undue hazards than we ought permit that among nonprisoners. Neither should we withhold from prisoners the minor compensations that serving as subject normally provides. One principle we surely wish to maintain is that prisoners not be in any way special targets for exploitation, and their not being special targets entails their being treated, in the matter of payment, just as nonprisoners are treated. They should be paid no more, no less.

How "more" or "less" ought to be calculated is a nice question. Is it equality of the absolute sum that is required? Or is it the same relative proportion of regular income that is called for? This is arguable. In my judgment it is the same dollar sum that should be used, both to be fair and to avoid the appearance of unfairness. The sums are in any event small; and adjusting them relatively entails the supposition of an "average regular income" of nonprisoner-subjects that must be wholly arbitrary.

It should be seen that even these small sums will be more alluring to prisoners than to most nonprisoners. If the payment be set at a regular standard, however, its allure is not the result of any deliberate effort by the researcher to twist the volition of the prisoner. Such

---

[3][D. Arnold Tannenbaum,] *Research in Prisons,* Survey Research Center, Institute for Social Research, Ann Arbor, Mich., University of Michigan, 1976, pp. 47 ff.

twisting would be coercive. Given reasonable restrictions that twisting can be avoided in the case of prisoners as it is in the case of nonprisoners.

I conclude that the argument against permitting prisoners to choose in this sphere, by virtue of their necessarily coerced condition, is simply mistaken. It confuses a wide sense of constraint (rightly characterizing the prison environment) with a different, narrow sense of constraint in the decision at hand—of which the prisoner can, with care, be entirely free. In the sense that one's condition coerces him, we are all coerced, and many of us as severely or more severely than prisoners. In the sense that choices before us, given our condition, may be made by us without ulterior manipulation in view of the merits of the case, the prisoner can, if fairly treated, be as free to choose as the rest of us.

Now it should be emphasized that prisoners and nonprisoners alike must be very carefully protected in making this choice—protected against "force, fraud, deceit, duress, over-reaching, or other ulterior form of constraint." Such protection against unfairness is a delicate and constantly ongoing business whose detail I cannot enter here. In the case of potential subjects in prisons, the fact of total custody and the evident potential for the abuses of power place upon the protecting body stringent demands for caution. Membership of that body, its procedures and powers, reviews and appeals—all are matters requiring utmost circumspection. But seeing to it that the right rules are well enforced is essentially an administrative matter, though a hard one. Mine has been a moral concern, about the rightness of the rule that would forbid all experimentation on prisoners. The common argument supporting that rule, I conclude, is grounded on mistake, on a misunderstanding of what is required for genuinely free consent.

IV. PROTECTION OR PATERNALISM?

The argument for that exclusionary rule is bad; the rule itself is worse. Reasons of two different kinds suggest that prisoners should be permitted to volunteer as subjects in medical experiments. Reasons of the first kind arise from the moral importance of protecting, for the prisoners, their right to give or withhold consent. Reasons of the second kind arise from the positive moral worth of the medical experimentation in which prisoners participate of their own volition. I deal briefly with the two categories in turn.

First, without urging participation in experimentation upon anyone we may insist that prisoners are morally entitled to permission to volunteer. Not to permit them to do so is to deny bluntly the autonomy of the prisoner in this sphere. Persons in full custody need to be protected, not patronized. They need to be guarded from abuse, but not treated as less than the full human beings they are. Prisons are commonly condemned, with much truth, as inhuman environments, demeaning, debasing, decivilizing. Perhaps we ought not have them at all. But since we do have them, and are likely to retain them for a good while into the future, we ought to seek to create within them a spirit in which—so far as is consistent with security and punishment—the humanity of the inmate is respected. One way to register this respect is to give to prisoners, within some feasible contexts, opportunities to make serious decisions about their own lives, just as nonprisoners must. To say of prison inmates that they cannot reach genuine decisions, that they are so cramped in mind that they are not even to be allowed to make effective choices in their personal lives, is to deny them a chunk of that capacity for self-direction that must be as precious to them as to anyone else. Such denial, it seems to me, is not justifiable. It is a usurpation of their self-direction of body and person that prison itself was never intended to effect. I am frankly dismayed by the presumption of well-meaning reformers in this sphere. They will preserve the gentle heifer of freedom in the prisons by shooting it in the head.

The voice of prisoners themselves on this question is not dispositive, but it is worth hearing. Of prisoners who have been subjects, 98 percent of those interviewed in a University of Michigan study were either very willing or somewhat willing to participate again in a similar project. Eighty-seven percent were very willing.[4] This suggests strongly that they would oppose the denial of the opportunity to do so. I know of no large-scale study of prison populations generally on the moral issue itself. But I submit that, were the question we discuss to be put before prisoners for vote: "Should prisoners be permitted to decide for themselves whether they choose to consent to be subjects in medical experiments?" it may be safely predicted that the endorsement of that right by prisoners would be overwhelming.[5]

Of course they want the opportunity for relief and earnings, in

---

[4]*Ibid.*, p. 57.

[5]In April, 1973, "96 of the 175 inmates of the Lancaster County, Pennsylvania, prison wrote to the local newspaper protesting the state's decision to stop all medical experiments on state prisoners" (*Wall St. J.,* April 2, 1974). Anecdotal evidence only, but not surprising.

exchange for discomfort or risk, when they think (based on an honest account of the facts) that they are getting a good deal. Their willingness to make the deal, the critic says, is only a product of their coerced condition. We have looked at that response and, I trust, put it behind us. Beyond any bargain or deal, many prisoners do genuinely want to be of service to medicine and to fellow human beings. The altruism is genuine for a good number; there is substantial evidence for the seriousness and generality of that motivation.[6] Surely it is presumptuous of the reformer to decide for prisoners that this self-described motivation is not genuine, or is too small a factor in their real set of motivations to allow them to decide for themselves. That, I submit, is heteronomy on stilts.

V. WHAT COUNTS AS MORAL?

The rule excluding prisoners from experimentation is bad for reasons of a second kind, having to do with the experiments themselves. The advantages accruing to society as a whole (prisoners included, of course) from the medical experiments taking place in prisons are very, very great. I shall not even begin to catalog the benefits that have resulted, and continue to flow, from such programs. "But," says the critic, "such benefits may not be taken as considerations bearing on the proposed exclusionary rule, since they are matters of utilitarian calculation, while the rule is a nonutilitarian protection of justice for prisoners." Allowing that the benefits are real, the critic insists that for judgment on this question the calculation of them cannot even be reached.

Again he errs. For utilitarian moralists his argument is utterly without sense, obviously. For those of us who are not thoroughgoing utilitarians this argument fails because it treats the process of experimentation, and the effort to acquire knowledge that can alleviate suffering and disease, as being purely nonmoral, instruments for the attainment of sheer utilities having nothing to do with justice or duty. Not so. There are strong moral reasons to engage in medical experimentation, to serve the vital interests of persons numerous but unidentified.

---

[6]While this study shows that money is the reason most commonly given by prisoner-subjects for volunteering, the second most common reason, cited by 27 percent of the many subjects interviewed, was "To help others, help society" (Tannenbaum, *op. cit.,* p. 47). Anecdotal but very persuasive support for this conclusion may be found also in "Why Prisoners Volunteer to Be Experimental Subjects" (J. C. McDonald, *J. A. M. A.,* vol. 202 (6), November 6, 1967).

Reasons supporting such activities may include crass considerations like the reduction of absenteeism in factories, and so on, but also surely include considerations of human pain and longevity that cannot be thought crass. To the extent that there lies upon any of us the obligation to advance inquiry of a beneficent character, a proposed rule that would hinder the fulfillment of that obligation is morally objectionable so far. If we allow that some (and perhaps all) of us have such obligations, the impact of the rule in question here upon the fulfillment of these obligations may certainly be reached in appraising that rule.

Is there a general principle of beneficence that does oblige us to be actively good? If there is, does that principle provide, perhaps, a prima facie obligation to advance (or not to obstruct) research aimed at knowledge to be used in healing the sick? I am not sure. It may be so. In any event we will want to insure that our rules do not unduly hinder any of us (including prisoners) who honestly believe that they have that beneficent obligation, or those of us whose special placement yields special duties.

The circumstances of the research investigator are special in this respect. The physician and the physician-researcher do take on, consciously and deliberately, the obligation to do what is reasonably within their power to ease pain, to heal, and to acquire the knowledge needed to promote these ends. The likely long-term consequences of the pursuit of such knowledge must therefore be weighed in the fully moral appraisal of any proposed principle that would restrict such pursuit.

What may mislead the critic here is the fact that while our duties to the subject in an experiment are reasonably precise—we must tell this person these things in this way—our duties to the unidentified beneficiaries of future experimentation are very imprecise. Toward them we have, as Kant would say, "imperfect" duties, because, although obliged to serve them, the form of our service is not specifiable in advance. But imperfect duties are as real as those of more perfect form. That understood, we can have little remaining doubt that the results of medical experimentation for which prisoners volunteer is morally relevant in deciding whether they should be permitted to volunteer.

Finally, there are benefits of other kinds, arguably nonmoral, that may also be worthy of consideration because they bear directly upon imprisonment, and the well-being of the prisoners concerned. Serving as genuinely voluntary subjects in medical experiments can and often does support the rehabilitative aims of the correctional institution. Studies have shown that such participation adds measurably to the prisoner's sense of self-esteem.[7] This becomes one of the few contexts in which he finds himself able to act purposefully in a larger world of serious affairs. In this role he can be full citizen, participant, taking some risks, gaining some advantages, being of service—in general grappling with serious matters in a way that supposes him to be the rational captain of his own fate. Rehabilitation in our prisons has not generally succeeded, as we know well. This device is no panacea, to be sure. But it does as much, perhaps more, to rehabilitate those it fully involves as any other activity in the prison. To eliminate it, out of regard for the prisoners, is to cut off our noses with theirs.

In sum: The reasons against permitting prisoners to give their consent are not sound. The moral reasons for permitting them to do so are forceful. The consideration of long-term benefits to all, and especially to the prisoners, that flow from the permission merely transforms an argument that is compelling into one that is more so.

VI. EPILOGUE

Two concluding notes: Wherever I refer to the advantages or permissibility of medical experiments with voluntary prison subjects, I suppose that the caution in selecting subjects, in informing them, and in safeguarding their honest volition has been maximal. Horror stories abound; they are instructive in many contexts, but not in this one. Our question concerns the principles that ought to govern experimentation when fairly and honorably conducted.

And last. Early on I observed that prisoners are archetypical of persons precariously placed. But there are other categories of persons who, by virtue of their jobs, or custodial status, or the like, are particularly vulnerable to manipulation. The cautions that are rightly introduced in proposing to prisoners that they volunteer as subjects must of course be mirrored, in appropriate form and degree, for others in analogous circumstances: servicemen on military duty, patients in public hospital wards, employees in drug firms and laboratories, even students in school or university classes—all are in need of special protection for reasons like (but of course not identi-

---

[7]For additional reading on this subject, see S. H. Wells, P. Kennedy, et. al., "Pharmacological Testing in a Correctional Institution," Springfield, Ill., Charles C. Thomas, 1974, and *Proceedings,* Conference on Drug Research in Prisons, National Council on Crime and Delinquency, 1973.

cal with) the reasons we are specially concerned about prisoners. By the same token, it is a mistake to assume that persons in such categories are incapable of giving their uncoerced consent, and that they therefore must not be permitted to do so. Of the larger class of the "precariously placed" the category of prisoners is the most extreme. Having dealt with it, I take myself—putting aside special situations —to have dealt, a fortiori, with all of the less extreme cases in the same family.

6

Informed Consent and the "Victims" of Colonialism

Samuel I. Shuman

Law School and Department of Psychiatry, Medical School, Wayne State University, Detroit, Michigan

I. THE COLONIAL RELATIONSHIP IN MEDICINE

Colonization has frequently resulted in paternalistic yet exploitative domination by the colonizers. Indeed, modern usage has extended the application of the term colonization to characterize a relationship in which the keepers necessarily compromise the autonomy of the kept. Among peers, even those who attempt to influence one another's decision making, there is no colonialism; in the colonial relationship, be it benevolent or malevolent, the keepers and the kept are not peers because the latter can never freely make their own decisions. It is the keepers' right to compromise the autonomy of the kept, whether or not the right is exercised, which distinguishes the colonial relationship. Justifying the right to compromise the decision-making autonomy of the kept is ultimately more important than whether individual keepers are benevolently paternal or brutally exploitative. Englishmen in the last century and earlier in this century justified their colonialism by arguing and even believing that they were bringing the benefits of white civilization to primitive people. In modern medical practice, one finds similar self-serving declarations which purport to justify society's right to compromise the decision-making autonomy of patients, especially if the patients happen to be children, prisoners, institutionalized subjects, students, or others who, because of their status, age, or alleged psychological or biological inadequacies, are "properly" subjected to someone else's decision-making power.

I am interested here in exploring some of the implications of socially sanctioned "medical colonialism," particularly as it affects children. I stress children because, in order to honestly examine questions about decision-making autonomy, about the ethical legitimacy of sometimes compromising that autonomy, and about the criteria to use when compromise is necessary, we have to be willing to apply the results of the examination to the most difficult, emotionally charged case, and I think that is the case of children. Furthermore, the issues are clearest in the case of children, because children have always been the kept. Anyone who has children and is at all self-conscious about the role of parent must be acutely aware of the colonialism inherent in it; furthermore, we have all been children, and thus subject to our "necessarily" colonialistic parents.

Decision-making competence for a biomedical intervention is not, however, a question which must be confronted only in the hard cases. Indeed, it is best to begin with the easier, more usual cases, because we have to recognize that even then the patient is the kept and the biomedical professionals the keepers. I stress the point that patients are always the kept, the victims or beneficiaries of the purportedly benevolent but nonetheless colonial relationship, because it is so often overlooked. Yet, in any relatively serious situation where a biomedical intervention is under consideration, the patient's decision-making autonomy and responsibility for the consequences of decision are almost inevitably compromised. This is true both because of the knowledge gap between almost all patients and the biomedical specialists and because of the emotional trauma which necessarily accompanies the situation where a serious choice must be made.

If the effects of the colonial relationship will be felt in any situation where a biomedical intervention is to be considered (and especially when the condition to be treated is serious), what mechanisms can be used to enhance the decision-making autonomy of the relatively normal adult? This is the so-called "easy case"—the patient is not a child, not mentally incompetent, not a prisoner, and not otherwise suffering disabilities which would make it obvious that he or she is subject to diminished autonomy. It is at this point that we must make the choice which will color everything else involved in dealing with the question of decision-making autonomy. Furthermore, the choices here are not ones where compromises are likely to be helpful. Rather, we shall have to choose between absolute individual autonomy or a model of compromised autonomy which can then be expanded to cover the more difficult cases. Put differently, if for the easy cases of normal patient populations we conclude that individual autonomy ought to be compromised— perhaps by interposing some institutional mechanism for determining access to a particular biomedical intervention, or by creating some other mechanism which forces a community-held value to be considered—then we will have contaminated the well at the outset. It is inevitable that the contamination will be even greater in considering the hard cases.

Because I find the interjection of institutional mechanisms both operationally difficult and morally unattractive, I want to begin by at least ruling out the interjection of any values other than those of the normal patient into the decision-making process. Taking this position does force the acceptance of greater anarchy in medicine than would be the case if individual autonomy did not reign as king. But, if such autonomy is the apex value in the hierarchy of all social, moral, and political values to be accommodated, then there can be no institutionalized procedure pursuant to which the choice of the individual normal patient can be vetoed.

Despite the seeming simplicity of this proposal, there are many complications. It seems simple only because a single value is posited as relevant for determining decisions, but this need not imply that implementation of the decision entails the suppression of all other considerations. For example, we may still wish to accommodate those legal and professional considerations which influence or even determine the kinds of disclosures which have to be made as to risks, benefits, and options. However, having labelled the patient "normal," and having satisfied the relevant requirements as to disclosure, the cardinal point remains: the final decision must be made only by the patient and by no other, and the patient's decision must be honored. If, for example, the patient concludes that he or she does not wish to be subjected to a particular procedure, even though the consequence of refusal is death, that decision must be absolutely respected. Using this model would prevent "Jehovah's Witness" cases where the patient's autonomy—for example, rejecting a blood transfusion—is compromised by the colonial judges. The model would make the use of humane sophistry, such as that of Judge J. Skelly Wright in the Georgetown College case,[1] impossible. Transfusions were ordered because the judge concluded that the patient did not come to the hospital to die, and therefore it was appropriate to order the intervention. The transfusion would not be deemed contrary to the religion of the patient since the patient did not herself request the transfusion but rather it was ordered by the judge.

II. DECISION-MAKING ACCEPTANCE AND DECISIONAL RESPONSIBILITY

As a moral choice, I would favor the anarchistic absolute autonomy position outlined above were it not that autonomy is effectively eroded by recognizing only the absolute autonomy of those previously labelled normal. What are workable criteria for determining who is an adequately normal decision-maker? As I have suggested, almost everyone is the victim of trauma and ignorance when that person must decide about possible alternative biomedical interventions. Having spent several years examining consent forms and consent procedures, and having on many occasions been required to consider whether a consent was adequate, my opinion is that there are probably no functionally manageable criteria for determining who should be deemed "normal" in this context. In other words, if we start classifying patients by appealing to such internal criteria as intelligence, problem-solving ability, and so on, rather than by appeal to objective criteria, I do not believe that we can find any manageable test for justifying the imposition of institutional restraints upon some patients. I am not suggesting that the clearly competent cannot be distinguished from the clearly incompetent. But, that is hardly the major problem. If the patient is clearly incompetent, there will almost surely be some intervening factor, such as a guardian. The hard cases are those where the patients do not come already "pre-packaged."

If, as I believe, there are no manageable mechanisms for deciding decision-making competence in terms of such individually variable internal criteria as intelligence, maturity, responsibility, and so, then we must next ask whether some other criteria are considered sufficiently relevant to decision-making competence to warrant the imposition of an institutional barrier without considering individual

---

[1]Application of the President and Directors of Georgetown College, Inc., 331 F2nd 1000, D.C. Cir., 1964. Compare A. Thompson, "She May Die If She Chooses," 72 Liberty 25, Jan./Feb. 1977.

competence. Unfortunately, at least for the present, the answer is clearly yes. For those labeled children, mentally incompetent, mentally disabled and institutionalized, prisoners, and so on, the law does impose restraints upon medical decision-making autonomy even though there has been no determination as to individual decision-making competence. We might wonder what it is that children, prisoners, and institutionalized populations have in common to warrant such restraints. There is at least this: generally, they themselves will not bear the responsibility for the consequences attached to a biomedical decision. With children, it will normally be the parents who bear that responsibility, and with institutionalized populations, it will be society generally. We might, therefore, be tempted to conclude that if responsibility for the decision will fall upon someone other than the patient, that person's decision-making competence properly may be compromised. It is the old idea that the person who pays the piper may call the tune.

This point is explicitly raised in a report prepared for the Commission on the Protection of Human Subjects:

> [P]rior to conducting a therapeutic procedure on a child, the consent of the parent is generally obtained. Indeed, there is case law that would indicate that the giving of such consent is a parental right that is not tied to any protective function. In the only case that analyzes the basis for the parental consent requirement, it is said: "This rule [that a minor cannot consent to medical treatment] is not based upon the capacity of the minor to consent, so far as he is personally concerned, within the field of the law of torts or law of crimes, but is based upon the right of parents whose liability for support and maintenance of their child may be greatly increased by an unfavorable result from the operational procedures upon the part of the surgeon. . . . [S]ince the parents of such a child are responsible for his nurture and training and are liable for his maintenance and support, others will not be permitted to interfere with such relationship or with matters touching the child's personal welfare.[2]

But, accepting this position raises a number of undesirable possibilities. First, if the person who pays the piper may call the tune, then may that person call any tune—for example, imposing an unwanted therapy? Secondly, if the person who pays may call, then why permit even a competent patient to make a decision if society or some-

---

[2]L. Glanz (primary author), "Legal States of Informed Consent In Human Experimentation; Children," Preliminary report prepared for the National Commission for the Protection of Human Subjects, N.I.H. Contract No. NO1-HU-6-2120, April 1, 1976 at 8, and quoting from Lacey v. Laird, 166 Ohio St. 12, 139 N.E. 2d 25, 1956.

one other than the patient will bear the responsibility for the patient's choice? These two questions alone suggest that simply judging by who bears the responsibility for consequences is unlikely to provide an acceptable basis for justifying colonialistic interventions on decision-making autonomy. Furthermore, even if some attractive rationale could be worked out to support the theory that autonomy is properly compromised when the patient is not responsible for consequences, there would still be very difficult cost-benefit problems. For example, suppose a prisoner asks for a surgical procedure on his or her brain which the prisoner believes will enable him or her to function in an open society without having further uncontrollable outbursts of aggression, and there is some medical evidence to support this belief.[3] Who will really bear the cost for the consequences? It may be that the procedure works, and the former inmate is releasable, thus saving the state $10,000 a year in direct prison costs. On the other hand, perhaps the long-term consequences of the surgery leave the inmate so docile that while he or she cannot compete in a free economy, he or she is sufficiently aggressive to produce children requiring state support. Society then pays not only for the former inmate, but for any dependents as well.

We are then in this position: *(1)* compromising medical decision-making autonomy by appealing to internal criteria which allegedly bear a functional relationship to decision-making competence is probably unmanageable; and *(2)* compromising autonomy where the consequences of a decision will fall most heavily upon someone other than the patient is probably both unjustifiable and unworkable. As is so typical in policy-making situations, we must choose not, as from among flavors of ice cream, the one we like best, but rather, as from among vegetables, none of which we happen to like. From among the options we do have available, and basing my opinion upon both philosophical considerations and my experience in dealing with actual cases at the practical level, I still favor maximizing decision-making competence even though the price may be that greater anarchy which could be avoided were institutional restraints more frequently imposed. As I have already suggested, ordinarily this means the decision of the patient cannot be vetoed.

---

[3]See Kelley, "Prisoner Access to Psychosurgery: A Constitutional Perspective," 9 Pacific L. J. 249, 1978.

III. AGE AND THE PRESUMPTION OF AUTONOMY

Although the two tests outlined above are unsatisfactory, it may be possible to establish specific objective standards to which appeal may be made in order to justify the infringement of medical decision-making autonomy. In my opinion, there are only two such objective standards. They are *(1)* age, and *(2)* a judicial declaration of incompetence, together with the appointment of a guardian. I do not regard incarceration alone, in a prison or elsewhere, nor institutionalization alone, a sufficient criterion by which to identify populations whose decision-making autonomy should be compromised. There is simply no empirical evidence to support any necessary connection between institutionalization *per se* and decision-making competence. Henpecked husbands and browbeaten wives are just as much subject to their colonial masters as are some institutionalized persons, and many prisoners are sufficiently aggressive and competent to make decisions about their own welfare. But, elsewhere, I have dealt at length with the problems of informed consent, decision-making competence, and autonomy in relation to institutionalized populations;[4] in the rest of this article, I would like rather to concentrate on these issues specifically as they concern children. Briefly, I believe that children (at least above the age of seven), absent appointment of a guardian following a judicial declaration of incompetence should, when a biomedical intervention is contemplated, be recognized as competent to make decisions which cannot be vetoed.

So badly stated, this proposal is likely to provoke heated reactions, only some of which are actually responses to the fundamental issue of decision-making autonomy for normal children. (At least, I have so far found this to be true.) It is thus probably best to first make clear what are only peripheral concerns. I formulated and first proposed my recommendation for children above seven before the National Commission for the Protection of Human Subjects issued its Report and Recommendations on Research Involving Children, but was gratified to find that seven is also considered as the appropriate cut-off age there, at least for nontherapeutic research. For therapeutic research, the re-

---

[4]I have dealt with this matter at length in the brief I submitted to the court in Kaimowitz v. Dept. of Mental Health, Civil No. 73-19434-AW, slip opinions (Circuit Court, Wayne County, Mich., July 10, 1973). The opinion of the court is reproduced in 2 Mental Disability Law Reporter 147, Sept.–Oct., 1976. The portion of my brief referred to above appears as an appendix in my book, *Psychosurgery and the Medical Control of Violence: Autonomy vs. Deviance* (Wayne State University Press, 1977). In several of the chapters in this book, I also discuss the problem of institutionalization and its effect upon competence.

fusal of a child of seven or older is not "controlling." Thus, for any therapeutic intervention, research or not, the Commission recommendation would continue to give parents the veto over the decision of the child even though seven or older. My proposed "rule of seven" is consequently very much broader than the position of the Commission which only allows the seven year old to have a nonvetoable right to refuse participation in nontherapeutic research.

The specific age for autonomy is more a question of empirical evidence than of moral judgments drawn upon the basis of that evidence. I do not regard myself as sufficiently knowledgable about the relevant data to mount a major defense for the age of seven rule. If one were to have read only Piaget, the age of autonomy would probably be 12 or 13.[5] According to Justice Douglas dissenting in Wisconsin v. Yoder, most relevant experts would give 14 as the age when the child's "moral and intellectual maturity approaches that of the adult."[6] In a careful law review note, the author concludes that 16 to 18 is the right cut-off age.[7] The National Commission includes, in its October draft on "Children As Research Subjects," a chapter entitled "Psychological Perspective: The Freedom and Competence of Children to Make Choices." It is the least satisfactory section of the Draft and furnishes no support whatsoever for the "age of seven" position taken by the commission.[8] The two page section on "Psychological Perspective" in the Final Report and Recommendation contains even less that is relevant to the question of how seven came to be the suggested cut-off age.

I must also admit that I have done no better in offering empirical data or literature to support my choice of seven. However, there are two factors which should be borne in mind: (1) I do not have available the

---

[5]J. Piaget and B. Inhalder, *The Psychology of the Child,* New York, Basic Books, 1969.

[6]Wisconsin v. Yoder, 406 U.S. 205 at 245, N.3, 1972.

[7]B. Konkle, "Nielsen v. The Regents: Children As Pawns or Persons?", 2 Hastings Constitutional Law-Quart. 1151, 1975.

[8]The report relied upon by the commission is L. Ferguson, "The Competence and Freedom of Children to Make Choices Regarding Participation In Biomedical and Behavioral Research," Jan. 30, 1976. The report was not based upon any independent research about decision-making competence, but does contain the following reference: "Much recent research on cognitive development . . . particularly carried out from the perspective of Piaget's theories, suggests that a number of critical shifts in cognitive capacities occur around age seven." (On page 15 in the Report). This is supported by a reference to the chapters of White, Stevenson, Berlyne, McNeill and Rohwer in P. Mussen, ed., *Carmichael's Manual of Child Psychology, Vol. 1,* New York, Wiley, 1970, 3rd ed. The above sentence and its reference to the Mussen volume is the basis for the commission's choice of seven as the appropriate age.

resources of the Commission, although I did conduct some not very scientific, anecdotal research; *(2)* the precise age is far from cardinal to my central thesis, which is primarily moral and political, not psychological. I have urged the age of seven rule because there are no adequate, manageable "internal" criteria for deciding autonomy and therefore some objective standard is necessary even though it is to some degree arbitrary. Professor Robert Bennett, writing in the *Virginia Law Review,* makes the point this way:

> The determination of the appropriate cutoff age should be left to courts, legislators, and those expert in child development. It is necessary only to pick some plausible age, since any age cutoff will be a statistical approximation at best. The present standard of a child capable of giving informed consent provides little guidance to a doctor and is probably irrelevant in cases tried to a jury. The impression of the jury or judge will be dominated by the appearance of the child at the time of trial, probably several years after the procedure was performed. Whether the child has matured, as children do, rapidly at the ages involved, or deteriorated due to the procedure, the factfinder will be severely disabled in judging whether he was mature enough to have given meaningful consent at a time then well past. The proper time for informed consent is when the practitioner deals with the parent about a medically controversial decision. On such occasions both the information and the consent are of real significance.[9]

IV. THE PRESUMPTION OF AUTONOMY VS. THE PRESUMPTION THAT PARENTS KNOW BEST

Because the precise age chosen is one of those peripheral concerns referred to above, I would not regard a recommendation of eight or nine as an attack upon important constitutional or moral rights. Furthermore, it is important to notice that children who are declared judicially incompetent and for whom a guardian has been appointed are not within the recommended age of seven. Finally, there is nothing in the recommendation requiring that parents be denied the opportunity to influence their children, bribe their children, or indeed, subject to the limitations on criminal abuse, abuse their children in order to make them comply with the parental belief regarding the particular intervention. My thesis, therefore, is hardly as radical as it appears at first blush. What all this means to me is that when the point is reached where

---

[9]R. Bennett, "Allocation of Child Medical Care Decision–Making Authority: A Suggested Interest Analysis," 62 Virginia L. Rev. 285 p. 325, 1976.

despite parental cajoling, bribery, or coercion, a child over seven still declines to submit to the allegedly necessary intervention, or insists upon having an intervention which is contrary to his or her best interests as seen by his or her colonial masters, there must be some "safety" mechanism. In our society, it is appeal to the courts for a declaration of incompetence which permits overriding the child's decision. The heart of my argument is that the decision of a normal child should not be vetoed except after judicial intervention; this is a fair compromise because when the family structure has so deteriorated that all of the usual mechanisms have not sufficed to obtain the child's compliance, then an agency other than the family must be relied upon to resolve the controversy.

If we examine actual life experiences, we seldom encounter cases where it is necessary to resort to the judicial relief valve in order to circumvent a child of seven who will not consent to a biomedical intervention allegedly required to sustain his or her life. Indeed, I find it extraordinary that adults so seldom take children seriously enough to actually talk with them to discover whether they have the competence necessary to make serious decisions. It has been my experience that children are extremely sensitive to their real needs, and in the overwhelming majority of cases, their judgment is as reliable as that of their parents. As the Washington court said in the Koome case, involving the abortion decision of a minor which by legislation was subjected to the veto of her parents, "the state's 'conclusive presumption' that the parents' judgment is better than the pregnant woman's cannot withstand constitutional scrutiny."[10] Even if it is unconstitutional to presume conclusively that adults (parents) always do know best concerning a medical intervention, the presumption is apparently constitutionally permissible in the case of a "purely moral" matter. In Ginsberg v. New York, the Supreme Court did sustain a New York statute which prohibited the sale to minors of "obscene" material salable to adults.[11] Relying upon Ginsberg, it might be argued that when the child's participation in research is nontherapeutic, the parental veto should be sustained (since the issue here is almost purely moral), but that when the intervention is therapeutic, then no such veto power is demanded even by Ginsberg. It is interesting to note that the National Commission comes out just the opposite way and recommends a parental veto for therapeutic research but denies it when the research is nontherapeutic.

---

[10]State v. Koome, 84 Wash. 2d 901 p. 908, 530 p. 2d 260 p. 265, 1975.
[11]Ginsberg v. New York, 390 U.S. 629, 1968.

It might be argued that on some other plane the Ginsberg decision and the Commission recommendation are quite consistent in that both rest upon the usual justification for benevolent colonialism —protect the kept from their incompetence. Kids will undermine their morality if allowed to purchase pornography just as they will undermine their health if allowed to "purchase" or refuse therapeutic medical interventions. Morality and health are too important to be left to children; therefore, adults must have a veto right. But, since a child's refusal to participate in nontherapeutic research cannot undermine his or her *physical* health, there need be no parental veto (when the child is seven or older). My argument that there is an inconsistency is based upon the belief that health and physical health are not the same, and it is this distinction which is crucial for understanding why both Ginsberg and the Commission are inconsistent with the very premises upon which both purport to rest their conclusions.

V. FAMILY INTEGRITY

In my opinion, both the recommendation of the Commission (allowing parental veto) and the decision in Ginsberg (also allowing parental veto) are wrong and wrong for the same reason. Both fail to respect that specific cardinal, moral, political, and social principle advanced by the Supreme Court and considered by the Commission in its October draft.

In Ginsberg, the Court states:

> First of all, constitutional interpretation has consistently recognized that the parents' claim to authority in their own household to direct the rearing of their children is basic in the structure of our society.[12]

The Court then goes on to quote from its earlier decision in Prince v. Massachusetts:

> It is cardinal with us that the custody, care and nurture of the child reside first in the parents, whose primary function and freedom include preparation for obligations the state can neither supply nor hinder.[13]

The Commission endorses this "cardinal" principle (in its October Draft on Research with Children):

---

[12]*Ibid.,* p. 639.
[13]Prince v. Massachusetts, 321 U.S. 158 p. 166, 1944.

> In the Anglo-American tradition, the state has protected and fostered the integrity of the family unit, and parents have enjoyed broad authority to make decisions regarding the care and upbringing of their children.[14]

Unlike the Draft of October, 1976, the chapter on "Deliberations" in the Commission's final Report and Recommendations (September, 1977)[15] does not contain any mention of the Anglo-American tradition of state protection for the integrity of the family unit; nor does the "Deliberations" chapter in the Final Report conclude, as did the Draft, with any statement about "family integrity" as one of the bases for the Recommendations. Instead, in the Final Report and Recommendations, the Commission says this:

> The permission that parents give for children's participation in research can be accepted as an exercise of their general role, as caretakers, to *guide* decisions [of their children]. Although some critics have challenged the right of parents to make decisions for their children to participate in research, the Commission is persuaded that the practical need for parents to manage the details of the child's life legitimately extends to such decisions.[16]

The point I have been urging is that when there is a parental veto, then parents do more than *guide* to a decision. Peers guide one another, only colonial masters can veto.

It is the failure to fully respect the cardinal moral, political and social principle of family integrity which leads me to argue that both Ginsberg and the Commission are wrong when they allow adults (parents) to veto the decision of children, even concerning the purchase of pornography, let alone concerning a biomedical intervention. (It is worth noticing that, consistent with the cardinal principle, neither Ginsberg nor any other Supreme Court decision prohibits parents from allowing their children free access to obscene material at home.) In order to see why I say they are wrong, we must examine both the presumption of Ginsberg and the Commission that morality and health are too important to be left to children, and their avowed adherence to the principle of family integrity. The "error" in the Ginsberg presumption is that sexual morality is all there is to morality and the related "error" of the Commission is that physical health is all there is to

---

[14]Draft of Oct. 1, 1976, on Children as Research Subject at 8. National Commission For the Protection of Human Subjects.

[15]Report and Recommendations; Research Involving Children, DHEW Pub. No. (OS)77-0004, Sept., 1977.

[16]*Ibid.,* p. 128–129. Italic added.

health. It is this unwarranted and unjustifiable constriction of the crucial concepts that makes it possible to allege, simultaneously, support for the family integrity principle and for the presumption that morals and health are too important to be left to children.

It is because I do believe that the "integrated" family does have the primary opportunity and responsibility for educating children that I find it inconsistent to create the legal presumptions against decisional competence in children over seven (or whatever is the cut-off age). On the one hand, the Supreme Court (at least in Ginsberg) and the Commission (at least concerning therapeutic research) commit themselves to the support of the integrated family because such a family does exercise its opportunity and responsibilities for the education of its children. Yet, on the other hand, even though the children are thus educated, they are still deemed so incompetent that parental veto is required for the really big issues—sex and good health. But, once we recognize that there are even bigger issues, or at least others that are of no less significance, then it becomes hard to see why the veto is either reserved for all big issues or for none.

At least as important as education for sexual morality is education for autonomy; indeed, it may well be the case that absence of the latter makes the former unlikely if not impossible. Similarly, if good health means psychological as well as physical health, it is difficult to see how the former is developed or insured by supressing what may well be its most critical component—autonomy. What I see in the two decisions I am criticizing is an almost classical illustration of the Catch-22 double bind: "Heads, I win: tails, you lose." On the one hand, the child is taught (by an integrated family) to be a morally healthy person, which must mean acquiring the capacity to make morally responsible choices, yet, on the other hand, the child is told he or she cannot be trusted if the matter is important.

The probably inevitable, intrinsic ambiguity of the message communicated by the "integrated family" is the reason I favor the age of seven rather than some later age. The later the cut-off age, the more deeply entrenched is this ambiguity. There may be no way to entirely avoid some ambiguity in the message unless we never allow adults to veto any "decision" made by a child of any age. Doing so might be logically consistent with the cardinal principal of family integrity, but I find the price for such consistency too high and, therefore, want to tolerate only as much message ambiguity as is necessary to avoid the "horror cases." I do not believe that allowing children over seven to buy any reading material which adults can buy comes close to being such a horror case, and, therefore, the message ambiguity of Ginsberg is not worth the gain. Similarly, if a child over seven has a functioning integrated family, it is very unlikely that that child will refuse life-saving procedures or insist upon those which are life-threatening. Therefore, giving the parents a veto is also not worth the increased message ambiguity generated by vesting such a veto in parents. If a horror case should occur, it would be because the family has not been functioning successfully—it was not an "integrated family" and thus it would be quite right to lay the case before a decision maker other than the family itself.

In its Final Report, the Commission stresses the importance of respect for the developing autonomy of children,[17] yet in the critical seventh recommendation, this autonomy is compromised and the child's right to refuse participation in nontherapeutic research is recognized only because there is no biomedical risk.[18] If the child wishes to participate, then parental veto is recognized. In other words, respect for developing autonomy is great so long as it doesn't cost anything! In the October Draft, the Commission suggests that:

> [I]nsofar as the responsibility of parents includes the moral education of their children, and their authority in this regard is constitutionally protected (again, within the limits of reason), then the exercise of that authority properly includes the instruction of children regarding their duties as members of the community. This instruction might very well extend to encouraging participation in nontherapeutic research.. . .[19]

Yet, in the Final Report, the family which has failed to teach the child what it believes is the right attitude about community membership is just the family which is given the veto right over the child, who perhaps *despite* the family has a morally preferable conception of community. The family has failed both to teach *and* convince the child that he or she ought not participate in the nontherapeutic research, and precisely because it has failed, it shall now have the right to veto the child's decision. Recommendation *(5)* permits only "nontherapeutic research which involves no more than minimal risk to children;"[20] consequently, the Commission's commitment to this fun-

---

[17]*Ibid.,* p. 129.

[18]*Ibid.,* p. 12–13. In its discussion of the Recommendations, the Commission states not that below seven the child's decision can be vetoed if the research intervention is therapeutic, but rather that "the objection of a small child may be overridden," at 16.

[19]Draft of Oct. 1, 1976, p. 9.

[20]Report and Recommendations, Sept., 1977, p. 7–8.

damental principle of "respect for developing autonomy" comes down to this: even if the subject cannot suffer more than minimal risk, his or her autonomy is to be respected only upon his or her reaching majority age, unless he or she wishes not to participate. Hardly a ringing defense of autonomy.

Although many will, no doubt, view my age of seven proposal as the consequence of an exaggerated commitment to developing autonomy, what concerns me is the ease with which that commitment can be pragmatically rendered insignificant by even a modest commitment to family integrity. Since this "integrated family" may not only educate, but may do so through bribery, reward, coercion, and also punishment, what we should question is whether autonomy will be permitted to develop unless the child is at least to some degree insulated from his or her integrated family.

VI. CAN THERE BE AN OVERLY INTEGRATED FAMILY?

If, under the protection of religious freedom, parents can educate their children in almost any way, even to the point their autonomy is virtually obliterated (as may well be the case, for example, with Amish females), the underlying basis for the "age of seven rule" would be eroded. If parents are allowed to choose an educational program which reinforces domestic socialization by conditioning the child to a blind acceptance of *whatever* the parents (or other authority figures) command, then there can be no justification for a rule considered precisely because normal children over seven are presumed autonomous. It is therefore worth questioning whether the 1972 decision of the Supreme Court in Wisconsin v. Yoder,[21] dealing with the education of Amish children, is compatible with the Court's more recent decision on the right of a minor to have an abortion.[22] In its abortion decision, the Court does not permit the parents to veto the decision of their unmarried daughter while the Yoder decision would permit parents to educate their child in such a way that she could never make any autonomous decision.

On the other hand, if some children can become minimally autonomous only by compromising their parents' right to choose their educa-

[21] Wisconsin v. Yoder, super note 6. For a discussion of this case, see A. Keim, ed., *Compulsory Education and the Amish: The Right Not To Be Modern,* 1975.

[22] Planned Parenthood of Central Missouri v. Danforth, 428 U.S. 52, 1976.

tional programs, then are we not really only making a substitution of one set of "religious" principles for another? In terms of constitutional protections, why should "faith" in the need for autonomous children prevail over the Amish faith in the need for submissive children—especially female children? Although I do believe the preference for autonomy is justifiable in terms of political considerations, as well as on the basis of what it means to be human, I shall not attempt that justification here.

Even if my undefended preference for autonomy is shared, however, someone may still argue that it is wrong to force some parents to compromise religious convictions by sending their child to a school which meets state requirements imposed to insure that the child will be pluralistic, free, and autonomous. In this case, the school officials become the source of coercive standards instead of the family. This is a criticism to which I am very sympathetic and for which I have no very satisfactory "answer." However, there are two relevant considerations. First, unlike the family, at least in theory the school is not a closed institution; the school officials are publicly accountable for how they "fertilize their crops." Parents are almost entirely immune, even in theory, from such accountability. Second, the Supreme Court has demonstrated concern over school officials who attempt to suppress the expression of nonconformist political views. In Tinker v. Des Moines School District, which arose when school officials prohibited children from wearing arm bands to express unpopular political sentiments, the Court held that the autonomy of children required that they be permitted to wear whatever they wished so long as doing so did not disrupt legitimate school functions.[23]

In this essay, I have made two proposals about the rights of children which might affect "family integrity": *(1)* that there be an objective (chronological age) criterion for determining what some, like Rawls, call the "age of reason" and what others call the age of competence. The Commission, in its Recommendations on psychosurgery, refers to a "mature minor; *i.e.* child with a certain capacity for rational judgment."[24] By whatever name, the central idea is that reason, competence, or rationality is a developmental phenomenon and therefore not capable of "mechanical" determination. My point has been that reason, competence, or rationality is an attribution, not a description, and hence necessarily reflects unavoida-

---

[23]393 U.S. 503, 1969.

[24]Report and Recommendations: Psychosurgery, p. 69. DHEW Pub. No. (OS)77-0001, March, 1977.

ble social value commitments, none of which easily lend themselves to objective or easily administrable testing; therefore, a statistical, objective, and hence admittedly arbitrary mechanical criterion is preferable.

(2) The second proposal was that the best available evidence be reviewed by some suitably constituted body, like the National Commission, to fix that statistical compromise. Unfortunately, the Commission has not done this, and in the absence of some such "national" determination, I proposed seven as the age of autonomy, reason, competence, and rationality for purposes of any biomedical intervention.

Now the question is: Do the two proposals I have made really erode "family integrity?"

As I indicated earlier, whenever I have advanced arguments in favor of recognizing the autonomy of children, my audiences' reactions have characteristically been excessively emotional. However, in light of the existing law on parental rights to "educate," I wonder if this reaction is warranted.

The constitutionally protected basic right of the parents to raise their children, to choose their education, and to determine their religion goes a long way in making both proposals symbolic, if not functionally irrelevant. Furthermore, as a practical matter, how frequently will a child have occasion to exercise the recommended right of autonomy? How often will a child even hear about a biomedical intervention which the parents do not wish to have revealed? How often will a child learn about a research proposal for which he or she might be a candidate, unless the parents tell him or her? Yes, there might be cases of pregnant minors and mentally disabled children, who though institutionalized, are bright enough somehow to learn that there is some research going on. But, do these few and marginal cases erode so well entrenched an institution as the family? Furthermore, when the "integrated family" is threatened by a child who insists upon exercising the right to autonomy, it is difficult to see how integration is further eroded since this family has not been successfully integrated.

In light of these considerations, one may now conclude not that the excessive emotionalism is unwarranted, but rather ask whether even making these proposals was warranted. For those who do not share my commitment to the psychological, moral, and political importance of individual autonomy, my answer will hardly be convincing: My two proposals are warranted not because they are likely to do much in the real world, but simply because they further support the symbolic significance of that informed consent which underlies all of consensual medicine.

VII. AUTONOMY FOR RESEARCH VS. AUTONOMY FOR THERAPY

Before concluding, I want to consider in this and in the next two sections, three rather "practical" problems related to the matter of pediatric research.

It is frequently suggested that a distinction be drawn between therapeutic and nontherapeutic interventions, and between risk and no-risk interventions or research, in determining the age at which a child shall be deemed to have a nonvetoable right of decision. Many persons would surely support the recommendations of the National Commission which rest upon these distinctions, but I am unable to embrace their suggestions enthusiastically. For one thing, there are so many difficulties inherent in distinguishing between therapeutic and nontherapeutic, research and nonresearch, that I fear losing the essential protection for absolute autonomy in the gaps between these distinctions. Furthermore, I find it hard to understand why a no-risk research intervention should require a higher age than a modest-risk therapeutic intervention. Indeed, it seems to me important to recognize that normal children above the age of autonomy may well be expected to have developed a sufficient sense of social responsibility that denying them the opportunity to participate in socially beneficial research would penalize their status as children unnecessarily. Neither the Constitution nor moral principles in general are intended to discriminate against children; if we discriminate about children, it should be to their advantage and I fail to see what advantage we bestow upon them by withholding the opportunity to do that which we deem so honorable for adults.

It might be argued that there are at least two cases in which it would be appropriate to institutionalize some mechanism beyond the judicial safety valve proposed earlier. One is if the child declines to give consent for an intervention without which his or her life would be threatened. The second is when the child does consent to a risk procedure having no therapeutic potential for him or her personally. Despite what some will view as an exaggerated commitment to individual autonomy, I would still grant no individual the right to veto the decision of the child above the age of autonomy who has not been judicially declared incompetent.

The more troublesome case is probably the second, in which the child consents to the nontherapeutic, risk research. But it should be recognized that before the child's consent may be solicited, the research proposal has presumably cleared all those review mechanisms which are required by HEW or other federal or state regulations. Pursuant to the usual procedure, the institutional review board (IRB), or what was formerly called the human experimentation committee, would have had to conclude that the risk was one which was appropriate for a child to take. Furthermore, once HEW does promulgate rules for research with children that reflect the Commission recommendations discussed above, no IRB will be permitted to approve research with children which puts children at more than minimal risk.

VIII. PROXY PERMISSION

It is important to recognize that there can be no informed consent when decisional autonomy is properly compromised because of age or a judicial declaration of incompetence. There is informed consent only when the patient/subject personally agrees to participate or at least does not refuse participation. If the decision is made by a proxy because the competence of the patient/subject is to be compromised, there cannot be informed consent. At the very best, there is what might appropriately be called "informed permission" to proceed with a procedure which would have been illegal without the informed permission by the proxy.

Although past cases have ignored the significance of the distinction between informed consent and informed permission, a rational justification for compromising decision-making autonomy must take account of it. Such justification must in particular recognize that while the proxy decision-maker has the legal capacity to decide, it does not necessarily follow that the proxy decides as he or she would have decided were he or she the patient/subject. In other words, there is a distinction between *(1)* actually substituting the judgment of the proxy decision-maker for that of the subject/patient; and *(2)* requiring that the proxy decision-maker decide as the subject/patient would have decided if the subject's/patient's competance were not compromised. For example, suppose that there is the opportunity for a Caucasian patient to participate in some biomedical research designed primarily to benefit blacks. It should not be within the capacity of the proxy decision-maker to decide as he or she personally would decide were he or she in the position of the patient. Rather, the proxy decision-maker's function should be limited to deciding as the patient would, were the patient able to make a decision. If the patient's deeply-entrenched prejudices against blacks is known by the proxy decision-maker, and the proxy should know of such prejudices if acting as proxy, then it would be entirely inappropriate for the proxy to consent to the participation of the patient in such research. Even though a morally mature, reasonable person might well have consented to such participation, if the specific potential subject is not similarly mature, even if otherwise reasonable, then it would be wrong for the proxy decision-maker to try to decide as would a reasonable, morally mature person. What I am arguing for, to put the distinction in political terms, is that the proxy must function not as the delegate of the patient, but as the patient's representative. The recognition of this feature of proxy decision-making will go a long way in solving some of the more serious problems which have encumbered the development of a morally defensible proxy mechanism.

Resort to this "representative rather than delegate" standard for proxy decision-making does generate a number of problems which are not relevant when all the proxy-decider need do is decide as a reasonable person would. If the proxy is allowed to substitute reasonable judgment for the judgment of the patient/subject, whether or not that patient/subject's judgment would have been similarly reasonable, there is no need to ascertain what the patient/subject would have thought if he or she were capable of thinking at the right time and at the right place. There will be new problems, for example, if the proxy must decide as the child would decide if the child were to survive to the age of autonomy; shall the proxy presume that the child's present familial environment will continue to that age? or need the proxy decide as would the child if the child were to be placed in a new environment— such as when a guardian other than the parents has been appointed? Furthermore, if there has been either a judicial declaration of incompetence or the child is so young that some adult may decide for the child, why should it follow that the child's wishes are respected at all in determining how the child would decide were the child of age?

All of these questions deserve more careful analysis than I will provide here, but the recommendation stands: even when decisional autonomy for a biomedical intervention is properly compromised because of incompetence or age, the proxy ought still try to fashion a decision which will accommodate as much of the life values of the subject as are ascertainable at the time the decision is made, while not being bound by those values which were precisely relevant in determining that the subject was incompetent. With very young children this recommendation will mean extrapolating into the future on the basis of unknown events, but if we must choose between (1) attempting to discover what the child would decide were he or she old enough and competent; and (2) imposing a decision which has no relation to the child's life style expectations, the first choice seems preferable. Because the proxy decision should reflect the child's social and moral values, parental proxy for young or incompetent children is more appropriate than a decision made by some independent, "neutral," and frequently uninformed proxy-decider. The presumption is that the parents are most likely to reflect the values which the child will have since they are normally the ones who will most affect the child's socialization.

It is entirely possible that there may be good reasons for trying to insulate some children from their most natural socializing forces, namely, their parents. However, a very different set of considerations is relevant here and ought not be the basis for coloring the proxy mechanism. The legitimate search for a social mechanism by which to insulate children from undesirable socialization processes should not be used to defeat the otherwise valid rule that parents are the normal proxy-deciders when children are either below the requisite age or incompetent. No single legal rule is likely to suffice for all the hard cases when moral issues are relevant, but it would be a disservice to contaminate what may be an adequate rule by trying to have it serve the double purpose of furnishing a rational proxy decision mechanism and also a basis for insulating children from indesirable familial influences. If parents are disqualified as proxies, then they should be disqualified for the same reason which justified the imposition of a restriction on the decision-making competence of the patient or subject in the first place —that is, judicial declaration of incompetence.

IX. THE PRESUMPTION OF AUTONOMY

There is a further aspect of informed consent which is particularly troublesome in connection with young children. It is the problem which confronts the doctor or researcher who has significant reservations as to the decision-making competence of the potential patient/subject. In this situation, there should be some institutional mechanism which will insulate the physician or investigator from liability for having made the decision as to the decision-making competence of the patient/subject alone. Mechanisms of the usual type involve informed consent committees, peer review committees, and the like. If such a committee determines that the subject is not competent, then the matter should be laid before a court to consider whether a guardian need be appointed. If the committee determines that the subject is competent, then the procedure may be initiated with the subject's consent. Providing for such a mechanism strikes what I think is a fair balance. There is a rebuttable presumption of competence for anyone who meets the age requirement and for whom there has not been a judicial declaration of incompetence. But, if the physician or investigator has any qualms about the decision-making competence of the patient/subject, then there will be a way for the investigator to resolve the difficulty without being required to take risks which ought not be a part of his or her function as the provider of medical services or as a medical researcher. The imposition of such a competence determination mechanism, if properly administered, will not unduly interfere with treatment or research. The time required to fulfill the requirements of the mechanism is more than compensated for by the freedom from potential liability which would otherwise always be present, particularly in the case of biomedical research.

X. SUMMARY AND CONCLUSION

In dealing with complex moral issues for which a legal rule is required, it is unlikely that any single, operationally manageable rule will be sufficient to cover all the complexities. Therefore, the task is to develop those principles which will lead to a rule and to identify that one which does more overall justice than an alternative rule. To support the rules I have proposed to govern autonomy and proxy consent, let me now try to identify more specifically the principles and policies which seem relevant. Among the relevant policies and principles are these: *(1)* For constitutional as well as other legal and moral reasons, individual autonomy ought not be unnecessarily compromised. Extraordinary circumstances, such as war or a medical disaster, might make compromise necessary. *(2)* If autonomy is to be compromised because of overriding communal benefits, then it cannot be compromised on the ground of the individual idiosyncrasies of particular patients or subjects, but only because of their membership in some class of persons who are deemed for whatever reason to be appropriately subjected to the demands required to satisfy the overriding social interests. This could mean, for example, that some experiments are deemed so important that regardless of consent, subjects are "conscripted" for service. In such cases, competence would clearly be irrelevant so long as the subject satisfied the profile relevant for the experiment. *(3)* If individual autonomy must be compromised on grounds other than overriding communal benefit, it must be because that individual patient/subject would suffer greater harm if his or her autonomy were not compromised. "Harm" here is not limited only to biological harm, but includes psychological harm and political disadvantage as well. *(4)* Autonomy is appropriately compromised because of age or judicially declared incompetence, because these two conditions are morally and legally reasonable bases for questioning whether an individual is an autonomous human being. Without either of these disabilities, an organism which satisfies the criteria for a biological human being is presumed to be autonomous. *(5)* Autonomous human beings have an absolute right to determine what shall be done to or with their bodies concerning a biomedical intervention, if the kinds of extraordinary circumstances (such as war, disaster) relevant to *(1)* above are absent. *(6)* When a human being is not autonomous because of incompetence or age, then proxy decision mechanisms may be necessary. *(7)* When a proxy intervention is appropriate, the proxy-decider ought to try to shape a decision which will come closest to that of the patient/subject and reflect the patient's/subject's lifestyle, values, and lifestyle expectations.

The rules I have recommended come closer to satisfying this range of principles and policies than do the recommendations of the National Commission or any alternative rules which I have seen in the literature or in judicial decisions. The rules also have the advantage of being understandable by the courts and society generally. Recommending an age for autonomy lower than seven might show greater respect for the principles of autonomy, but there may be sufficient psychological evidence to conclude that below the age of seven anatomical entities which look like human beings are not yet autonomous human beings. As I have already admitted, it may also be argued that seven is too young, but if we must err here, I prefer to take some chances on the side of autonomy until there is more convincing evidence that some higher age is necessary.

Nothing I have said about children over seven or competent adults prevents either from doing what is in fact now so frequently done, and that is to allow the doctor, in "consultation" with the patient to actually make the decision. Indeed, the case Roe v. Wade[25] and its recent progeny, Planned Parenthood v. Danforth[26] and Belicotti v. Baird,[27] very strongly support the view that even in the case of a minor, no one has the right to veto the decision of the subject/patient about a biomedical intervention. While these cases are concerned specifically with abortion, I fail to see why that most extreme case ought to be protected under privacy or other provisions squeezed out of the Constitution while other less extreme cases would not receive at least as much

---

[25]410 U.S. 113, 1973.
[26]Supra note 22.
[27]Belicotti v. Baird, 428 U.S. 132, 1976.

protection. Therefore, if the abortion decision of the patient made in consultation with the physician is subject to no governmental veto nor veto by any other individual, including the spouse of a married woman or the parents of a minor, it is difficult to understand why, for other biomedical interventions, a different, lower level of protection should be accorded to the autonomy of the patient. Without pressing the "right to life" aspect of abortion—that is, without focusing heavily on the fact that in abortion a "potential" life is terminated—if autonomy of the mother in the abortion case is sufficient to preclude a veto by the state as decided in Roe v. Wade, or by the husband or parents of a minor, as in Planned Parenthood, why would the state or any individual have the veto right when the intervention involves only the body of the individual patient/subject and not also the body of another potential human being?

In conclusion, I wish to call attention to a too-often ignored aspect of the informed consent situation, but one which is particularly relevant for me. I am convinced that informed consent has a primarily symbolic function in affording much-needed recognition to the integrity of the personality of the individual patient/subject. Indeed, in large measure, it is because of the importance of this symbolic function that I stress autonomy even at the price of "anarchy." In acknowledging this symbolic function of informed consent, I do not mean to suggest that we need not be meticulously careful in maximizing the real opportunity for intelligent decision-making. I am, rather, suggesting that the modest empirical evidence which is available strongly supports the conclusion that no matter what is done in this field in terms of disclosures, time spent by the physician, opportunity to question, opportunity to read literature, opportunity to consult independent experts, as so on, the overwhelming majority of patient/subjects are not likely either to become more competent or better decision-makers when the question concerns a biomedical intervention. Furthermore, I believe this will be true even when the doctor makes those more elaborate disclosures which may be required as a result of Canterbury v. Spence and its progeny.[28]

To a considerable degree, it is because I do not believe that the patient/subject's decision is likely to become significantly "better" regardless of any "practical" requirements (greater disclosure of risks, options, and so on) that I am so willing to "allow" even young children to have the same nonvetoable right as competent adults. In other words, I take this position not so much because children over seven will decide

---

[28]Canterbury v. Spence, 464 F.2d 272, D.C. Cir., 1972.

as well as adults, but perhaps more because most adults do not, in fact, decide significantly "better" than most children. If this heavily pessimistic premise is rejected, for example by arguing that some or even many adults do make "good" biomedical decisions given the appropriate (post-Canterbury) disclosures, then all that should be concluded is that some adults as well as some children ought not have their autonomy recognized. Such an argument only reintroduces decision-making competence as the criterion for recognizing autonomy, and then we are back to the very beginning. However, and to the contrary, having rejected competence as the test for recognizing autonomy, and frankly acknowledging that autonomy deserves recognition not because of its functional instrumental relevance but because of its symbolic importance, we are strongly compelled to recognize the autonomy of almost everyone—even children.

In the Report accompanying its final recommendations on prisoners, the National Commission states: "To respect a person is to allow that person to live in accord with his or her deliberate choices."[29] Obviously, I agree. The difference is that, unlike the Commission, at least as judged by its recommendations on children, I cannot understand why a child is not a person. If a child is a person, why does that person not possess the right to make choices?—even if, in the context of contemporary American family life, that right to choose is often only symbolic.

---

[29]Report and Recommendations: Research Involving Prisoners at 6. DHEW Pub. No. (05)76-131, Oct., 1976.

7

Morality and Medical Experimentation

Alister Browne

Erindale College, University of Toronto, Toronto, Canada

Experiments have been and are being carried out in the service of medical research on a vast scale. I want to discuss the morality of some of these experiments. In the first part of my essay, I shall discuss experimentation on human subjects; in the second part, experimentation on nonhuman subjects. The sorts of experiments I shall be talking about throughout are those which may be termed "pure experiments" —that is, experiments performed on subjects not for their own benefit, but for the benefit of future patients. While there are other valuable kinds of experiments, these seem to me to be the most important for experimental medicine.

I. EXPERIMENTS ON HUMAN SUBJECTS

There can be no serious doubt that experiments on human beings have contributed substantially to medical progress. Numerous surgical procedures, vaccines, medications, anesthetics, and diagnostic techniques, for example, have been developed and refined by such experimentation. On the other hand, experiments with human beings frequently involve elements of risk and unpleasantness. Many subjects have died, many more have been disabled, and still more have suffered both physically and mentally. Given this, the question arises: Under what conditions, if any, can we rightly use human beings as experimental subjects?

In the history of experimental medicine, many experiments have been performed on human beings without their knowledge or consent; individuals have, in effect, been conscripted for experimental purposes. The experimentalists have frequently tried to justify this by arguing that the suffering excluded by so proceeding far outweighed the suffering occasioned. For example, Professor H. von Hubbenet, who had done particularly comprehensive experiments on nonconsenting human beings pertaining to the contagiousness of syphillis in its secondary stage, published his findings with the following comment:

> [The publication of these observations] will perhaps restrain others, even with such a skeptical nature as my own, from making further experiments, often leading to the complete wrecking of the lives of the persons subjected to them. It would add considerably to my peace of mind in respect to the victims' fate, if these experiments were to spread the conviction that the secondary stage is contagious. If they lead to the establishing of such an important truth, the sufferings of a few individuals were not too high a price to be paid by mankind for the attainment of such a truly beneficial and practical result.[1]

Whether or not there is anything in principle wrong with this type of argument is a question that I shall come back to later. But, for the time being, I think that it can be fairly said that not even the most radical utilitarian will say that this sort of practice ought to be widespread. It is generally agreed that consent of the subject is typically a necessary condition for legitimate experimentation.

Introducing the notion of consent, however, does not put an end to our moral problems. For one thing, there are religions which hold that individuals do not have the right to consent to certain types of experiments. For example, the Roman Catholic Church holds that our bodies are not our property but that they are, in some sense, owned by God. And, since this is so, as Pope Pius XII put it, "one has no right to involve his physical or psychic integrity in medical experiments when they entail serious destruction, mutilation, wounds, or

---

[1]Quoted in V. Veressayev, *The Memoirs of a Physician* (1916). Cited in J. Katz with A. M. Capron and E. S. Glass, eds., *Experimentation with Human Beings,* New York, Russell Sage Foundation, 1972, p. 288.

perils."[2] This is certainly a conclusion that one can embrace without fear of refutation; for, so far as I can see, there is no way of refuting the view on which it rests that does not beg the question. On the other hand, that conclusion cannot be held up as an unchallangeable requirement of morality; for, there is likewise no nonquestion-begging way of establishing the view which forms its basis. However, there is one thing which can be said here with firmness: there should be no legislative prohibitions against experiments on consenting human beings. Given the divergence of moral views that there are on the matter, and the impossibility of settling the crucial issue in dispute, individuals should be left free to follow their consciences—to consent to or to refuse to consent to such experiments as they see fit.

But, even if we agree with this, we are now confronted with another question: When can it be said that a subject has, in the appropriate sense, consented to an experimental procedure? It is useful to begin to answer this by considering an account of a cancer experiment allegedly performed with consent. It was found that if live cancer cells were injected into patients who did not have cancer, the injected cells died out completely within three weeks. This was contrasted with another finding: If live cancer cells were implanted into patients with advanced cancer who had a short life expectancy, the implanted cells lived much longer in them—from three to eight weeks. This suggested that cancer patients have some immunological defect. But this hypothesis was not firm; there remained the possibility that the immunological defect was not due to the cancer *per se,* but to their associated gross debility. In order to rule out this possibility, doctors injected live cancer cells into 19 noncancer patients who were suffering from chronic debilitating diseases. None of these patients did, in fact, develop cancer. The doctors who carried out the experiment agreed that there was no written consent, but that the patients were verbally informed that this was a cancer experiment and that the injections might produce localized lumps. However, it was also acknowledged that the patients had not been informed that the injections consisted of live cancer cells, as it was felt, according to a spokesperson, that imparting such knowledge would adversely affect the patients' emotional and physical conditions. The hospital executive director said: "They were told that they were to get cells to test their immune reactions to cancer. There was no need to specify the nature of the cells because they were harmless."[3]

---

[2]"The Moral Limits of Research and Treatment" (1952). Cited in J. Katz, et al., *op. cit.,* pp. 549–550.

[3]M. H. Pappworth, *Human Guinea Pigs,* Boston, Beacon, 1967, pp. 124–125.

One thing that must be said about this experiment is that it was conducted without the consent of the subjects. The subjects agreed to participate in an experiment described as having features $F_1 \ldots F_n$; they were subjected to an experiment having features $F_1 \ldots F_{n+1}$. To say that by consenting to the former experiment they thereby in any way consented to the latter is a travesty of both logic and morality. The moral to be drawn from this is that persons can be said to have consented to an experiment only if they have been given an adequate description of the experiment. What constitutes such a description is difficult to specify in detail, but a general answer can be given: subjects must be told everything that might affect their decision to participate. If they have not been told that, they have not been put in a position to give informed consent.

Insistence on the notion of informed consent, however, will rule out, as illegitimate, a whole range of experiments that are frequently conducted. For one thing, we will have to forego all those (perhaps very valuable) experiments which are valid only if the subjects do not know that they are being experimented on. For another, since consent given without understanding is no more informed consent than consent given without information, we will have to forego any experiments making use of uncomprehending subjects such as the ignorant, the mentally defective, and, unless they have made prior provision (for example, by authorizing experimentation in certain circumstances, or by appointing a proxy to give such authorization), also the comatose and the senile.

There is another aspect to the notion of consent, not yet touched on, which diminishes still further the sorts of subjects that can be rightly used for experimental purposes. Suppose a thief holds a knife to your throat and says "Your money or your life" and suppose you give the thief your money. There is a sense in which you consented to give up your money. But, the sense in which you did, though it is informed, is not fully voluntary. We would say that there was an element of coercion or duress present; that you did not freely give your consent. Similarly, one may want to say that the consent required for experimentation on human subjects must not only be informed, but also voluntary; there must be no element of coercion or duress. This position is widely accepted. But, it now becomes a rather difficult and subtle matter to determine just when a subject consents freely. For example, can it be said that prisoners who are offered certain benefits (such as early parole) in return for consenting to experimental procedures are entirely free from all elements of coercion? Or the extremely poor who are offered financial reward? Or the sick, who (perhaps feeling that they have no use left in life, or that they have a debt of gratitude to repay) are approached by their doctors? Though voluntary consent may be obtained from individuals in all these categories on occasion, any claim that they have given such consent is open to some question; for, they are all in situations which make them especially liable to coercion of a sort that is always difficult to avoid and often difficult to detect. Thus, if we are to be strict about using only those subjects who have given their consent completely freely, without suspicion of any element of manipulation or coercion, we ought to draw on such individuals as the exception rather than the rule.

So, insisting on the notion of voluntary informed consent does have a certain amount of moral bite. It has the consequence that the bulk of human subjects used for experimental purposes must be drawn from those of us who are healthy and not in any state of medical, legal, financial, or social dependency. For these are the only individuals from whom voluntary informed consent can be unproblematically obtained. Since volunteers from this class are likely to be difficult to enlist, most medical experimentation must be done, if it is to be done, as it has always been done, on nonhuman animals. I now turn to examine such experiments. I want to do this partly because they raise important and interesting moral issues, and partly for another reason. The position I have just outlined concerning the conditions under which experimentation with human beings is morally permissible is one that can be defended on utilitarian or non-utilitarian grounds. It will emerge from what follows that if we endorse experimentation with nonhuman animals, then the position just outlined must be held on utilitarian grounds; this will entail that that position cannot be held in an absolutist way, but rather must be held as one that is always *sub judice,* overturnable in principle by considerations of utility. If, on the other hand, we deny that experimentation with nonhuman animals is morally permissible, then we can hold the above position in an absolutist way. But if we do so, we then have to accept the severe curb that this will put on experimental medicine.

II. EXPERIMENTS ON NON-HUMAN SUBJECTS

Let me begin by giving some examples of the ways in which animals are sometimes used for experimental purposes:

1. Researchers for Technology Inc., San Antonio, Texas constructed a pneumatically driven piston to impact an anvil attached to a special helmet called HAD I producing impact to the heads of 13 monkeys. But

they found the blows were insufficient to cause concussion, so they made a more powerful device called HAD II which they used on the same 13 monkeys and found that it caused cardiac damage, haemorrhages and brain damage from protrusion of plastic rings which they had implanted under the monkeys' skulls.

Monkey number 49-2 was again subjected to HAD II six days later, then 38 days later was struck multiple blows until she died.

Some of the animals who temporarily survived suffered subsequent fits and the researchers were impressed to find that after the experiments the monkeys' behaviour "was distinctly abnormal. The usual post-acceleration behaviour in the cage was that of hanging upside down cowering in a corner."[4]

2. At the National Institute for Medical Research, Mill Hill, London, W. Feldberg and S. L. Sherwood injected chemicals into the brains of cats—"with a number of widely differing substances, recurrent patterns of reaction were obtained. Retching, vomiting, defaecation, increased salivation and greatly accelerated respiration leading to panting were common features." . . . The injection into the brain of a large dose of Tubocurarine caused the cat to jump "from the table to the floor and then straight into its cage, where it started calling more and more noisily whilst moving about restlessly and jerkily . . . finally the cat fell with legs and neck flexed, jerking in rapid clonic movements, the condition being that of a major (epileptic) convulsion . . . within a few seconds the cat got up, ran for a few yards at high speed and fell in another fit. The whole process was repeated several times within the next ten minutes, during which the cat lost faeces and foamed at the mouth." This animal finally died thirty-five minutes after the brain injection.[5]

These are not isolated cases. The scale on which experiments with nonhuman animals are carried out is vast. For example, in Great Britain in 1969 over 5 million such experiments were performed; no figures are kept in the United States on these matters, but estimates range from 20 million to 200 million. Most of the experiments, it must also be said, are conducted without anesthetics.[6] Even if only 1 per cent of the experiments cause animals severe pain (and that is an unrealistically low figure), that is still an alarming amount of suffering.

Is there any justification for this? One does not have to be overly-sentimental toward animals to say that in many cases there is not.

---

[4]R. Ryder, "Experiments on Animals," in T. Regan and P. Singer, eds., *Animal Rights and Human Obligations,* Englewood Cliffs, N. J., Prentice-Hall, 1976, p. 38.

[5]*Ibid.,* p. 44.

[6]*Ibid.,* pp. 33–34. For still more cases of animal experimentation, see P. Singer, *Animal Liberation,* New York, Random House, 1975, and R. Ryder, *Victims of Science,* London, Davis-Poynter, 1975.

When, as is all too frequent, the end is trivial, and nontrivial pain is inflicted on the animals, then there is a firm case for saying that the experiments are immoral. But, of course, the end is not always trivial; when it is not, one may think that matters stand differently. In particular, one may think that if by conducting experiments which involve inflicting suffering on animals we can exclude a vastly greater amount of suffering in human beings, and if we cannot bring about that end with a lesser cost of suffering, then we are morally entitled to proceed.

The first thing I want to say about this principle is that I do not think that there is a special kind of suffering known as human suffering which is intrinsically more evil than another kind of suffering known as animal suffering. It would be discrimination of the most blatant sort to say that human suffering is intrinsically worse than animal suffering merely on the basis of physiological differences. So, if the claim is to be made, the difference in intrinsic value must be consequential on some other feature or features that human beings possess but animals do not. Natural candidates for this role are things like rationality, creative ability, intelligence, concept of self, ability to use moral concepts, moral autonomy, and so forth. Nonetheless, there are difficulties in appealing to such characteristics for this purpose. To begin with, it is not the case that all human beings possess them; certain mentally defective human beings do not. So, even if we were to grant that no animals possess them, the most that we could say is that the suffering of some or most human beings is intrinsically worse than the suffering of some or all animals. But, even that limited claim is doubtful. We commonly believe that we ought not to, and typically do not, count the suffering of one human being as more or less intrinsically evil than the equal amount of suffering of any other human being, regardless of however much they may differ with respect to the above sorts of characteristics. But if variations in these things are irrelevant to the valuation of suffering within the human species, they should, likewise, be irrelevant to cross-species comparisons of the value of suffering. The upshot of this is that unless one can find some characteristic, appropriately linked to the value of suffering, which human beings as a class possess but which animals do not, one is committed to asserting the equal intrinsic value of animal and human suffering. What such a characteristic could be, I do not know.

I thus conclude that, to paraphrase Bentham, quantity of suffering being equal, animal suffering is as bad as human suffering. If this is right, then it follows that it should be a matter of indifference whether the suffering one aims to reduce *via* experimentation is human or animal suffering. It also follows that we cannot endorse inflicting suffering on animals, but exclude doing the same to humans on the ground that animal suffering is less important than human suffering. This suggests that the principle we began by discussing ought to be stated without reference to animals or human beings. If, however, we do so restate it, the result is a principle which entails that if it is morally all right to use animals in experiments in certain ways, then there is nothing in principle wrong with using human beings in experiments in exactly the same ways. That implication, no doubt, would commonly be regarded as morally outrageous. Nonetheless, if we are going to block it and say that it is morally defensible to use animals for experiments in ways in which we cannot use human beings, then we had better be able to point out some morally relevant difference between the two species which would justify this difference in treatment. Otherwise, we could rightly be accused of an analogue of racism and sexism, speciesism: the treating of one species differently from another when there is no morally relevant difference between them. Can we do this?

Suppose that there is a race of beings which are like us in that: they can experience pain to a considerable degree; they look just like us; they mate and have families; and they have some kind of social organization. But, also suppose that they are unlike us in that: they do not communicate by means of engaging in anything that we would describe as linguistic activity; they are much weaker than we are in the sense that they could not defend themselves against organized and concerted attacks by us—they are, in short, in our power; and they are much less intelligent than we are. Would it be morally all right to use these beings for experimental purposes? If we say "yes," then unless some further differentiating features are forthcoming, I do not see why we cannot rightly use certain mentally defective human beings for experimental purposes; for, there are mental defectives who would satisfy the description I have given.

Now, suppose that this race were slightly different. Instead of looking just like us, its members were covered with hair, had protruding mouths, longish arms, and tails. And, just to give them a name, suppose we called them "monkeys." If it is not morally right to experiment with the race I earlier described, it could not be morally right to experiment with monkeys, because these physiological differences could not be morally relevant differences. Conversely, if it is morally all right to experiment with monkeys, then it must be morally all right to experiment with that imaginary race. But if so, then it should also seem morally all right to experiment on certain classes of human beings without their consent.

The same consequences seem to me to hold if we modified the race still further, for example by saying that they walked on four legs rather than two, were easily domesticated as house pets, and were fond of chewing on bones. Nor need we confine our attention to the higher animals to run this sort of argument. If we compare animals lower down on the chain—say guinea pigs, white mice, or even fruit flies— to really defective human beings—say those who have monitorable brain activity, but who are nonetheless irreversibly unconscious—it is going to be hard to cite any morally relevant feature that the latter possess but which the former do not. It will also be impossible, in the absence of some differentiating intrinsic feature, to take the higher ground here and say that human beings have a right to be treated as ends in themselves, never merely as means, but animals do not. For, that alleged right, if it is not to be based on some shaky intuition, must be based on a morally significant distinction between animals and human beings.

Thus, it seems hopeless to find a justification for using animals for experimental purposes while at the same time maintaining an absolute prohibition against using any nonconsenting human beings for the same purposes. The most that one could hope to find is some characteristic or set of characteristics which would enable us to endorse the use of some or all animals while maintaining an absolute prohibition against the similar use of some or most nonconsenting human beings. Candidates for such characteristics are not scarce; features such as rationality, creative ability, intelligence, concept of self, capacity to make moral judgments, moral autonomy, and so forth, immediately come to mind. But, even granting that these are characteristics which most human beings possess, but which all animals lack, or lack in some required degree, I do not think that any of them will singly or jointly do the required job. I do, indeed, think that it is generally wrong to use beings possessing such characteristics without their consent; I do not, however, think that any cogent grounds can be provided for saying that it is always wrong to do so. There is no a priori connection between these features and the absolute prohibition in question; so, any alleged connection must be consequentialist. But, if the connection is consequentialist, then it will not support an absolute prohibition.

If this is right, then it is, indeed, the case that the principle introduced near the beginning of this section ought to be stated without reference to animals or human beings; moreover, some further qualifications need to be added in order for it to accurately represent the case. In particular, if one is to endorse experimentation on animals, one needs to hold that: If, by inflicting suffering on some innocent beings (which would not otherwise suffer), we can exclude a vastly greater amount of suffering in other innocent beings, and cannot bring about that end with less suffering, then we are morally entitled to do so. But, now one may have some qualms about accepting this principle. For, if one does accept it, then one is committed to the view that there is nothing wrong in principle with experimenting on innocent human beings without their consent to prevent vast amounts of suffering. The only criticism that could be made of a person doing so would amount to the claim that the person made a miscalculation in the estimates of suffering. Still, it seems to me that unless one is prepared to accept at least this principle, one cannot endorse the use of animals for experimental purposes.[7] Thus, the conclusion of the inquiry so far seems to be that either it is morally all right to experiment on human beings without their consent or it is morally wrong to experiment on animals. Neither of these views seems readily acceptable.

Is there any way of avoiding these undesirable alternatives? In view of what has gone before, one can, I think, say it is morally all right to experiment with animals and yet resist the slide to "so it must be morally all right to experiment with nonconsenting human beings" only by citing certain untoward consequences of so treating human beings which do not accrue from so treating animals. There are such consequences. The capacity to suffer varies in proportion to the complexity of a being. A being that has highly developed characteristics such as rationality, a concept of self, creative ability, a moral sense, and so on, is susceptible to pain at more points, and, in some instances, to greater degrees than a being that lacks these characteristics altogether, or possesses them to a lesser extent. So, given that normal human beings are enormously more complex than any animals in this regard, there is some reason for generally giving them preferential treatment; they are likely to suffer more than animals from the same treatment.[8]

---

[7] I say "at least," for the offered principle seems to me the weakest one to which a person could appeal to try to justify animal experimentation. One may, of course, adopt a stronger version of the principle—for example, one which omits the word "vastly," or is formulated in terms of duty rather than moral permissibility. But, such variations in strength would only cause variations in the number of occasions on which we could legitimately use nonconsenting human subjects for experimental purposes. This will still not affect my main point, namely, that one cannot endorse animal experimentation without embracing a principle which entails that experimentation on nonconsenting human beings is not always wrong.

[8] On occasion, however, the fact that human beings possess such features would militate toward the opposite conclusion. By possessing such characteristics, they may be able to understand the nature of the experiment, and thus be able to avoid anxiety and fear that could not be quelled in animals. It may thus turn out in certain cases that experimentation on humans would occasion less suffering than the same experimentation on animals. If so, then we surely ought to favor using humans as experimental subjects.

There are also consequentialist grounds for giving preferential treatment to defective human beings. Human beings typically can envisage a future for themselves. Since no human being is immune from being reduced by some mishap or disease or age to a vegetating state, if experimentation on defective human beings were allowed, certain anxieties and fears about a possible future would naturally be aroused. Human beings also typically fit into networks of social relationships and dependencies such that anything which adversely or beneficially affects them also affects their near connections. To experiment on human beings (however defective they may be) would be very likely to arouse substantial feelings of horror and disgust in others. Neither of these considerations, it seems to me, can be applied to the case of animals with the same force. Animals (especially the so-called higher animals) can indeed experience horrors of anticipation or distress at the loss or sufferings of a fellow creature. But, there does not seem to be any real parity between what they suffer and what human beings would. Still, it must be acknowledged that if, as I allege is the case, these are the only sorts of reasons we can cite to justify treating members of the different species in question differently, and if it is the case that it is morally all right to experiment with animals, then if the untoward effects of experimenting on human beings could be avoided, there would be nothing wrong with doing so.

Nothing I have said, however, does show that it is morally right to use animals for experimental purposes. At most, my argument only shows that it would generally be worse to experiment on human beings without their consent. But, it is compatible with this to say that both sorts of experimentation are morally wrong. So, the question arises: Is it ever morally justifiable to use animals for experimental purposes? I have already isolated the weakest principle that anyone who wishes to answer this in the affirmative must subscribe to. A full-dress defense of that principle is beyond the scope of this essay, but I do want to indicate that I think it ought to be accepted. I take it to be uncontroversial that suffering is a bad thing and that, other things being equal, we are morally entitled to reduce it whenever possible. But it is, of course, far from uncontroversial that we can rightly use any means to reduce suffering. There are philosophers who hold that certain actions are wrong whatever the consequences. These philosophers would thus say that suffering ought not be reduced if to do so required an act of this forbidden type. Now if one is to balk at the principle in question, one has to claim that inflicting suffering on nonconsenting innocent beings (whether they be animal or human) is such an act. To make that claim, however, one needs to argue that those beings possess some feature or set of features which is connected in a nonconsequentialist way with a prohibition against using such beings without their consent. What could such a feature or set of features be? That question may not be uncontroversially rhetorical but I cannot provide any plausible answer to it. Thus, I think that the principle in question ought to be accepted.

Since I accept the principle in question, I do think that it is morally all right to use animals in experiments in certain circumstances, specifically when there is good reason to think that by so doing we can thereby exclude vastly greater suffering. And since, as I earlier argued, it is generally worse to use human beings for the same purposes without their consent, we ought not do so as long as animals are available. Still, I want to acknowledge that according to the position I am endorsing, the only thing that makes it wrong to experiment with human beings without their consent results from certain contingencies of consequences, not any prohibition of principle. It may be difficult to imagine cases in which we could firmly say that such experimentation is morally acceptable; but that, I submit, is just because the consequentialist case against it is so very strong.[9]

---

[9] I am indebted to my commentators Barbara Mishkin and (especially) Louis Katzner for helpful critiques. I am also grateful to Marylou Browne and Richard Sikora for having read and commented on earlier drafts of this essay. In developing the argument of Part II, I have profited greatly from a fine paper by T. Regan, "The Moral Basis of Vegetarianism," *Can. J. of Phil.* 5, pp. 181–214.

8

The Moral Admissibility or Inadmissibility of Nontherapeutic Fetal Experimentation

Stephen Toulmin

University of Chicago, Chicago, Illinois

I. THE ALTERNATIVE VIEWPOINTS

Before there is any question of discussing the practical limits or controls needed in any policy for a restricted program of fetal experimentation, a prior ethical question must be faced:

> Is the use of experimental procedures on a human fetus, or on fetal tissues and organs, morally admissible at all in situations where those procedures are "nontherapeutic"—that is, not immediately directed to the individual medical benefit of the affected fetus or mother?

Papers before the National Commission for the Protection of Human Subjects of Biomedical and Behavioral Research give answers to this question that range all the way from advocating a total ban on all nontherapeutic fetal experimentation, by way of various carefully-qualified middle-of-the-road positions, to the view that any such research is morally admissible, provided only that it aims at improved medical knowledge.[1] If the former view is accepted, the question of practical restrictions and controls does not (of course) even arise. If the latter view is accepted, there would be no need for any special controls over fetal research, beyond those that apply to all human experimentation. So, my first task here will be to present the arguments advanced in support of these two extreme positions.

The Case Against Special Controls

The case for the most liberal position toward fetal experimentation is argued by Joseph Fletcher. As I understand the case, Fletcher accepts an overriding moral claim in favor of the pursuit of biomedical knowledge, and sees nothing in the obstetric situations characteristic of fetal research to limit the scope of that claim, beyond a requirement of maternal consent in the case of fetuses (whether *in utero* or *ex utero*) which are still alive:

> In fetal research, whether with live or lifeless fetuses, what we are after is the ability to save life and lift its quality. Our goal is useful medical knowledge . . . We must be delivered from the kind of ethics which let "principles" . . . nullify useful know-how in medicine's effort to save and improve life.[2]

The chief thrust of Fletcher's argument is directed against those who would reject such a liberal policy, and would place restrictions on biomedical research in the name of general or universal "principles." He construes their argument as part of a political campaign to impose on medical scientists, against their own feelings and better judgments, limitations that are required only by adherents to a "doctrinaire and rule-oriented" system of ethics. In reply, Fletcher pleads for a "pragmatic and value-oriented" approach to the issues in dispute, based not on a "categorically rigid" insistence on hard-and-fast rules or principles, but on a readiness to consider problems "situationally" or case by case: an approach that will be "nondogmatic, flexible, particularized, value-oriented." He is evidently confident that, in all cases involving a "tension between life-saving research . . . and prohibitions on fetal

---

[1] The original version of this essay was prepared for the National Commission for the Protection of Human Subjects of Biomedical and Behavioral Research.

[2] Joseph Fletcher, "Fetal Research: An Ethical Appraisal," The National Commission for the Protection of Human Subjects of Biomedical and Behavioral Research, *Research on the Fetus: Appendix,* Washington, D. C., U.S. Department of Health, Education, and Welfare, 1975, pp. 3–12.

research," such a situational approach will certainly lead us to favor medical science.

With all respect, I cannot agree that this conclusion follows, even on Joseph Fletcher's own grounds. The distinction between "rule-oriented dogmatism" and "value-oriented pragmatism" is not (as I understand it) a distinction that cuts between rival systems of ethics. Rather, it cuts between alternative ways in which any ethical system can be applied to actual cases. Whatever considerations are appealed to as morally relevant to a case in question can be advanced in either a dogmatic or a pragmatic spirit; but the task of demonstrating that specific considerations are or are not morally relevant to a particular case is a separate matter. As a result, the case for restricting fetal research is not met by merely pointing out that advocates of restriction frequently present their case in a dogmatic or absolutist spirit. On the contrary, it must be shown that the specific considerations appealed to by the restrictionists lack the moral relevance to the fetal research situation that they claim. Otherwise, the case for restriction can equally well be advanced in a "situational" manner, and in a "pragmatic and value-oriented" spirit. (As I read it, this is just what Sissela Bok does in her paper.)

In my view, Joseph Fletcher has not succeeded in demonstrating the impossibility of arguing a case for limitations and controls in precisely such "situational" terms. The problem for his approach is that "situations" are not self-describing. With the most flexible and value-oriented spirit in the world, we might still acknowledge, for example, that a woman has a genuine moral stake in the disposal of her own aborted issue, even after it is unquestionably dead, and so regard Fletcher's guidelines for fetal research as disregarding her legitimate interest. Different characterizations of the fetal research situation can thus lead to different moral conclusions about the admissibility of such research, and Fletcher's argument comes to an end (it seems to me) before the operative issues have been addressed, whether in a pragmatic spirit or any other.

To put the point in Fletcher's own vocabulary, the Commission's terms of reference call for guidance, precisely, over the questions: *(1)* which of the alternative particularized descriptions of the fetal research situation properly balances all the values and benefits that constitute authentically relevant moral features of that situation; and *(2)* on what conditions the categorical present claims, benefits and interests of individuals may properly be set aside in favor of hypothetical future benefits to "science" or "humanity" in general.

The Case for a Total Ban

At the opposite end of the spectrum is the conclusion that fetal experimentation is justifiable only when its aim is immediately therapeutic, and so should be "limited to procedures which have as their aim the enhancement of the life-systems of the fetuses"—that is, the particular fetuses which are being experimented on, not fetuses in general. On this view, all nontherapeutic fetal experimentation should be banned as morally inadmissible. All of the arguments advanced in support of such a ban concede that the fetus is—at any rate, after a certain point in pregnancy—a creature of a kind that is entitled to primary rights, but otherwise they take two rather different forms. There are those that deny that any third parties can have the right to give proxy consent for such experimentation on behalf of the fetus, and there are those that deny the medical scientist's right to pry into "the secrets of the Almighty," or to "compromise the dignity" of present human life for the hypothetical benefit of future human beings. Both Paul Ramsey[3] and Seymour Siegel[4] advance arguments of the former type. Siegel alone puts major weight on the latter. LeRoy Walters also argues, more generally, that there are genuine risks of brutalization involved in permitting exceptions to the rule that hypothetical and general future benefits may not be sought at the price of categorical and particular present suffering.

Let me cite Seymour Siegel's paper first:

> [T]he burden of proof is always upon those who wish to subordinate the interests of the individual presently before us for the sake of those who will come later. Experiments for the "good of medicine" or for the sake of the "progress of knowledge" are not automatically legitimated, if they cause harm to people now, because someone in the future might benefit. What comes in the future is what the Talmudic literature calls "the secrets of the Almighty." This does not mean that we have no responsibility toward the future. However, we have a greater responsibility to those who are now in our care. These reflections do not, of course, preclude the scientist's search. These are intended to make him more cautious in his search.[5]

---

[3]Paul Ramsey, "Moral Issues in Fetal Research," *Research on the Fetus: Appendix,* pp. 6–11.

[4]Seymour Siegel, "Experimentation on Fetuses Which are Judged to be Non-Viable," *Research on the Fetus: Appendix,* p. 7–1.

[5]*Ibid.,* p. 7–1.

When considered in the light of its historical origin, the Talmudic appeal to the sanctity of Divine "secrets," together with Siegel's call for caution in the face of "the indeterminacy of the future," must indeed be understood—on the face of the words—as precluding not just therapeutic fetal experimentation, but biomedical research of all kinds. In this respect, Siegel's preliminary argument, like Fletcher's, does not seem to me sufficiently fine-grained, as it stands. Is fetal research in his view on all fours with all nontherapeutic biomedical research? Or, are there special limitations on fetal, as contrasted with later, medical experimentation? If the latter is the case, then what are the morally relevant considerations distinguishing the two classes of research? Do these have predominantly to do with the problems of consent, as in Ramsey's argument? Or, are there other considerations? It would be helpful if he could spell out more exactly what the crucial moral factors are.

What guidance does Siegel give us, in fact, about the conditions on which fetal research might have been morally admissible, despite the general burden of proof against incautious research projects? As I read his view, adult patients of sound mind do have the right to consent to nontherapeutic experimentation on their own bodies since the act of giving informed consent protects their human dignity from compromise. If that is the crucial factor, then Siegel's case for a ban on nontherapeutic fetal research becomes the same as Ramsey's. Both men agree that the problem of obtaining adequate fetal consent to such experimentation is insuperable, and so conclude that fetal experimentation is admissible only if its aims are directly therapeutic for the particular fetus under examination.

Taking all the available literature together, then, it is clear that the central arguments for or against a total ban on nontherapeutic fetal research are those which turn on the admissibility of proxy consent, by the mother, the father or other third parties. These arguments will, of course, be fully convincing either way only to those who accept the notion that the fetus itself can have morally relevant "claims" or "interests" in its own right. (The denial of primary rights to the "previable" fetus entails that no question of proxy consent can arise, so that, on that alternative position, only the mother's own primary consent can come up for question.) Over this central issue, the cases presented by Paul Ramsey for, and Father Richard McCormick against, a total ban carry particular weight.

Rather than attempting to condense their close arguments still further, at the price of distorting them, let me simply recall the precise point at which the two men part company. Granted that it is out of the question for the fetus to give direct consent to being made the object of nontherapeutic experimentation, Ramsey holds that there is no ground on which any third party can legitimately give consent on its behalf, either vicariously or as a proxy:

> I myself tend to believe that any use of the fetal subject, children, the unconscious, the dying or the condemned would be an abuse. . . . Seizing the "golden opportunity" afforded by abortion to exact—and falsely to "presume"—acts of charity from the fetus as a human research subject . . . can only mean a terrible distortion of medical ethics to date, and of the Jewish-Christian Tradition which was the foundation of its regard for the sanctity of human life.[6]

Ramsey's position has the merit of cutting along a clean line. Like Siegel, he would have fetal experimentation permitted only when it was directly "related to promoting the life of the [particular] fetus." Richard McCormick, by contrast, seems prepared to allow third parties (specifically, the parents) a right to "vicarious" or "proxy" consent on behalf of the fetus, as on behalf of a child, on certain strict conditions. How, then, does his argument rebut Ramsey's unqualified case against nontherapeutic fetal research? It does so (as I understand) by claiming that vicarious consent can be justified, provided that it is directed at the question:

> What may it be presumed that the fetus ought reasonably to consent to, if it were capable of understanding what is at issue, and taking this decision for itself?[7]

Since the fetus is a human creature, and so potentially a rational being, there are certain things to which it ought to be prepared to consent, in virtue of that potential rationality; and suitably qualified third parties (for example, the mother) are accordingly qualified to give its vicarious consent in these terms.

Father McCormick supports this conclusion by appeal to considerations from "the natural-law tradition" to the effect:

> . . . that there are certain identifiable values that we ought to support, attempt to realize, and never directly suppress because they are definitive of our flourishing and well-being.[8]

---

[6]Ramsey, *op. cit.,* p. 6–11.

[7]This is a referrence to an earlier draft of Richard McCormick, "Experimentation on the Fetus: Policy Proposals," the final version of which is in *Research on the Fetus: Appendix,* pp. 5–1 to 5–11. All future references here to McCormick are to his earlier draft.

[8]McCormick, *op. cit.*

As he notes, this is not a position that depends on any specifically theological dogma:

> Knowledge of these values and of the prescriptions and proscriptions associated with them is, in principle, available to human reason. That is, they require for their discovery no Divine revelation.[9]

Nonetheless (I would comment), this is not a position that has won universal agreement. Many people would argue in reply, for instance, that we do not have a self-evident obligation to act rationally all the time, and that we cannot reasonably impose such an obligation by proxy on a fetus. Carrying this line of criticism further, Paul Ramsey himself replies that McCormick's argument actually imposes on the fetus an obligation to perform an implied act of charity that, in an adult, would represent at best an act of supererogation; and he finds this morally repugnant.

Speaking for myself, although I cannot wholly support Paul Ramsey's position, I have great respect both for his conclusion, and for the force of the arguments by which he supports it. If members of the Commission hold that the fetus is entitled to primary rights, and if they decide to recommend that the present ban on nontherapeutic fetal research be continued, they can accordingly do so with the confidence that such a recommendation can be given a firm ethical foundation.

The Case for a Restricted Program of Fetal Research

There remains an intermediate position, which would permit a resumption of nontherapeutic fetal research on a restricted basis and subject to carefully designed institutional controls. Among those who have prepared papers for the Commission, both supporters and opponents of the view that the fetus can have primary rights (for example, Sissela Bok and Richard McCormick) have argued for variants of this intermediate position; and, despite the force of Paul Ramsey's advocacy, I would personally be inclined to join with this intermediate group.

For those who deny the fetus primary rights, the case for placing restrictions and controls on nontherapeutic fetal experimentation must rest, of course, on the interests of other parties—on the direct interests of the parents in the disposal of an aborted fetus, on the agony of mind to be expected in parents from the fear of casual experimentation on their issue, and on the general risk of brutalization in society, if medical

---

[9]*Ibid.*

research workers are permitted to handle human beings and human tissues in a callous or arrogant manner. Sissela Bok's paper accordingly gives prominence to the question at just what point in fetal development these dangers become realistic, so that the use of the whole previable fetus for nontherapeutic research should cease to be permissible. For those who would accord the fetus primary rights, on the other hand, it remains necessary to reply further to Paul Ramsey's arguments. In my opinion, this can be effectively done, if we make one small modification to the statement of Father McCormick's case. We can follow him in requiring that proxy consent be directed toward the question:

> What may it be presumed that the fetus ought reasonably to consent to, if it were capable of understanding what is at issue, and taking this decision for itself?[10]

We can alternatively pose the operative question in the form:

> What may it be presumed that the fetus could not reasonably object to, if it were capable . . . ?

This emendation does little to alter the practical substance of McCormick's proposal, but it does avoid the objection of imputing "obligations" to the fetus, in virtue of its "rational nature," and it does underline the force of McCormick's requirement (in the case of nontherapeutic experimentation on children) that such research should be attended by: "no discernible risk, no notable pain, no notable inconvenience, and . . . promise of considerable benefit."[11] For, to declare that nontherapeutic fetal experimentation, in order to be morally permissible, must be of a kind that the fetus itself, if cognizant, "could not reasonably object to," suggests, on the one hand, that such experimentation should be limited to, for example, kinds of innocuous research investigations that might be conducted incidentally on infants in a postnatal clinic, and would, at the other extreme, certainly rule out any idea of, for example, stockpiling aborted human fetuses in tissue or organ "banks." Accordingly, I conclude: Whatever view the members of the Commission take about the fetus' entitlement to primary rights, if they decide to recommend that the present ban on nontherapeutic fetal experimentation be relaxed in favor of a restricted program of fetal research, subject to careful controls and safeguards, they can again do so with the confidence that such a recommendation can be given a firm ethical foundation. Either way, however, the task of striking a balance

---

[10] *Ibid.*
[11] *Ibid.*

between the risks of such research, and the benefits to be foreseen from it, remains a highly delicate one; and the key task of the Commission must be to devise appropriate safeguards and controls.

For those who support a moderate position of this kind, therefore, the substantive problem immediately becomes one of striking a balance between the risks to which the fetus, the mother, and society would be exposed as a result of nontherapeutic fetal experimentation, and the benefits that would presumably accrue to medical science, and to humanity at large.

II. IMPLICATIONS OF THE MODERATE CONSENSUS

Any policy for the licensing of nontherapeutic fetal experimentation on a limited basis must be based *(1)* on an analysis of the actual risks and potential benefits involved, and *(2)* on the establishment of appropriate institutional safeguards to monitor and control the application of that policy. The papers on the ethics of fetal experimentation that are before the Commission provide significant consensus about what we might call the "moral boundary conditions" within which any such policy should be framed, in case a restricted program of nontherapeutic fetal research is resumed. I shall draw attention to the key elements in that consensus here, while adding some additional comments of my own.

The Risks of Fetal Experimentation

In assessing the risks attendant on fetal experimentation, we should consider separately three groups that are apparently at risk: the fetuses themselves, the mothers, and society at large.

As to the fetuses, from certain points of view, it might appear paradoxical that we should consider their interests at all. Father McCormick's paper on "Proxy Consent in the Experimental Situation," for instance, links the exercise of parental consent partly (though not entirely) to the child's prospect of survival. Nothing should be done, by way of an experimental procedure, which might reasonably be supposed to risk having deleterious effects on the child's future welfare. To that extent, it would seem, the consequential arguments can hardly be extended, as they stand, to a fetus which is due to be aborted. Yet, the papers submitted to the Commission generally agree that such a fetus may nevertheless be exposed to two significant types of risk. First, there is the risk of discomfort or pain during the experimental procedure, in the event that its development is sufficiently advanced; and second, there is the risk of deformed birth, in case the mother withdraws her consent to the abortion after the experimental procedure has actually taken place.

Several papers mention the risk of pain and discomfort to the fetus in passing, but none of them, in my view, pays close enough attention to the topic. It seems somehow to be assumed that the question of sentience is directly linked to that of "viability," and discussion of fetal pain tends to switch, almost immediately, to that of the fetus' capacity for autonomy or survival. So, let me underline here the fact that these two issues are, on the face of it, quite independent. The question whether or not a fetus is capable of surviving *ex utero* after being aborted has no obvious or direct bearing on the question of whether or not it is capable of experiencing pain and discomfort if subjected to experimental procedures either *in utero,* before abortion, or *ex utero,* after abortion, but before death. If it were clear that some fetuses are, in this respect, "sentient" by, say, the sixth month of pregnancy, then there would be an equally clear moral objection to employing painful nontherapeutic experimental procedures on them at that stage, for, in these circumstances, the use of such procedures would be quite straight-forwardly cruel. At just what stage in fetal development sentience may reasonably be supposed present, however, is a question about which I have found regrettably little solid evidence. At what stage, for instance, is the central nervous system sufficiently consolidated for sentience to be a possibility? (Evidently, much of the motor activity of the fetus is purely reflex in character, but this is presumably less completely the case the nearer the fetus approaches to full term.) I suggest that these are questions about which the Commission should obtain testimony from impartial experts. For, there are certainly some kinds of fetal experimentation whose permissibility would have to be made dependent, not on the "viability" of the fetus, but on its *sentience.*

The other class of risks capable of affecting fetuses that are due to be aborted springs from the possibility that the mother may change her mind about the abortion after the experimental procedure is complete, and the fetuses may subsequently be born deformed. Two different proposals have been made concerning these risks. Sissela Bok suggests an insurance scheme, to compensate mothers who are left with the task of bringing up a deformed child, in consequence of such a fetal experiment. Paul Ramsey refers (disapprovingly) to the view that experiments should be undertaken only as a part of a single operative procedure, designed to terminate with the abortion. This would normally obviate the possibility of the mother's revoking her consent after the experiments have taken place. I feel that both suggestions deserve serious consideration by the Commission, though I am personally inclined to think the latter proposal is the more satisfactory one. In a case of this kind, after all, the financial burden is the least of the agonies a mother will be exposed to, and it would be preferable to design our operative procedures in a way that spared her the other, more painful, psychological and personal burdens. At the same time, Sissela Bok's proposal does have the merit of drawing attention to the important question (also referred to by Joseph Fletcher) of who is to take responsibility for the future welfare of those fetuses, or premature infants, whose lives are preserved after a late abortion, by medical intervention against the wishes of the mother, especially when they are too frail or deformed to be suitable subjects for adoption. (In a suitable social and political environment, a case might be made for regarding such children as "wards of the State," and for assigning them to publicly-financed foster homes, rather than obliging their mother to raise them, even with the help of insurance benefits.)

The risks of nontherapeutic fetal experimentation to the mother are not in dispute, and it is generally agreed by the members of the present panel that the proposal to perform such experiments should never be made the reason for delaying a planned abortion. On the one hand, the experimental procedures themselves may be a direct source of pain and discomfort; on the other hand, they may have longer-term medical consequences; and, either way, any delay in the abortion is generally undesirable. There is much to be said, therefore, in favor of Paul Ramsey's argument that—if there are to be fetal experiments at all—they should, at most, be combined with the actual abortion procedures.

In addition to the possible physiological effects of fetal research on the mother, however, these risks have another side also, to which I feel the papers before the Commission give too little attention. The psychological aspects of pregnancy and abortion are a subject about which too little is known; but we do at least know enough to recognize that it would be morally wrong to disregard a woman's psychological investment in a pregnancy, and in the issue of that pregnancy. Whatever the circumstances in which a pregnancy is terminated, the mother should have confidence that the issue will be handled and disposed of, both before and after death, in a respectful and humane way; the lack of such an assurance would be a legitimate source of grief and guilt. This represents, therefore, an additional element to be taken into account in judging the potential damage to be guarded against in fetal research. (I shall return to this topic at the end of this essay.)

More attention is paid in the papers to the risks affecting society at large, in case nontherapeutic fetal research is permitted, either at all, or without being subject to adequate controls. In this respect, the fear is one of "brutalization"—that is, a fear that any relaxation in the general feelings of reverence and concern toward the tissues and remains of the dead and dying could give the color of extenuation to other forms of callousness, violence and human indifference. It may be questioned whether, applied to fetal research in particular, these fears are in fact realistic; every apprentice physician is exposed to the dissecting room as part of the normal training and, by the time he or she is medically qualified, his or her attitudes to human tissues and cadavers will have been effectively formed and tested. So, it is not clear that a properly regulated program of fetal research can, in this respect, have any novel effect on the attitudes of physicians and medical researchers.

On the other hand, the existence and currency of these fears is itself a matter of importance and moral relevance, as well as being a significant element in the social context of the Commission's proceedings. The sources of this fear are not hard to trace. Over the last 25 years, the public's image of the physician has changed. Traditionally, the general practitioner of medicine was one of those people—along with the local priest or minister, and perhaps the family lawyer—to whom the individual could turn for advice, in absolute confidence that any advice received was concerned wholly with his or her personal welfare. The family doctor had no perceptible conflict of interests: his or her whole position was dependent on the capacity to act as a fully-committed personal advisor. Even after a patient was admitted to the hospital, he or she could still look to the family doctor to represent his or her interests unhesitatingly, and to rescue him or her, if the need arose, from the hospital's bureaucratic toils. The new alliance between attendant physicians and medical research scientists has brought that implicit confidence into question. As a result, many people today actively feel something less than certain that the medical advice they get is purely directed at their own individual benefit, or that it is not, in part, motivated by other concerns, such as by the research interests either of the attendant physician or of that physician's colleagues. (This uncertainty has been only aggravated by the growing shift in the locus of medical practice, from the bedside or private consulting room, to the hospital clinic.) So, the current public image of the physician is in the course of being transformed from the friendly and totally trustworthy one of the "family G.P.," to the intimidating and psychologically opaque one of the "white-coated" scientist.

No doubt, this transformation in public attitudes has gone too far, and I am not in any way claiming that it is justified. Still, this change itself has made it possible for public feelings about abortions and fetal experimentation to be inflamed beyond a realistic level, to the point that the collaboration between attendant physicians and biomedical scientists can sometimes be made to appear an "unholy alliance" for promoting scientific knowledge, in disregard of patients' interests. Given the resulting disquiet, the actual *fear* of brutalization becomes as relevant a feature of the ethical situation as the objective *risks* of brutalization; any procedures for supervising human experimentation in general, and particularly fetal experimentation, must take this fear into account. For this reason among others, the general public has a legitimate moral interest in being adequately represented on the ethical and human experimentation committees of all hospitals in which nontherapeutic fetal experimentation is to be undertaken. Such lay representation will, of course, not just protect the public against the possibility of overenthusiasm or malpractice on the part of research workers, but also protect the research scientists themselves against uninformed or ill-motivated outside criticism.

There is one other source of public disquiet, which takes us beyond the scope of the Commission's immediate recommendations, though not beyond its topics of discussion. Let me simply mention this in passing. Some years ago, it was demonstrated at Cambridge University that a newly fertilized human zygote could be kept alive *in vitro* for a period of days, during multiple cell-divisions. This demonstration drew widespread public attention. The resulting outcry about "test-tube" babies played on fears and hostilities toward science that have roots in the Middle Ages, if not in antiquity. This episode is relevant to the present controversy about fetal research. If we carry the discussion of "viability" to its final conclusion, the question indeed arises whether it will not eventually be possible to engage in "zygote culturing," and even to bring an embryo to full term outside the mother's womb. If this were ever practicable, there might well be situations in which it was both medically desirable and ethically permissible to bring a child into life by *in vitro* gestation. But, another application of the same techniques would also make it possible to mass-produce human tissues and embryos for use in scientific experimentation. It is my sense of the matter that people of most persuasions find the prospect of such "zygote farming" morally repugnant. Whatever their position on the "personhood" issues, they would see such a practice as encouraging unacceptably casual and arrogant attitudes toward the control of human life.

The Benefits of Fetal Experimentation

Surely, none of those who have prepared papers for the Commission on the ethics of fetal research has any doubt about the positive value of improving medical knowledge. The implication apparent in some speeches at the National Academy of Sciences discussion, that those who raised moral objections to unsupervised, nontherapeutic fetal experimentation are "against science," is accordingly beside the point. The question is not whether our medical knowledge about pregnancy and fetal development ought to be improved by all legitimate means at our disposal, but rather how far this can be done without lapsing into morally unacceptable procedures. So, it should go without saying, here, both that fetal experimentation holds out the promise of genuine and substantial benefits to "medical science"—both directly, to pediatrics and obstetrics, but also to general physiology, pathology and medical therapeutics—and that those benefits can reasonably be expected to carry over to "humanity" in general, as the new techniques of biomedical science become incorporated into actual medical practice. If ethical questions must, nevertheless, be raised about these benefits, those questions have to do with the sad, yet realistic, need to satisfy ourselves that these beneficial results are being achieved in fact, and are not being sidetracked into directions to which legitimate objections might be taken. So, it is desirable to introduce, at this point, a word of caution about the intended beneficiaries of fetal research—namely, "medical science" in the first place, and "humanity" in the second.

As to medical science: the same public disquiet that shows itself in fears that fetal experimentation might encourage "brutalization" also extends to hesitations about the personal motives underlying the medical scientist's own research. The suspicion is that, in some cases, the legitimate theoretical goals of medical science may eventually become partly confused in the minds of those human agents who are personally engaged in fetal experimentation with the satisfaction of their intellectual curiosity or the personal achievement; thus, a proprietary attitude toward their own research may lead them to expose fetuses or fetal organs to experimental manipulation *praeter necessitatem*. (This anxiety, too, was reportedly evident in the National Academy of Sciences discussion.) Once again, these hesitations may well be groundless in all but a tiny minority of cases. But, in so delicate a field as that of fetal research—as in all matters involving the possibility of delicate conflicts of interests—it is not enough that justice should in fact be done; it must also be seen to be done, in a visible and verifiable manner. Once again, therefore, I am led to conclude that the general public has a legitimate moral interest in being represented by lay assessors on hospital ethical and human experimentation committees. Such lay assessors could satisfy themselves, on the public's behalf, that nontherapeutic fetal experiments were being approved only in cases in which it had been demonstrated that their results held genuine promise of contributing substantially to the legitimate therapeutic goals of science, and that no alternative ways were available to arrive at the same discoveries. Once again, also, the fact that experimental protocols had been scrutinized by lay assessors would protect biomedical scientists from uninformed outside criticism, as effectively as it would reassure the public about the actual conduct of fetal experiments.

The claim that better medical science is a good for humanity in general also needs qualifying in one significant respect. We may, of course, discount loose and uncritical claims of this kind when they are made by a public spokesman for medical research in the context of advocacy of increased funding for biomedical science; but, even Richard McCormick's account of "what any rational being ought to want, and so ought to be ready to promote," takes it for granted that the improvement of medical science is beneficial to all of humanity. In an ideal world, this might well be the case. But, we should take a moment to inquire who will, in fact, be the primary beneficiaries of the therapeutic advances made possible by fetal research.

Many of the panel members, notably LeRoy Walters and Paul Ramsey, have pointed out the limitations to the claim that categorical suffering on the part of a child or a fetus is justified by hypothetical benefits to children or fetuses in later generations. It is one thing for, say, a father to make a sacrifice now, of which his own children can expect to be the beneficiaries after his death; but it is quite another matter for an individual to suffer pain now, in order to do hypothetical good to some unidentifiable class of possible beneficiaries at some indeterminate future time. What is morally questionable about such appeals to charity is not just the hypothetical character of the resultant goods; we must also satisfy ourselves that there is no evident systematic differentiation between the class of those who are to suffer now and the class of those who are to benefit later.

E. H. Carr, the historian, has wisely commented on the political demand that the Russian people of the 1920's should have "sacrifice[d] their present comfort for the benefit of future generations," pointing out that all such demands are in practice intrinsically inequitable; the class that pays is always other than the class that benefits. If we are to justify nontherapeutic fetal research in similar terms, we must, therefore, be sure that we are not building any comparable inequity into our practice.

At once, certain reservations suggest themselves. Suppose, for the sake of argument, that the class of pregnant women predominantly involved in fetal experimentation were taken from the poorest members of the population, while the class of those who predominantly benefitted from the resulting therapeutic advances were taken from the richest. The effect of this would be to introduce a substantial and morally relevant inequity into the actual practice of fetal research.

This supposition, whose racial implications do not need to be made explicit, is not an entirely idle one. There is an evident suspicion—as discussed again below, in connection with the problem of consent—that "free" hospital abortions, especially second-trimester abortions, may in some cases be "traded" to indigent parents, in return for consent to participate in fetal experimentation. As before, the significant issue here is not whether this suspicion is well-founded, but the fact that it arises at all. For the reasons already indicated, therefore, I myself would hope that the proposed National Council for the Protection of Human Subjects will accept responsibility for monitoring the social incidence of human experimentation in general, and of fetal experimentation in particular. A well-documented assurance that the burden of human experimentation was not being borne unduly by any one section of the population would both provide the public with legitimate peace of mind, and shield fetal research workers from any charge that their research was conducted in an inequitable or discriminatory manner.

Balancing Risks Against Benefits

Father McCormick has indicated that, in his view, the possibility of justifying nontherapeutic fetal experimentation depends on an appropriate balance of risks against benefits. He offers us two complementary criteria: *(1)* the risks involved must be low, and the prospective benefits high enough to outweigh them, and *(2)* there must be no alternative route to the same results. These propositions might win support from a majority of panel members. (Even Paul Ramsey suggests at one point that his opposition to McCormick's position might weaken, if the criterion of "low risk" were applied stringently enough.) Furthermore, these criteria have the merit of covering quite generally all types of experimental procedure applicable to the complete fetus itself, whether *in utero* or *ex utero* before death. But there are some significant differences between the panelists when it comes to spelling out the rules governing their actual application in practical situations.

Thus, Sissela Bok recommends that the United States follow the

British guidelines in laying down a specific term and/or weight as the index of "fetal viability," and in ruling that "the use of the whole previable fetus [in non-therapeutic experimentation] is permissible, provided that only fetuses weighing less than 300 grams are used."[12] This recommendation appears to me too undiscriminating to meet McCormick's requirements. Let me set aside for the moment the question whether "viability"—which Bok admits to be a "fluid and shifting concept"—is the relevant issue at this point. Quite aside from that, I question whether it is morally appropriate to draw only a hard-and-fast line, dividing one class of fetuses which may not be used in nontherapeutic experiments at all from another class of fetuses which may, it seems, be used in any scientifically justifiable experiment. Surely, the question whether the use of a fetus in nontherapeutic experiments is permissible at all is not the only question; we must ask also what kinds of experiments are permissible for a fetus with given characteristics. So, while there may be reasons for laying down some definite upper size-limit, above which aborted fetuses may not be made the subject of any experimentation, it will probably also be necessary to balance off "risks" and "benefits" further, by establishing guidelines governing what types of procedures may or may not be undertaken on fetuses at different stages of development below that upper limit. In the event that a restricted program on nontherapeutic fetal research is resumed, indeed, one may foresee that the actual practices of human experimentation committees in research hospitals will come to be based, not on any single, hard-and-fast "index of permissibility," but rather on a more discriminating body of "case law" and "precedents." It should be one responsibility of the National Council for the Protection of Human Subjects to keep a watchful eye on the development of that "case law."

The problems that arise over the use of "the whole previable fetus" are less severe, however, than those that arise over the use of organs, tissues, and so on, from aborted fetuses, in place of, say, animal organs, tissues, and so on, in cancer research and similar fields of inquiry. We face serious practical difficulties with this question, as well as difficulties of medical ethics, in determining a "cut-off" point beyond which such use is impermissible and in setting appropriate criteria of "fetal death." If the experimental use of fetuses below 300 grams in weight is approved, it is presumably also supposed that a fetus must be clearly dead before organs or tissues may be removed for study. Yet, what tests of

---

[12]This is a reference to an earlier draft of Sissela Bok, "Fetal Research and the Value of Life," the final version of which is in *Research on the Fetus: Appendix*, pp. 2–1 to 2–18.

"fetal death" are envisaged? As Bok points out, the proposed DHEW guidelines 46.307 *(d)* and *(e)* are substantially more restrictive in this respect than the British Peel Commission recommendations; in particular, paragraph *(e)* states that "experimental procedures which would terminate the heartbeat or respiration of the abortus will not be employed."[13] Bok herself would remove this latter restriction, and would permit researchers to perform experiments which might accelerate the death of the fetus. On this issue, I personally favor 46.307 *(e),* and consider the further problems raised by suspending it too serious to set aside. It could be argued, no doubt, that a "previable" (and so, presumably nonsentient) 250-gram abortus, which has no hope of surviving more than a short time anyway, has "nothing to lose" by meeting an accelerated death at the hands of an experimenter, so that dismemberment should not be regarded as involving an "injury" to such a fetus. But, while I share Bok's sense that the risk of causing pain to the fetus is the most weighty consideration, I still find it hard to go along with her acceptance of the Peel Commission's less restrictive recommendations. Even in the case of a 250-gram fetus, I myself still feel the force of the analogy with McCormick's argument that we cannot properly consent by proxy to, for example, a child's giving up a kidney for a transplant operation.

Rather, the questions at issue here appear to me strictly parallel to those which arise in obtaining suitable hearts, or other complete organs, for transplantation operations. On the one hand, the success of such operations depends on the availability of organs that are still (so to say) "fresh"; on the other hand, in the case of heart transplants particularly, this has on occasion meant removing the organ from a (euphemistically called) "Donor" at a time when the actual death was still problematic. The question at just what point it should be permissible to remove organs from a dying patient, for transplantation to another patient, has been much argued over the last 10 years. (I refer particularly to the 1968 Beecher report in which the loss of brain function in an irreversible coma is suggested as marking a significant point of transition on the passage from life to death.) Like Ramsey, Walters and Siegel, I believe that "the criteria for ascertaining death in the fetus should be consistent with the criteria applied to other organisms," and more specifically, with the criteria relevant to human organ transplantation operations.

The difficulty of deciding under what circumstances the removal

[13]"Protection of Human Subjects," Department of Health, Education, and Welfare, *Federal Register* 39, no. 165, August 23, 1974.

of fetal organs or tissues for study would be permissible is particularly acute, for a reason that may at first sight appear merely technical. The abortion procedures commonly used in the early months of pregnancy —at a stage when the fetus is clearly presentient and "previable"— gravely damage or destroy the fetus and its organs. It is only in cases of hysterotomy, or comparable procedures, that an entire live fetus is recovered from an abortion. The stage in pregnancy at which these more drastic procedures are justifiable approaches the point at which legitimate questions can be raised about "viability" and sentience. Evidently, if it were a simple matter to obtain experimental material from the detritus of a simple six-week miscarriage or an early D and C—in which case it would probably be inappropriate for the mother to claim any serious "psychological investment" in her issue—the difficulty would not arise with the same force. As matters stand, however, the point in fetal development at which we have unambiguously crossed the line dividing the detritus of a D and C, on the one hand, from a sentient being, on the other, is inconveniently close to that at which destructive procedures of abortion have to give way to nondestructive procedures, such as hysterotomy. At any rate, it is only in the case of hysterotomies and the like that the question of experimental dismemberment becomes an active one, and the fetuses available for this purpose seem, all of them, to be within significant range of sentience and "viability."

III. THE PROBLEM OF CONSENT

The other practical topic discussed at length by the panel is that of consent, and consent procedures. What parties can claim authentic legal or moral interests in the issue of an abortion, whether spontaneous or induced? And what sorts of consent procedures should be required, in order to respect those interests and give the various parties proper opportunities to exercise any corresponding "rights" in the disposal and handling of that issue? I will summarize the outcome of these discussions under three heads: Fetal Consent, Maternal Consent, and The Interests of Third Parties.

Fetal Consent

Evidently, the question of fetal consent is a purely theoretical one, but it is one over which, as we have already seen, a good deal turns, particularly in respect to the mother's own standing in the matter.

Granted that there is no question of obtaining consent for non-therapeutic experimentation directly from a fetus, as one can from an informed adult, two questions arise. Is it *(1)* necessary and *(2)* possible to obtain a satisfactory equivalent in the form of vicarious or proxy consent? Three main answers are represented in the papers before the Commission. In the first place, we can declare fetal consent both indispensible and unobtainable (as Paul Ramsey does); and so condemn all such experimentation as unethical. In the second place, we can declare fetal consent unnecessary (as Sissela Bok does), on the grounds that the fetus itself has no legal or moral standing and therefore no formal "interests" in the case; in this instance, we can then give the mother primary rights of consent directly, rather than vicariously or as a proxy. Or, in the third place, we can accept fetal consent as necessary, but infer or presume it (as Richard McCormick does), on the basis of proxy decisions taken vicariously by the parents, who are considered to have the interests of the fetus at heart. Given the borderline nature of the present case, all three positions seem to me to run into some difficulties on a theoretical level. For practical purposes, however, the differences between them become significant only when we turn to consider what other parties have authentic claims and how they should be exercised.

Maternal Consent

As to the mother's rights of consent or veto, we have one clear starting point. In the case of a full-term infant, there can be no doubt of the mother's right to approve or veto the use on her infant of any experimental procedure, particularly a nontherapeutic one. We may, therefore, take as our starting point the question under what circumstances, if any, a mother could forfeit that right to have a say in the treatment or disposal of her issue.

In the Senate sub-committee testimony and elsewhere, there has been eloquent advocacy of the view that a mother forfeits this right simply by choosing to have an abortion, so that she should not have any right of veto over the use of the resulting fetus for experimental purposes. By electing an abortion, it is argued, the woman "puts her own welfare before that of the fetus," and so destroys the presumption on which proxy consent depends: namely, that she "has the interests of the fetus at heart."

This view finds no serious support from the panel, but its weaknesses are worth spelling out here since they embody some influential confusions. Four different counter arguments can be offered against it, all of which tend to strengthen the presumption in favor of a maternal veto on nontherapeutic fetal experiments.

(1) The argument for forfeiture rests on a false assumption. Very rarely can the decision to terminate a pregnancy be represented as merely being the mother's choice "to put her own welfare before that of the fetus." It is commonly an agonizing decision, in the course of which many considerations are weighed, including the fetus' own interests. (The argument, "it would not be right for me to bring this child into the world in my present circumstances," is not necessarily a self-deceiving one.) Whatever one may think about the mother's motives in one or another particular case, the argument offered gives no grounds for an automatic forfeiture of rights just by the very decision in favor of abortion.

(2) All question of motives apart, the mother retains the normal psychological stake in her issue, which demands respect whether the pregnancy is terminated naturally or by surgical intervention. This psychological investment is, of course, not a mere matter of conventional sentiment. It is associated with physiological, particularly hormonal, changes which are disrupted at abortion with consequences that should not be lightly disregarded or dismissed as morally irrelevant. (LeRoy Walters cites an interesting side argument at this point: the right of parental consent for medical or surgical procedures on children is derived from the parent's continuing personal and financial stake in the child's future—the parents will have to go on taking responsibility for the child after treatment, whatever its outcome, so they should have the chance of vetoing it—in which case the right of consent would again lapse on abortion which spares the parents any need to take subsequent responsibility for the fetus. But here too we can reply that the parent's psychological stake in the child goes far beyond that created by future caretaking responsibilities, so forfeiture again does not follow.)

(3) The analogy advanced by supporters of the forfeiture argument —that a mother who chooses an abortion is like a parent who abandons a child—does not serve the required legal purpose. Although abandonment of a child no doubt calls into question a parent's fitness to retain custody of that child, few jurisdictions would treat it as entailing automatic, much less irreversible forfeiture of all parental rights. By abandoning a child, one loses, at most, only some parental rights. Law and custom alike require us to respect the wishes of parents or other next-of-kin, especially in respect to the disposal of the dead, whatever may have been the state of personal relations between the deceased and the survivors.

(4) Most significantly in the context of the present discussion, even if a mother could forfeit or renounce her rights and responsibilities toward her offspring in any way, those rights and responsibilities would

in no case fall automatically to the nearest medical research scientist, or even to the attendant physician. Rather, the offspring would merely become a ward of the State, which would have the responsibility of acting *in loco parentis.* So, the onus of obtaining consent to non-therapeutic experimentation would not be removed; its locus would merely shift from the mother to the competent authority of the State.

Accordingly, there appears to be no basis for the suggestion that hospitals should be free to assume full rights and responsibilities over the issue of abortions, in disregard of the mother's wishes. This conclusion is not affected by the Peel Commission's argument that it would cause "unnecessary suffering" to obtain consent for experimentation from the mother, under the circumstances of an abortion. (That is a comparatively straightforward matter of consent procedures, and I shall return to the question below.) While maternal consent may not by itself be sufficient to authorize the use of a fetus for experimental purposes, it should normally be a necessary requirement. Further, a maternal veto should, in all cases, be treated as final.

The Interests of Third Parties

Can any other parties, besides the mother, plausibly claim any interest in the disposal of an aborted fetus? In different ways, claims of five other parties need to be considered.

(1) Where the abortion takes place within a marriage, the father can claim certain moral and even legal rights in respect to all his offspring—including aborted ones. Some of these moral rights, at least, might also be extended to a presumed father, even when conception has taken place out of wedlock. (In both cases, too, some degree of psychological investment can reasonably be argued.) On the other hand, in many out-of-wedlock pregnancies, the father may be unidentifiable, unavailable or indifferent, so that his interest in the offspring may reasonably be regarded as having lapsed. As a general guideline to the subject of paternal consent, therefore, one could suggest the twofold rule: *(a)* where a father is either present or in effective touch with the mother, he should also have the right of veto over nontherapeutic experimentation on his offspring, and *(b)* where the father is neither present nor in effective touch with the mother, no special effort need be made to obtain his consent.

(2) We may consider the attendant physician at the delivery and also the research scientist who proposes to perform an experiment on the fetus. In both respects, the relevant moral issues seem

to be well taken care of by the Peel Commission's recommendation, 4(iii):

> The responsibility for deciding that the fetus is in a category which may be used for this type of research rests with the medical attendants at its birth and never with the intending research worker.[14]

In particular, the medical research scientist should not normally play any direct part in the decision either to abort or to approve the issue of an abortion as suitable for any particular class of research.

(3) A specific public interest is involved, notably, in insuring that the "separation of powers" between the attendant physicians and the research scientist is respected and observed. Here again, we must not ignore the element of distrust or disquiet that has grown recently—the suspicion that hospital physicians and research scientists are to some extent "in collusion"—even if we consider it without foundation. The more groundless this distrust may be, indeed, the easier it will be to accept a simple procedural provision that can set it at rest. For this purpose, one might recommend that the proposed lay assessors on the human experimentation committees of research hospitals (referred to earlier) should have the further responsibility of satisfying themselves that decisions about abortion, and about making an aborted fetus available for experimentation, are, in fact, being made in accordance with these general rules.

(4) In addition to this general public interest, there is a specific State (or Federal) government interest in the disposal of aborted fetuses. The issues that arise in this connection involve somewhat technical problems of law, rather than ethical problems. But evidently, the existing responsibilities of the Registrar of Births and Deaths, and of the Coroner, whether in respect to births, deaths, and/or stillbirths, together with the rules about the timing and legal implications of registration, must extend in certain respects, and on certain conditions, to aborted fetuses. In a situation where ambiguities in the law have already led to criminal prosecutions, indeed, the legal rules in question are in urgent need of clarification. This is particularly urgent if, as Sissela Bok proposes, the Commission follows the Peel recommendations in permitting fetal experiments in which the death of a "previable" fetus is accelerated by the experimental procedure itself. Over this delicate point, a clearer set of rules and sympathetic cooperation between a

---

[14]"The Use of Fetuses and Fetal Material for Research," Department of Health and Social Security, Scottish Home for Health Department, Welsh Office, Report of the Advisory Group, Her Majesty's Stationery Office, London, 1972.

research hospital and the local coroner's office could do as much to protect the legal standing of fetal experimenters as it does to insure that the State (or Federal) government's rules are being respected.

Consent Procedures

In general, the point at which the Peel Commission's recommended code of practice appears, at this distance, to be vaguest and least satisfactory is over the procedures for obtaining and documenting parental consent to fetal experimentation. Three points need to be made:

(1) I referred earlier to the Peel Commission argument that, in cases where "the separation of the fetus from the mother leads to the termination of its life," to seek parental consent for the use of a fetus in experimentation "could be an unnecessary source of distress to parents." I feel this argument would carry weight only if the consent were deferred until after the abortion. There is no evident reason, on the other hand, why consent for the experimental use of tissues or organs from the fetus should not be given or denied before the abortion, at the same time, and on the same document, as consent to the operation itself. (The Peel Commission, in fact, goes on to make a very similar proposal.) Apparently, the consent or denial would have a different legal standing in different situations; for example, it might have binding legal force only in case the fetus were delivered alive. But, one might hope that hospitals would not be too ready to disregard parental wishes, even where these were not legally binding.

(2) There is an evident risk involved, nonetheless, in the use of such a combined form. The Peel Commission's requirement 3(iv) that there be no monetary exchange for fetuses or fetal material must be understood as covering not merely open monetary exchanges, but also "barter deals." There is a need to guard against the possibility that indigent parents might come to regard consent to the experimental use of tissues as an implicit "price" for obtaining a free hospital abortion. It is both ethically and socially important that any such "payment in kind" be clearly brought under the scope of any recommendation against "monetary payment" for the use of fetuses or fetal material.

(3) Something much more specific needs to be laid down about the form of consent proposed and about the manner and circumstances in which maternal or parental consent is to be obtained. Consent or denial of consent must be directly documented on a form which, if needed, would be available to a competent Court for review. Furthermore, wherever possible, consent should not be given just in the presence of

the attendant physician alone, but to the satisfaction of a third party representing the public interest. (A hospital social worker, acting on behalf of the lay representative or representatives on the human experimentation committee of the hospital, would be a suitable person.) One needs only a limited exposure to the problem of consent to understand that "informed consent" is an ideal rather than an easily attained result. In so delicate a situation as that of a mother consenting to the use of her aborted fetus for experimentation, however, it is certainly desirable that every reasonable step be taken to insure that her consent is as clearly and fully informed as is practicable, not least, because care taken at this stage may serve to alleviate, later on, the psychological shock and grief which are probably an inevitable consequence of the abortion and everything associated with it.

9

Justice in Fetal Experimentation

Natalie Abrams

Philosophy and Medicine Program, New York University Medical Center, New York, New York

One of the most difficult questions in regard to fetal experimentation is the relationship between the regulations guiding such research and the issue of abortion, particularly the Supreme Court ruling on abortion in Roe v. Wade.[1] The following essay is a discussion of a few of the problems which are involved in this relationship. Section I briefly comments on the issue of the fetus' status and the implication of this for abortion and fetal research. Section II discusses a distinction made in the Health, Education, and Welfare regulations between fetuses to be aborted and those to be carried to term. Two arguments are made here. The first concerns the implication of the regulation for fetuses in nonmedical situations. The second claims that the distinction itself is illegitimate and does not adhere to ordinary principles of justice or fairness, nor to the standards adhered to in other medical contexts. Section III then discusses alternative ways of removing the suspect distinction and equalizing treatment for all fetuses. Finally, Section IV connects the above to the problem of consent in fetal research.

---

[1]Roe v. Wade, 93 Supreme Court 705, 1973.

I. FETAL STATUS

It has been argued that if abortion is permissible, it is irrational to forbid fetal experimentation, on the assumption that if it is all right to kill the fetus, there can be no objection to using the fetus to gain valuable information. Certainly, the harm the fetus would be subjected to in research is less than death.[2] Another way of considering this argument is in terms of the "personhood" question or the right to life of the fetus. If the fetus is not considered a "person" or at least a being with some protectable rights, certainly there is no problem of abortion and/or fetal experimentation. The first question to be answered, then, is whether definite inferences can be drawn from the Supreme Court ruling and/or from the permissibility of abortion concerning the "personhood" or the rights of the fetus. If one looks simply at what the Supreme Court states about this question, one would have to conclude that the abortion decision does not specifically answer the "personhood" issue:

> We need not resolve the difficult question of when life begins. When those trained in the respective disciplines of medicine, philosophy, and theology are unable to arrive at any consensus, the judiciary, at this point in the development of man's knowledge, is not in a position to speculate as to the answer.[3]

However, the decision itself seems to contradict the overt statement. Surely, if the fetus in the first two trimesters were considered by the court to be a person with protectable human rights, including the right to life, how could the decision in favor of abortion have been reached? How could a woman's right to privacy override another's right to life?

At first glance, this way of thinking seems correct. If one assumes that all people have a right to life, that the fetus is a person and therefore also has this right, then abortion would seem to be impermissible. A very persuasive argument against the necessary connection between these

---

[2]This argument is given by Marc Lappe and Willard Gaylin in "Fetal Politics: The Debate on Experimenting with the Unborn," *Atlantic Monthly* 235, May, 1975, pp. 66–73.

[3]"The 1973 Supreme Court Decisions on State Abortion Laws: Excerpts from Opinions in Roe v. Wade," in *The Problems of Abortion,* Joel Feinberg, editor, California, Wadsworth, 1973, p. 184. It might be interesting to consider the argument that if the Supreme Court really wanted to refrain from making a statement about the fetus' status, perhaps abortion should have been allowed only subsequent to viability. It would only be then that a decision in favor of the woman's right to privacy would not be identical to nonprotection of the "right to life" of the fetus. Abortion after viability would not entail fetal death.

propositions is given by Judith J. Thomson.[4] Basically, her argument
rests on the assumption that a right to life does not entail a right to be
given whatever is needed to maintain that life and also does not entail an
absolute right to be killed, but rather entails only a right not to be killed
unjustly. The crucial issue is, then, whether, assuming the fetus has a
right to life, abortion is in fact unjust killing. Thomson maintains that, at
least in certain cases, abortion is not unjust killing and that, therefore,
there is no simple connection between the fetus' right to life and its right
not be aborted. For the purposes of this discussion, it is not necessary to
examine Thomson's argument in detail. It is being cited here to support
the claim that a decision in favor of abortion does not necessarily or
automatically imply that the fetus is not a person and/or that it does not
have protectable rights, perhaps even including the right to life. Consequently, it is not "irrational," as would follow from Gaylin and Lappe's
reasoning, to permit abortion and yet to forbid and/or restrict fetal
experimentation. In the rest of this essay, I shall work on the assumption
that the fetus in question does have the right to some protection and that
permitting abortion does not automatically imply that there should be
no restrictions on fetal research.

II. FETUSES TO BE ABORTED VS. FETUSES TO BE CARRIED TO TERM

In light of this assumption, it then becomes important to consider the
new guidelines in the HEW regulations on the "Protection of Human
Subjects."[5] In these guidelines, a crucial distinction is made between the
class of fetuses to be aborted and nonviable fetuses ex utero versus the
class of fetuses to be carried to term. Whereas in earlier guidelines,[6] all
fetuses were to be treated equally and to receive the same protection,
the new provisions[7] do not require equal protection for all fetuses.
Rather, the new guidelines:

---

[4]Judith J. Thomson, "A Defense of Abortion," *Phil. and Public Affairs,* vol. 1, no.
1, Fall, 1971.

[5]"Protection of Human Subjects," Department of Health, Education, and Welfare,
Federal Register, vol. 40, no. 154, August, 1975.

[6]"Protection of Human Subjects," Department of Health, Education, and Welfare,
Federal Register, vol. 38, no. 221, November, 1973.

[7]*Federal Register,* vol. 40, no. 154, pp. 33547–33548, especially guidelines 5 and
6.

... would permit nontherapeutic research on the fetus in anticipation of abortion and during the abortion procedure, and on a living infant after abortion when the infant is considered nonviable, even though such research is precluded by recognized norms governing human research in general ... Under these recommendations, the fetus (to be aborted) and nonviable infant will be subjected to nontherapeutic research from which other humans (and fetuses) are protected.[8]

The assumption behind these regulations is that somehow, when a fetus is to be aborted or when it cannot survive outside the mother, it no longer deserves the same protection as it would have received were it to be carried to term.

Two main problems arising in connection with this new regulation will be discussed. The first concerns the implications of a woman's right to change her mind. From the above quote, it may appear as if *any* nontherapeutic research can be done with a fetus in anticipation of abortion—that is, prior to the abortion procedure itself. In fact, however, the ruling concerning fetuses anticipating abortion is the same as the ruling for fetuses to be carried to term except for the statement that research which presents "special problems related to the interpretation or application of the guidelines may be conducted if approved by a national ethical review body." The implication here is that certain experiments which would not be allowed on a fetus to be carried to term and which might involve greater risk *may* be approved for fetuses anticipating abortion. For the most part, however, research prior to abortion is restricted to that involving minimal or no risk.

As Ramsey points out, the primary reason for not permitting risky experimentation prior to the abortion procedure itself is that if the woman wanted to change her mind about the abortion and carry the fetus to term, she would be confronted with the possibility of giving birth to a defective child as a result of the experimentation. Two solutions to this problem were possible. One approach would have been to require a woman to go through with an abortion once she allowed her fetus to be used in nontherapeutic research. This approach, however, might certainly have been interpreted as a violation of her right to privacy. The second approach, which was in fact chosen, was not to restrict her right to change her mind, but to restrict her right to subject a fetus to certain kinds of risks as a result of an experiment and then to carry it to term. This right was restricted by forbidding most risky experimentation until the abortion procedure was already in progress

---

[8]David W. Louisell, "Dissenting Statement," *Federal Register,* vol. 40, no. 154, p. 33548.

and there was no question that the woman could not reverse her decision. In effect, therefore, a woman's right to change her mind was considered more important than her right to subject her fetus to a possible harm. If, however, it is not a violation of privacy to restrict the risks to which a woman may subject her fetus in experimentation, does it not follow that it might also be justifiable, if not required, to limit other risks which a woman might take with her fetus to be carried to term? In other words, if it is considered permissible to restrict non-therapeutic experimentation prior to abortion (to that involving minimal risk or to that approved by a review body) because a woman cannot forfeit her right to change her mind and the fetus should be protected from potential harms should it be carried to term, does it not follow that it might be equally permissible to restrict her participation in other, perhaps far riskier, activities, such as dangerous physical sports, the taking of drugs, smoking, and so on? Whether it be medical experimentation or these other non-experimental activities, the fetus can run equal risks of being harmed. It might be argued that there is an important difference between these situations in that research restrictions are not on the woman, but rather on the researcher, whereas restrictions on non-experimental activities fall on the mother. This distinction, however, would be analogous to claiming that an anti-abortion law would not restrict a woman's rights if it simply forbid physicians from performing abortions rather than the woman's right to undergo an abortion. In both the abortion and experimentation situation, third parties are necessary.

Furthermore, an important similarity between these nonexperimental and experimental risks should be noted. In both situations, the harm to the fetus is not intentional (that is, it would be a side-effect or an unintended consequence). Double-effect arguments could therefore not be used to make a moral distinction. In both cases, the activities in question create a risk of harm rather than produce the harm as a certain and desired end of the activity. Therefore, it cannot be argued that medical experimentation can be restricted because it would produce a harm to another directly and deliberately. Rather, medical experimentation is similar to the other activities mentioned in that they both increase the probability of harm to another. Therefore, it is not clear what the difference between these medical and nonmedical risks would be and how the restriction of one class of activities can be justified without the restriction of the other. Limiting most non-therapeutic research prior to abortion to that involving minimal risk would seem to have implications for restricting other activities of the woman.

Once the abortion procedure has begun, however, the usual restrictions on nontherapeutic research no longer apply, since the woman no longer retains the option to reverse her decision. The problem which arises here concerns the distinction between fetuses to be aborted and fetuses to be carried to term. No restrictions concerning risk pertain to fetuses during the abortion procedure. However, research on fetuses to be carried to term is limited to that involving minimal or no risk. Justice or fairness usually demands that when two classes of individuals are to be treated differently—namely, to receive different degrees of protection —it must be possible to cite a "relevant" distinction between the two classes to warrant the different treatment.[9] In the new fetal research guideline, the only basis for differential treatment is the fact that one group of fetuses is to be aborted. However, is the fact that one group is going to die in itself a "relevant" criterion upon which to base a difference in treatment?

The decision whether a distinction is "relevant" given a particular activity should be partially based upon the ultimate purpose of the regulation. For example, making a distinction between ambulance drivers and ordinary drivers in terms of legal speed limit can be considered legitimate in relation to the ultimate purpose of speed restrictions—that is, to save lives.[10] Is the fact that certain fetuses are going to die "relevant" to the ultimate purpose of the activity in question, namely fetal experimentation? Assuming that the end or purpose of nontherapeutic fetal research is to gain valuable information which can then be used to help other fetuses, the fact that certain fetuses are going to die does not appear pertinent. Either class of fetuses, those to be aborted or those to be carried to term, would be equally useful for the experimentation.[11] It does not seem, therefore, that dying fetuses are necessarily any more valuable research material given the purpose of research. More importantly, the purpose of regulations concerning fetal research is to offer protection to experimental subjects who may be improperly used for the benefit of others. Here, it might even be claimed that fetuses who are dying would be more in need of such protection. It should be noted that protection, here, is not simply protection from physical injury or harm. It also includes protection from being treated "as an object" and in ways which fail to respect the "fetus' dignity" and which are "inconsis-

---

[9]Joel Feinberg, *Social Philosophy,* New Jersey, Prentice-Hall, 1973, pp. 99–100.
[10]*Ibid.,* p. 105.
[11]Perhaps certain fetuses are better research material for certain experiments since they may be suffering from the illness to be studied. However, this fact is not necessarily related to whether or not the fetus is to be aborted.

tent with its human genetic heritage."[12] Furthermore, the commission claims as one of its own principles "to provide for fair treatment by avoiding discrimination between classes or among members of the same class."[13] Therefore, neither the purpose of the research nor the purpose of the regulations warrant distinguishing between fetuses to be aborted and those to be carried to term.

In addition to the importance of the goal or purpose of the activity in the determination of "relevance," there is also the issue of whether or not the factor in question was or could have been voluntarily acquired by the classes to be distinguished.

> Differences in a given respect are "relevant" for the aims of distributive justice . . . only if they are differences for which their possessors can be held responsible; properties can be the grounds of just discrimination between persons only if those persons had a *fair opportunity* to acquire or avoid them.[14]

Race, sex, and I.Q. would obviously be considered irrelevant according to this requirement, since they are not voluntarily acquired. Similarly, whether one is wanted or desired by another person, certainly in the case of a fetus, is not at all a voluntary choice of the fetus, nor something for which the fetus is responsible. It should not, therefore, be a relevant factor in distinguishing fetuses and allocating degrees of protection.

Of the possible bases for distinguishing classes of individuals,[15] only the principle of need seems relevant to the case of fetuses. Certainly, there would be no basis for a consideration of merit. In terms of need, the fetus to be aborted has an equal claim to protection to the fetus to be carried to term. In fact, the Commission itself believes that "those groups which are most vulnerable to inequitable treatment should receive special protection."[16] One might even claim, as Bernard Williams does, that "it is a matter of logic that particular sorts of needs constitute a reason for receiving particular sorts of goods."[17] When the need which should be the basis for a just distribution of a good is not operative—that is, when the need itself is not sufficient to secure the

---

[12]*Federal Register,* vol. 40, no. 154, p. 33545.

[13]*Ibid.*

[14]Feinberg, *op. cit.,* p. 108.

[15]Feinberg distinguishes five different principles: *(1)* the principle of perfect equality; *(2)* the principle of need; *(3)* the principle of merit and achievement; *(4)* the principle of contribution (or due return); and *(5)* the principle of effort (or labor), *Ibid.,* p. 109.

[16]*Federal Register,* vol. 40, no. 154, p. 33545.

[17]Bernard Williams, "The Idea of Equality," in *Justice and Equality,* Hugo A. Bedau, ed., New Jersey, Prentice-Hall, 1971, p. 129.

good—Williams claims that it is an "irrational" state of affairs.[18] The
present guideline which distinguishes between the amount of protection
allocated to fetuses to be aborted and fetuses to be carried to term would
consequently be "irrational" according to Williams' argument, since
the desires of the mother, rather than need, is operative. Hence, without
a "relevant" characteristic to distinguish the class of fetuses to be
carried to term and those to be aborted, they should receive equal
protection.[19]

Another possible approach to this question might be to argue that
it is not unreasonable to sacrifice fetuses to be aborted, since they will
be dying anyhow. Certainly this argument would not stand up legally.
An offender cannot use as a defense the fact that the person one has
injured would have died or suffered the harm even without one's intervention. Nor is it possible to argue that a fetus to be aborted cannot be
wronged since it is going to die and cannot be harmed for life. First,
the charge of battery consists of "unconsented touching," with or without harm. An individual can be wronged without being harmed. (This,
of course, assumes no consent. The issue of consent will be discussed
below.) Secondly, as noted above, the protection in question is not
simply in terms of physical injury, but concerns respect for human
dignity.

Furthermore, this approach would not be consistent with the guiding principles in other medical contexts.[20] The only situations in which
it is considered permissible to sacrifice the best interests or the wishes
of particular patients are those in which protection of their interests or
desires would injure other people and *(1)* the injury to the third party
constitutes a harm and not simply a deprivation of a benefit[21] (for

---

[18]*Ibid.,* p. 129.

[19]A legal analysis of the application of the 14th amendment's equal protection
clause to fetal experimentation is needed here. Without this, however, it appears that
although the "equal protection" clause does not require absolute equality or precisely
the same advantages, it does seem to rule against absolute deprivation of the particular
right in question (here this would be protection of the fetus). See San Antonio Independent School District v. Rodriguez, 411 U.S. 1, 1973. Furthermore, the disadvantaged
class here, fetuses to be aborted, can be easily defined and identified and would be
suffering an absolute rather than a relative deprivation, since there are no restrictions
in terms of risk or harm to the fetus during abortion. For an interesting comparison
of the San Antonio Case and Roe v. Wade, see "Forward: Toward a Model of Roles
in the Due Process of Life and Law," Laurence H. Tribe, *Harvard Law Review,* vol.
87, Nov. 73, No. 1.

[20]Michael M. Martin, "Ethical Standards for Fetal Experimentation," *Fordham
Law Review,* vol. 43, April, 1975, p. 596.

[21]*Ibid.*

example, quarantine and innoculation cases); or *(2)* the third party to benefit is in a special close relationship to the individual to be compromised (for example, the mother in an abortion case or a sibling in an organ donor case)[22]; or *(3)* violation of the expressed wishes of the individual actually acts to preserve the individual's life (for example, cases of compulsory medical treatment).[23] None of these qualifying characteristics apply to the fetal situation. First, by not doing fetal research and advancing medical knowledge, future fetuses will not receive the treatment which perhaps they could have received had the experimentation been done. The loss of this good, such as new medical treatment, however, certainly cannot be seen as an injury or infliction of harm, but rather must be seen as deprivation of a benefit. (On the other hand, nonreceipt of standard medical care might be rightfully claimed as a harm or injury). Secondly, the class to benefit from the research consists of other future fetuses. Not only are these fetuses not in a special relationship to those to be sacrificed, but the fetuses to benefit cannot claim any greater status as "persons" who might perhaps be worthier of more protection. All fetuses have the same "personhood" or lack of "personhood" status. Thirdly, overriding the interests of the fetus in the research context in no way ultimately works to benefit the fetus by preserving its life. The only acceptable reasons for sacrificing the interests of an individual or using coercion in the medical context are, therefore, not applicable to the fetal situation.

III. EQUALIZING TREATMENT FOR ALL FETUSES

Equalizing the distribution of being a subject in nontherapeutic research among dying fetuses has been suggested as a possible means of making the situation fair or just. Alexander Capron has suggested that any experimentation on fetuses to be aborted should be randomized in order to avoid the exploitation of one group (racial, economic, and so on).[24] The assumption here is that randomly distributing the burdens among the class of fetuses who would be medically fit for the research makes the experiment more fair or just. But, "is it the case that the sacrifice of the individual to the social good is morally permissible, if

[22]Charles Fried, *Medical Experimentation, Personal Integrity and Social Policy,* New York, American Elsevier, 1974, p. 23.

[23]Martin, *op. cit.,* pp. 558–559.

[24]Paul Ramsey, *The Ethics of Fetal Research,* New Haven, Yale University Press, 1975, pp. 97–98.

only the burden of the sacrifice is fairly distributed?"[25] As discussed above, the usual conditions allowing the sacrificing of an individual for another or for the social good are not present in the fetal research situation. In addition, randomly distributing the status of research subject among a group of possible subjects is only fair based on the assumption that being a "possible" subject is also fairly distributed. However, it is a "fallacy to see some fairness in the fact that sickness may be an arbitrary, random event."[26] The only circumstance which makes a fetus eligible to be a possible subject is the special fact that the fetus is to be aborted. This would be no different from claiming that experimentation on diabetics is permissible as long as the subjects are chosen at random. What is being overlooked is that being a diabetic, or a dying fetus, is not itself randomly distributed.

One alternative way of equalizing treatment might be to allow risky nontherapeutic research on all fetuses (whether they were to be aborted or carried to term). However, this would not rectify the situation. For, the use of all fetuses would have to be based on some notion that they owe a debt to society. Yet, how could it be argued that fetuses have obligations to society without also claiming that present children and adults do as well? Consistency would require that everyone participate in nontherapeutic research. More importantly, owing a debt to society must be founded on the belief that one has in some way benefitted or will benefit from society. Although this is undoubtedly true for all people as well as for fetuses to be carried to term, it is difficult to see how it could be applied to dying fetuses. What sense could be made out of the claim that they have benefitted from and therefore have an obligation to society? The argument that fetal research can be justified by reference to social obligations would strangely work to exempt dying fetuses from research and allow research on the fetuses to be carried to term.

A very interesting and important question arises from the belief in equalizing treatment. If one accepts in principle the imperative to equalize protection in the fetal research situation, what in practice would it actually mean to "equalize" the treatment of fetuses to be aborted and those to be carried to term? At least two different approaches could be appropriate. First, equalization might mean that only those experiments which would be acceptable to perform on fetuses to be carried to term are acceptable for fetuses to be aborted. Alternatively, equalization might mean that the same criteria must be

---

[25]Fried, *op. cit.,* p. 60.
[26]*Ibid.,* p. 65.

applied to both classes of fetuses—that is, they may both be subjected to experimentation only if the research involves "minimal or no risk." According to this latter interpretation, experiments might be permissible with fetuses to be aborted which would not be permissible with fetuses to be brought to term, provided the level of harm was minimal. This view, of course, works on the assumption that the phrase "minimal or no risk" could apply differently to the two classes of fetuses.

A conclusion concerning which interpretation is warranted cannot be reached here. However, a few points should be noted. First, if the criterion of "minimal or no risk" can mean different things for the two classes of fetuses, there must be a distinction between the classes which would warrant the different interpretations. To a certain extent, this places the argument back to an evaluation of the relevant differences between the classes. Secondly, it has been emphasized here, as well as in the Federal regulations, that the protection in question is not simply protection from physical harm, but includes respect for human dignity. It is only on the assumption that the fetus is worthy of this latter kind of respect that the regulations were necessary. Third, unless one wants to argue that abortion is the ultimate infringement of human dignity and once this is accepted, anything else is permissible, certain restrictions, even on the fetus to be aborted, must be maintained. The problem then becomes what, in practice, does it mean to respect the fetus' dignity? Assuming equal respect is due to all fetuses, whether they are to be aborted or carried to term, the difficult issue still remains as to what practices satisfy or fail to satisfy this imperative. It is the recognition of the imperative as such that I am arguing for here and that has not been recognized in the Federal guidelines.

IV. CONSENT IN FETAL RESEARCH

The problem of consent for fetal research is also complicated by the abortion issue. There does not seem to be any difficulty in allowing the mother the right of proxy consent in most situations of fetal research. However, assuming proxy consent is permitted based on the belief that the mother will act in the best interest of the child, does a woman who voluntarily aborts her fetus also retain the right to proxy consent? The present HEW guidelines maintain that a woman who voluntarily aborts does not thereby give up all interest in the fetus.[27] She is, therefore, regarded as a legitimate source of consent. Ramsey argues, on the other

---

[27]*Federal Register,* vol. 40, no. 154, p. 33528.

hand, that "interest" in the fetus is not the point. "Possessing the moral authority to consent is not a matter of strong or weak feelings."[28] Whereas abortion is based on the right to privacy, proxy consent, Ramsey argues, is based on a claim to care, which the mother who aborts does not have.

Perhaps it might be argued that a just distinction can be made between the class of women who carry to term, spontaneously abort, or abort in the so-called "best-interest" of the child and the class of women who voluntarily abort in their own best interest.[29] Again, it would be necessary to indicate a "relevant" basis for the distinction. In terms of the goal or purpose of regulations concerning proxy consent, it might be successfully argued, as Ramsey does, that voluntary abortion in itself is, in some cases at least, an indication of not acting in the child's best interest.[30] In terms of whether or not the distinction between the classes is based on a voluntary characteristic, certainly whether or not women have abortions is within their control. On the basis of this, a legitimate distinction might therefore be drawn between these two groups and proxy consent allowed by the former but not by the latter class of women. A legal guardian might even be appointed to act in the best interest of the voluntarily aborted fetus.[31]

The above argument was developed to support the claim that there is no basis for discriminating fetuses to be aborted and those to be carried to term in relation to the degree of protection they should receive in the medical context. The permissibility of abortion, in itself, does not automatically imply that the fetus has no protectable rights. In addition, limiting most risky fetal experimentation to a time coincident with the abortion procedure, in order to protect the woman's right to reverse her decision, has implications for possibly restricting other non-experimental risks to which a woman can subject her fetus. The distinction between fetuses to be aborted and those to be carried to term has been shown to be suspect. Justice requires that such a distinction be based on "relevant" characteristics. However, the fact that some

---

[28]Ramsey, *op. cit.*, p. 92.

[29]No doubt this distinction would be hard to make in practice. It is extremely difficult for a woman herself to sort out her feelings in order to decide whether she is aborting a defective child because in some sense the child's life would not be worth living, or because she wants to protect herself from the burden of caring for such a child.

[30]For an interesting view of abortion in terms of abandonment and not acting in the child's best interest, see Raymond M. Herbenick, "Remarks on Abortion, Abandonment, and Adoption Opportunities," *Phil. and Public Affairs,* vol. 5., no. 1, Fall, 1975.

[31]Ramsey, *op. cit.*, p. 97.

fetuses are going to die and/or are not wanted by the mother does not constitute a "relevant" ground for just differential treatment. This follows from the failure of either characteristic to be important in terms of the research goal or the goal of the regulations and from the involuntary nature of the distinguishing features. Also, sacrificing dying fetuses would not be consistent with the principles adhered to in other medical contexts.

Simple equalization of protection, however, is not the final answer. Applying a regulation equally does not in itself guarantee that the regulation is acceptable.

> If we treat everybody unfairly by the relevant noncomparative standard, but equally and impartially so, we have done an injustice to each that is barely mitigated by the equal injustice done all the others.[32]

Equalizing treatment of all fetuses by allowing risky experimentation on all of them would hardly be an acceptable approach. To be consistent, we would have to allow risky nontherapeutic experimentation on everyone, including children. Furthermore, required participation would have to be based on a conception of social obligation and would, in fact, work to exempt dying fetuses from research since they would receive no benefits from society and hence would have no obligations. Restricting nontherapeutic fetal research to that involving minimal or no risk for *all* fetuses would therefore, seem to be the only permissible regulation.[33]

---

[32]Feinberg, *op. cit.,* p. 98.

[33]The actual meaning of the phrase "minimal" or "no risk" has to be studied in more detail. For example, should it mean that there has to be minimal or no risk of any harm or rather should the possible harm itself be minimal, although there might be a high risk of suffering it?

10

Euthanasia, Killing, and Letting Die[1]

James Rachels

Department of Philosophy, University of Alabama in Birmingham

I. INTRODUCTION

The former editor of *The New England Journal of Medicine,* Dr. F. J. Ingelfinger, observes that:

> This is the heyday of the ethicist in medicine. He delineates the rights of patients, of experimental subjects, of fetuses, of mothers, of animals, and even of doctors. (And what a far cry it is from the days when medical "ethics" consisted of condemning economic improprieties such as fee splitting and advertising!) With impeccable logic—once certain basic assumptions are granted—and with graceful prose, the ethicist develops his arguments. . . . Yet his precepts are essentially the products of arm-chair exercise and remain abstract and idealistic until they have been tested in the laboratory of experience.[2]

---

[1]A shortened version of this paper (less than one-half the length), with the title "Active and Passive Euthanasia," appeared in *N.E.J.M.,* vol. 292, no. 2, pp. 78–80, January 9, 1975.

[2]F. J. Ingelfinger, "Bedside Ethics for the Hopeless Case," *N.E.J.M.,* vol. 289, no. 17, p. 914, October 25, 1973.

One problem with such armchair exercises, he complains, is that in spite of the impeccable logic and the graceful prose, the result is often an absolutist ethic which is unsatisfactory when applied to particular cases, and which is, therefore, of little use to the practicing physician. Unlike some absolutist philosophers, "the practitioner appears to prefer the principles of individualism. As there are few atheists in fox holes, there tend to be few absolutists at the bedside."[3]

I must concede at the outset that this essay is another exercise in "armchair ethics," in the sense that I am not a physician but a philosopher. Yet I am no absolutist, and my purpose here is to examine a doctrine that *is* held in an absolute form by most doctors. The doctrine in question is that there is an important moral difference between active and passive euthanasia, such that even though the latter is sometimes permissible, the former is always absolutely forbidden. This is an absolute which doctors hold "at the bedside" as well as in the seminar room; and the "principles of individualism" make little headway against it. But I will argue that this is an irrational dogma, and that there is no sound moral basis for it.

I will *not* argue, simply, that active euthanasia is all right. Rather, I will be concerned with the *relation* between active euthanasia and passive euthanasia: I will argue that there is no moral difference between them. My conclusion, then, will have this form: *if* you have no objection to passive euthanasia, then you should have no objection to active euthanasia either, for there is no moral difference between the two. It follows that whenever euthanasia of *any* sort is permissible—even passive euthanasia—we are morally free to choose which form of euthanasia to employ, depending on the needs of the particular case at hand. This is an important result, because in some cases it turns out that active euthanasia is very much preferable to passive euthanasia, rather than the reverse.

I am aware that this will at first seem incredible to many readers, but I hope that this impression will be dispelled as the discussion proceeds. The discussion will be guided by two methodological considerations, both of which were touched on in the editorial previously quoted. The first has to do with my "basic assumptions." My arguments are intended to appeal to all reasonable people, and not merely to some small group which is already disposed to agree; therefore, I try not to rely on any assumptions that cannot be accepted by any reasonable person. None of my arguments—I hope—depend on morally eccentric premises. Second, Ingelfinger is surely correct when he says that we

---

[3]*Ibid.*

must be concerned as much with the realities of medical practice as with the more abstract issues of moral theory. As he notes, the philosopher's precepts "remain abstract and idealistic until they are tested in the laboratory of experience." Part of my argument is precisely that when "tested in the laboratory of experience," the doctrine in question has terrible results. I believe that if this doctrine were to be recognized as irrational, and rejected by the medical profession, the benefit to both doctors and patients would be enormous. At the end of this essay, I will mention some of these benefits. In this sense, my paper is not intended as an "armchair exercise" at all.

II. ACTIVE AND PASSIVE EUTHANASIA

"Active euthanasia," as the term is used, means taking some positive action designed to kill the patient, for example giving a lethal injection of potassium chloride. "Passive euthanasia," on the other hand, means simply refraining from doing anything to keep the patient alive. In passive euthanasia, medication or other life-sustaining therapy is withheld, or a doctor refuses to perform surgery, and so on, and lets the patient die "naturally" of whatever ills already afflict him.

Many doctors prefer to use the term "euthanasia" only in connection with *active* euthanasia, and they use other words to refer to what I am calling "passive euthanasia"—for example, instead of "passive euthanasia," they may speak of "the right to death with dignity," or some such. One reason for this choice of terms is the emotional impact of the words: it *sounds* so much nobler to defend "death with dignity" than to advocate "euthanasia" of any sort. And, of course, if one believes that there is a great moral difference between active and passive euthanasia—as most doctors do—then one may prefer a terminology which puts as much psychological distance as possible between the two. However, I do not want to become involved in a pointless dispute about terminology, because nothing of substance here depends on which label is used. I will stay with the terms "active euthanasia" and "passive euthanasia" because they are the most convenient; but, if you prefer a different terminology, you may substitute your own throughout, and my arguments will be unaffected.

The belief that there is an important moral difference between active and passive euthanasia obviously has important consequences for medical practice. It makes a difference to what doctors are willing to do. Consider, for example, the following familiar situation. A patient who is dying of incurable cancer of the throat is in terrible pain which can no longer be satisfactorily alleviated. The patient is certain to die within a few days, but decides that he does not want to go on living for those days since the pain is unbearable. So, the patient asks the doctor to end his life now and the family joins in the request. One way that the doctor might comply with this request is simply by killing the patient, for example by giving a lethal injection. Most doctors would object to administering the lethal injection, not only because of the possible legal and personal consequences, but because they think such a course of action is wrong. And this is understandable: the idea of killing someone goes against very deep moral feelings; besides, as we are often reminded, it is the special business of doctors to save and protect life, not to destroy it. Yet, even so, the physician may sympathize with the dying patient's request, and feel that it is entirely reasonable for the patient to prefer death now rather than after a few more days of agony. The doctrine that we are considering tells the doctor what to do: it says that although the doctor may *not* administer the lethal injection—that would be "active euthanasia," which is forbidden—he *may* withhold treatment and let the patient die.

It is no wonder that this simple idea is so widely accepted, for it seems to give the doctor a way out of the dilemma, without having to kill the patient, and without having to prolong the patient's agony. The idea is not a new one. What *is* new is that the idea is now being incorporated into official statements of medical ethics; what was once done unofficially is now becoming official policy. The idea is expressed, for example, in a 1973 policy statement of the American Medical Association, which says (in its entirety):

> The intentional termination of the life of one human being by another—mercy killing—is contrary to that for which the medical profession stands and is contrary to the policy of the American Medical Association. The cessation of the employment of extraordinary means to prolong the life of the body when there is irrefutable evidence that biological death is imminent is the decision of the patient and/or his immediate family. The advice and judgment of the physician should be freely available to the patient and/or his immediate family.[4]

---

[4]This statement was approved by the House of Delegates of the A.M.A. on December 4, 1973. Similar statements have been endorsed by other medical associations; for example, the governing council of the New York State Medical Society approved a statement with similar wording almost a year before the A.M.A. statement was adopted. It is worth noting that some state medical societies have also advised *patients* to take a similar attitude toward the termination of their lives. In 1973, the Connecticut State Medical Society approved a "background statement" to be signed by terminal patients which includes this sentence: "I value life and the dignity of life, so that I am

Before going on, I want to say something about the notion of "extraordinary means" as it is used in this statement. The Judicial Council which composed the statement did not explain exactly what is meant by this phrase, but I think that its meaning is reasonably clear. The explanation is historical. The problem of when to suspend treatment did not take on its present urgent form until advances in medical technology made it possible to keep a great many hopeless patients alive indefinitely by the use of respirators, intravenous feeding, and so forth. The result of these advances is that it is no longer a serious option for doctors to keep every patient alive "for as long as possible"; for, if they did, the hospitals would quickly overflow with "human vegetables" whose maintenance would be humanly pointless and socially disastrous. So, the problem of when to suspend treatment, and allow the patient to die, is thought of in these terms; hence the reference to the use of "extraordinary means to prolong the life of the body."

However, the doctrine which is formulated in these terms is also taken to apply to other cases, in which physicians of conscience feel that medical treatment is pointless, even though the treatment in question is not "extraordinary." For example, when a mongoloid infant is born with an intestinal blockage, the doctor and parents may agree that there will be no operation, so that the baby will die; whereas, if the same infant were born without the obstruction, it certainly would not be killed.[5] This is a clear application of the doctrine that passive euthanasia is all right, but that active euthanasia is forbidden. However, the treatment required to save the baby—abdominal surgery—can hardly be called "extraordinary" by today's medical standards. Again, suppose a baby is born with multiple deformities including an opening in its esophagus which must be repaired to prevent death. In some such cases, the doctor and parents have chosen not to operate, relying on the permissibility of "passive euthanasia," even though the surgery in question is not "extraordinary" by current standards.[6]

Clearly, then, doctors interpret the doctrine as applying to a far

---

not asking that my life be directly taken, but that my life not be unreasonably prolonged or the dignity of life be destroyed."

[5]A discussion of this type of case can be found in Anthony Shaw, " 'Doctor, Do We Have a Choice'," *The N. Y. Times Mag.,* pp. 44–54, January 30, 1972. Also see Shaw's "Dilemmas of 'Informed Consent' in Children," *N.E.J.M.,* vol. 289, no. 17, pp. 885–890, October 25, 1973.

[6]On February 15, 1974, a Superior Court judge in Portland, Maine, ordered a doctor to proceed with an operation in a case of this type. Otherwise, the surgery would not have been performed. The baby died anyway a few days later. See "Deformed Baby Dies Amid Controversy," *The Miami Herald,* p. 4-B, February 25, 1974.

wider range of cases than those in which truly extraordinary or heroic measures are required to prolong life. They are right to do this, for (excepting the question of how best to allocate scarce or expensive resources), the moral questions are the same no matter whether the life-preserving measures are "extraordinary" or not. As Paul Ramsey points out:

> The same sort of question can be raised about many quite standard or routine procedures. Suppose that a diabetic patient long accustomed to self-administration of insulin falls victim to terminal cancer, or suppose that a terminal cancer patient suddenly develops diabetes. Is he in the first case obliged to continue, and in the second case obliged to begin, insulin treatment and die painfully of cancer, or in either or both cases may the patient choose rather to pass into diabetic coma and an earlier death? . . . Or an old man slowly deteriorating who from simply being inactive and recumbent gets pneumonia: are we to use antibiotics in a likely successful attack upon this disease which from time immemorial has been called "the old man's friend"?[7]

Thus, it appears that the much-debated distinction between extraordinary and ordinary means of prolonging life has little relevance to the moral issues raised by the distinction between active and passive euthanasia; for, those issues force themselves upon us regardless of whether or not the contemplated life-preserving measures are extraordinary.

III. THE MORAL EQUIVALENCE OF KILLING AND LETTING DIE

Not every doctor agrees that the active/passive distinction is morally important. Over 20 years ago, Dr. D. C. S. Cameron of the American Cancer Society said that "actually the difference between euthanasia and letting the patient die by omitting life-sustaining treatment is a moral quibble."[8] I want to argue now that Cameron was right.

In the first place, in any case in which euthanasia seems desirable, it is because the doctors and/or the family think that the patient would literally be better off dead—or at least, no worse off dead—than continuing the kind of life that is available. (Without this assumption, even

[7]Paul Ramsey, *The Patient as Person,* New Haven, Connecticut, Yale University Press, 1970, pp. 115–116.

[8]D. C. S. Cameron, *The Truth About Cancer,* Englewood Cliffs, N.J. Prentice-Hall, 1956, p. 116.

passive euthanasia would be monstrous.) But, as far as this main question of ending the patient's life is concerned, it does not matter whether the euthanasia is active or passive: *in either case, the patient ends up dead sooner than he or she otherwise would.* And, if the results are the same, why should it matter so much which method is used?

Moreover, we need to remember that, in cases such as that of the terminal cancer patient, the justification for allowing the patient to die, rather than prolonging his life for a few more hopeless days, is that he is in horrible pain. But, if the doctors simply withhold treatment, it may take the patient *longer* to die, and so he will suffer *more* than he would if given a lethal injection. This fact provides strong reason for thinking that, once the initial decision not to prolong a patient's agony has been made, active euthanasia is actually *preferable* to passive euthanasia, rather than the reverse. To say otherwise is to endorse the option which leads to more suffering rather than less, and is contrary to the humanitarian impulse which prompts the decision not to prolong the life in the first place.

But many people, including many doctors, are convinced that there is an important moral difference between active and passive euthanasia because they think that, in passive euthanasia, the doctor does not really *do* anything. No action whatever is taken; the doctor simply does nothing and the patient dies of whatever ills already afflict him. In active euthanasia, however, doctors *do something* to bring about the patient's death. They kill him. Thus, the difference between active and passive euthanasia is thought to be the difference between doing something to bring about someone's death, and not doing anything to bring about anyone's death. Of course, if the matter is conceived in this way, passive euthanasia seems preferable to active euthanasia, even though the outcome may be the same in both cases. Paul Ramsey, who denounces the view I am defending as "extremist" and who regards the active/passive euthanasia distinction as one of the "flexibly wise categories of traditional medical ethics," takes just this view of the matter. He says that the choice between active and passive euthanasia

> is not a choice between indirectly and directly willing and doing something. *It is rather the important choice between doing something and doing nothing,* or (better said) ceasing to do something that was begun in order to do something that is better because now more fitting.[9]

This is a very misleading way of thinking, for it ignores the fact that in passive euthanasia the doctor *does* do one thing which is very

---

[9]Ramsey, *op. cit.,* p. 151.

important: namely, he or she lets the patient die. We may overlook this obvious fact—or, at least, we may put it out of our minds—if we concentrate only on a very restricted way of describing what happens: "The doctor does not administer medication or any other therapy; the doctor does not instruct the nurses to administer any such medication; the doctor does not perform any surgery," and so on. Of course, this description of what happens is correct, as far as it goes; these are all things that the doctor does not do. But, the point is that the doctor *does* let the patient die, when he or she could have saved that patient, and this must be included in the description, too.

Here, we must remember some elementary points, which are so obvious that they would not be worth mentioning except that overlooking them is a source of so much confusion in this area. The act of letting someone die may be done intentionally and deliberately, just as the act of killing someone may be done intentionally and deliberately. Moreover, the doctor is *responsible* for the decision to let the patient die, just as the doctor would be responsible for giving the patient a lethal injection. The decision to let a patient die is subject to moral appraisal in the same way that a decision to kill him would be subject to moral appraisal: it may be assessed as wise or unwise, compassionate or sadistic, right or wrong. If a doctor deliberately let a patient die who was suffering from a routinely curable illness, then the doctor would certainly be to blame for what he did, just as the doctor would be to blame if he had needlessly killed the patient. Criminal charges against him would then be appropriate. If so, then it would be no defense at all for the doctor to insist that, *really,* he didn't "do anything" but just stand there. We would all know that the doctor did do something very serious indeed, for he let the patient die.

These considerations show how misleading it is to characterize the difference between active and passive euthanasia as a difference between doing something (killing) for which the doctor may be morally culpable, and doing nothing (just standing there while the patient dies) for which the doctor is not culpable. The real difference between them is, rather, the difference between *killing* and *letting die,* both of which are actions for which a doctor, or anyone else, is morally responsible.

Now we can formulate the problem more precisely. The reason why so many people think that there is an important moral difference between active and passive euthanasia is precisely that they think *killing someone is morally worse than letting someone die.* But, is it? Is killing, in itself, worse than letting die? In order to investigate this issue, we may consider two cases which are exactly alike except that one involves killing where the other involves letting someone die. Then we can ask whether this difference makes any difference to our moral assessments. It is important that the cases be *exactly* alike, except for this one difference, since otherwise we cannot be confident that it is *this* difference which accounts for any variation in our assessments of the two cases.

So, let us consider this pair of cases:

(i) Smith stands to gain a large inheritance if anything should happen to his six-year-old cousin. One evening while the child is taking his bath, Smith sneaks into the bathroom and drowns the child, and then arranges things so that it will look like an accident.

(ii) Jones also stands to gain if anything should happen to his six-year-old cousin. Like Smith, Jones sneaks in planning to drown the child in his bath. However, just as he enters the bathroom, Jones sees the child slip and hit his head, and fall face down in the water. Jones is delighted; he stands by, ready to push the child's head back under if it is necessary, but it is not necessary. With only a little thrashing about, the child drowns himself, "accidentally," as Jones watches and does nothing.

Smith killed the child, while Jones "merely" let the child die. That is the only difference between them. Did either man behave better, from a moral point of view? Is there a moral difference between them? *If the difference between killing and letting die were itself a morally important matter, then we should say that Jones' behavior was less reprehensible than Smith's.* But do we really want to say that? I think not. In the first place, both men acted from the same motive, personal gain, and both had exactly the same end in view when they acted. We may infer from Smith's conduct that he is a bad man, although we may withdraw or modify that judgment if we learn certain further facts—for example, that Smith is mentally deranged. But, would we not also infer the very same thing about Jones from *his* conduct? And would not the same further considerations also be relevant to any modification of this judgment? Moreover, suppose Jones pleaded, in his own defense, "After all, I didn't *do anything* except just stand there and watch the child drown. I didn't kill him; I only let him die." Again, if letting die were in itself less bad than killing, then this defense should have at least some weight. But, it does not. Such a "defense" can only be regarded as a grotesque perversion of moral reasoning. Morally speaking, it is no defense at all.

Thus, it seems that when we are careful not to smuggle in any further differences which prejudice the issue, the mere difference be-

tween killing and letting die does not itself make any difference to the
morality of actions concerning life and death.[10]

It may be pointed out, quite properly, that the cases of euthanasia with which doctors are concerned are not like this at all.
They do not involve personal gain or the destruction of normal
healthy children. Doctors are concerned only with cases in which
the patient's life has become or will soon become a positive burden
to him. However, the point is the same in these cases: the difference
between killing and letting die does not, *in itself,* make a difference,
from the point of view of morality. If a doctor lets a patient die, for
humane reasons, that doctor is in the same moral position as if he

---

[10]Judith Jarvis Thomson has argued that this line of reasoning is unsound. Consider, she says, this argument which is parallel to the one involving Smith and Jones:

> Alfrieda knows that if she cuts off Alfred's head, he will die, and, wanting him
> to die, cuts it off; Bertha knows that if she punches Bert in the nose he will die
> —Bert is in peculiar physical condition—and, wanting him to die, punches him
> in the nose. But what Bertha does is surely every bit as bad as what Alfrieda does.
> So, cutting off a man's head isn't worse than punching a man in the nose.

From "Killing, Letting Die, and the Trolley Problem," *The Monist,* vol. 59, p. 204,
1976. Thomson concludes that, since this absurd argument doesn't prove anything, the
Smith/Jones argument doesn't prove anything either.

However, I think that the Alfrieda/Bertha argument is not absurd, as strange as
it is. A little analysis shows that it is a sound argument and that its conclusion is true.
We need to notice first that the reason why it is wrong to chop someone's head off is,
obviously, that this causes death. The act is objectionable because of its consequences.
Thus, a different act with the same consequences may be equally objectionable. In
Thomson's example, punching Bert in the nose has the same consequences as chopping
off Alfred's head; and, indeed, the two actions are equally bad.

The Alfrieda/Bertha argument presupposes a distinction between the act of chopping off someone's head, and the results of this act, the victim's death. (It is stipulated
that, except for the fact that Alfrieda chops off someone's head, while Bertha punches
someone in the nose, the two acts are "in all other respects alike." The "other respects"
include the acts' consequences, the victims' deaths.) This is not a distinction we would
normally think to make, since we cannot in fact cut off someone's head without killing
him. Yet in thought the distinction can be drawn. The question raised in the argument,
then, is whether, *considered apart from their consequences,* head-chopping is worse than
nose-punching. The answer to *this* strange question is "No," just as the argument says
it should be.

The conclusion of the argument should be construed like this: The bare fact that
one act is an act of head-chopping, while another act is an act of nose-punching, is not
a reason for judging the former to be worse than the latter. At the same time—and this
is perfectly compatible with the argument—the fact that one act causes death, while
another does not, *is* a reason for judging the former to be worse. Since normally
punching someone in the nose does not cause death, we normally have a reason to judge
that less harshly than chopping off a head, which does cause death. So, surprisingly,
the Alfrieda/Bertha argument turns out to be perfectly acceptable.

or she had given the patient a lethal injection for humane reasons. If the decision was wrong—if, for example, the patient's illness was, in fact, curable—then the decision would be equally regrettable no matter which method was used to carry it out. And, if the doctor's decision was the right one, then which method was used is not in itself important.

The A.M.A. statement isolates the crucial issue very well; the crucial issue is "the intentional termination of the life of one human being by another." But then the statement goes on to deny that the cessation of treatment *is* the intentional termination of a life. This is where the mistake comes in, for what is the cessation of treatment, in these circumstances, if it is not "the intentional termination of the life of one human being by another?" Of course, it is exactly that, and if it were not, there would be no point to it.

IV. COUNTER-ARGUMENTS

Our argument has now brought us to this point: we cannot draw any moral distinction between active and passive euthanasia on the grounds that one involves killing while the other only involves letting someone die, because that is a difference which does not make a difference, from a moral point of view. Some people will find this hard to accept. One reason, I think, is that they fail to distinguish the question of whether killing is, in itself, worse than letting die, from the very *different* question of whether most actual cases of killing are more reprehensible than most actual cases of letting die. Most actual cases of killing are clearly terrible—think, for example, of all the murders reported in the newspapers—and we hear of such cases every day. On the other hand, we hardly ever hear of a case of letting die, except for the actions of doctors who are motivated by humanitarian reasons. So we learn to think of killing in a much worse light than we think of letting die; and we conclude, invalidly, that there must be something about killing which makes it *in itself* worse than letting die. But this does not follow; for it is not the bare difference between killing and letting die that makes the difference in these cases. Rather, it is the other factors—the murderer's motive of personal gain, for example, contrasted with the doctor's humanitarian motivation—that account for our different reactions to the different cases.

There are, however, other more substantial arguments that may be advanced to oppose my conclusion. I will consider two of them:

The first argument attempting to establish a moral difference between killing and letting die focuses specifically on the concept of *being the cause of someone's death.* If we kill someone, then we are the cause of that person's death. But, if we merely let someone die, then we are not the cause of death; rather, the person dies of whatever condition he or she already has. The doctor who gives the cancer patient a lethal injection has personally caused the patient's death, and will have this on his conscience; whereas, if the doctor merely ceases treatment, the cancer, and not the doctor, is the cause of the death. This argument has been advanced many times. Ramsey, for example, urges us to remember that "In omission no human agent causes the patient's death, directly or indirectly."[11] Also, writing in the *Villanova Law Review* for 1968, Dr. J. Russell Elkinton said that what makes the active/passive distinction morally important is that in passive euthanasia "the patient does not die from the act (e.g. the act of turning off the respirator) but from the underlying disease or injury."[12]

This argument will not do, for two reasons. First, just as there is a distinction to be drawn between being and not being the cause of someone's death, there is also a distinction to be drawn between letting someone die and not letting anyone die. It is certainly desirable, in general, not to be the cause of anyone's death; but, it is *also* desirable, in general, not to let anyone die when we can save them. (Doctors act on this precept every day.) Therefore, we cannot draw any special conclusion about the relative desirability of passive euthanasia just on these grounds. Second, the reason why we think it is bad to be the cause of someone's death is that we think that death is a great evil—and so it is. However, if we have decided that euthanasia—even passive euthanasia—is desirable in a given case, then we have decided that in *this* instance death is no greater an evil than the patient's continued existence. And if this is true, then the usual reason for not wanting to be the cause of someone's death simply does not apply. To put the point just a bit differently: there is nothing wrong with being the cause of someone's death if the death is, all things considered, a good thing.

The second argument appeals to a favorite idea of philosophers, namely that our duty not to harm people is generally more stringent than our duty to help them. The law recognizes this when it forbids us to kill people, or steal their goods, but does not require us in general to save people's lives or give them charity. This is said to be not merely a point about the law, but about morality as well. We do not have a

---

[11]Ramsey, *op. cit.,* p. 151.
[12]J. Russell Elkinton, "The Dying Patient, the Doctor, and the Law," *Villanova Law Review,* vol. 13, no. 4, p. 743, Summer, 1968.

strict moral duty to help some poor person in Ethiopia—although it might be kind and generous of us if we did—but we *do* have a strict moral duty to refrain from doing anything to harm that person. Killing someone is a violation of our duty not to harm people, whereas letting someone die is merely a failure to give help. Therefore, the former is a more serious breach of morality than the latter; and so, contrary to what was said above, there is a morally significant difference between killing and letting die.

This argument has a certain superficial plausibility, but it cannot be used to show that there is a morally important difference between active and passive euthanasia. For one thing, it only seems that our duty to help people is less stringent than our duty not to harm them when we concentrate on certain sorts of cases: cases in which the people we could help are very far away, and are strangers to us; or cases in which it would be very difficult for us to help them; or cases in which helping would require a substantial sacrifice on our part. Many of us feel that, in *these* types of cases, it may be kind and generous of us to give help, but we are not morally required to do so. Thus, we feel that when we give money for famine-relief we are being especially big-hearted, and we deserve special praise—even if it would be immodest of us to seek such praise—because we are doing more than we are strictly speaking required to do.[13]

However, if we think of cases in which it would be very *easy* for us to help someone, who is close at hand, and in which no great personal sacrifice is required, things look very different. Think again of the child drowning in the bathtub: *of course* a man standing next to the tub would have a strict moral duty to help the child. Here, the alleged asymmetry between the duty to help and the duty not to harm vanishes. Since most of the cases of euthanasia with which we are concerned are of this latter type—the patient is close at hand, it is well within the professional skills of the physcian to keep him alive, and so on—the alleged asymmetry has no relevance.

It should also be remembered, in considering this argument, that the duty of doctors toward their patients *is* precisely to help them; that is what doctors are supposed to do. Therefore, even if there were a general asymmetry between the duty to help and the duty not to harm, it would not apply in the special case of the relation between doctors

---

[13]For my purpose in this essay, I do not need to consider whether this way of thinking about "charity" is justified. There are, however, strong arguments that it is morally indefensible: See Peter Singer, "Famine, Affluence, and Morality," *Phil. and Public Affairs,* vol. 1, no. 3, pp. 229–243, Spring, 1972.

and their patients. Finally, it is not clear that killing such a patient *is* "harming" him, anyway, even though in other cases it certainly is a great harm to someone to kill him. For, as I said before, we are going under the assumption that the patient would be no worse off dead than he or she is now—without this assumption we would not even consider *passive* euthanasia—and if so, then killing the person is not harming him. For the same reason, we should not classify letting such a patient die as a failure to help. Therefore, even if we grant that our duty to help people is less stringent than our duty not to harm them, nothing follows about our duties with respect to killing and letting die in the special case of euthanasia.

V. PRACTICAL CONSEQUENCES

This is enough, I think, to show that the doctrine underlying the A.M.A. statement is irrational. There is no morally important difference between active and passive euthanasia; if one is permissible, then so is the other. If this were merely an intellectual mistake, having no significant consequences for medical practice, the whole matter would not be very important. But the opposite is true: the doctrine has terrible consequences. For, as I have already mentioned—and as doctors know very well—the process of being "allowed to die" can be relatively slow and painful, while being given a lethal injection is relatively quick and painless. Dr. Anthony Shaw describes what happens when the decision has been made not to perform the surgery necessary to "save" a mongoloid infant:

> When surgery is denied (the doctor) must try to keep the infant from suffering while natural forces sap the baby's life away. As a surgeon whose natural inclination is to use the scalpel to fight off death, standing by and watching a salvageable baby die is the most emotionally exhausting experience I know. It is easy at a conference, in a theoretical discussion, to decide that such infants should be allowed to die. It is altogether different to stand by in the nursery and watch as dehydration and infection wither a tiny being over hours and days. This is a terrible ordeal for me and the hospital staff—much more so than for the parents who never set foot in the nursery.[14]

Why must the hospital staff "stand by in the nursery and watch as dehydration and infection wither a tiny being over hours and days?"

---

[14]Shaw, " 'Doctor, Do We Have a Choice?'," p. 54.

Why must they merely "try" to reduce the infant's suffering? The doctrine which says that the baby may be allowed to dehydrate and wither, but not be given an injection which would end its life without suffering, is not only irrational but wicked.

The same goes for the case of the person with cancer of the throat. Here there are three options: with continued treatment, the patient will have a few more days of agony; if treatment is stopped, but nothing else is done, it will be a few more hours; and with a lethal injection, the patient will die at once. Those who oppose euthanasia in all its forms say that we must take the first option, and keep the patient alive for as long as possible. I myself cannot accept this view; I think that it is inhumane and it serves no decent human end. However, I can see a kind of integrity in this position. The morally decent position, it seems to me, is that we should administer the lethal injection so that he may die without further suffering. But, the *middle* position—that, although the patient need not suffer for days before dying, he must nevertheless suffer for a few more hours—is sheer nonsense from both the point of view of logic and of morals. It is a "moderate" view that incorporates the worst, and not the best, features of both extremes.

Let me mention one other practice that we would be well rid of if we stopped thinking that the distinction between active and passive euthanasia is important. About one in 600 babies born in the United States is mongoloid. Most of these babies are otherwise healthy—that is, with only the usual pediatric care, they will proceed to a "normal" infancy. Some, however, are born with congenital defects such as intestinal obstructions which require immediate surgery if the baby is to live. Sometimes the surgery is withheld and the baby dies; but when there is no defect requiring surgery, the baby lives on.[15] Now surgery to remove an intestinal obstruction is not difficult; the reason why it is not performed in such cases is, clearly, that the child is mongoloid and the parents and doctor judge that because of *this* it is better for the child to die.

But notice that this situation is absurd, no matter what view one takes of the lives and potentials of such a baby. If you think that the life of such an infant is worth preserving, then what does it matter if it needs a simple operation? Or, if you think it better that such a baby not proceed to a "normal" infancy, then what difference does it make that it happens to have an unobstructed intestinal tract? In either case, the matter of life or death is being decided on irrelevant grounds. It is the mongolism, and not the intestines, that is the issue. The matter

---

[15]See the articles by Shaw cited in footnote 5.

should be decided, if at all, on *that* basis, and should not be allowed to depend on the essentially irrelevant question of whether the baby's intestinal tract is blocked.

What makes this situation possible, of course, is the idea that when there is an intestinal blockage we can "let the baby die," but when there is no such defect, there is nothing we can do, for we must not "kill" it. The fact that this idea leads to such results as deciding life or death on irrelevant grounds is another good reason why the dogma should be rejected.

Doctors may think that all of this is only of academic interest, the sort of thing which philosophers may worry about, but which has no practical bearing on their own work. After all, doctors must be concerned about the legal consequences of what they do, and active euthanasia is clearly forbidden by the law. They are right to be concerned about this. There have not been many prosecutions of doctors in the United States for active euthanasia, but there have been some. Prosecutions for passive euthanasia, on the other hand, are virtually nonexistent, even though there are laws under which charges could be brought, and even though this practice is much more widespread. Passive euthanasia, unlike active euthanasia, is by and large tolerated by the law. The law may sometimes compel a doctor to take action which he might not otherwise take to keep a patient alive;[16] but, of course this is very different from bringing criminal charges against the doctor after the patient is dead.

Even so, doctors should be concerned with the fact that the law and public opinion are forcing upon them an indefensible moral position, which has a considerable effect on their practices. Of course, most doctors are not now in the position of being coerced in this matter, for they do not regard themselves as merely going along with what the law requires. Rather, in statements such as the A.M.A. policy statement that I quoted, doctors are endorsing the dogma as a central point of medical ethics. In that statement, active euthanasia is condemned not merely as illegal but as "contrary to that for which the medical profession stands," while passive euthanasia is approved. However, if my arguments have been sound, then there really is no moral difference between the two; and so, while doctors may have to discriminate between them to satisfy the law, they should not do any *more* than that. They should not give the distinction any added authority and weight by writing it into official statements of medical ethics.

---

[16]See, for example, the case cited in footnote 6.

11

Moral Agency and Negative Acts in Medicine[1]

Martin Benjamin

Medical Humanities Program, Michigan State University, East Lansing, Michigan

The philosopher's term "moral agency" refers to a person's capacity to make various choices and decisions and to be responsible, morally, for the foreseeable consequences. Determining the nature and extent of moral agency is, therefore, an important aspect of ascribing responsibility for various states of affairs. In what follows, I argue that the conduct of physicians and their patients often presupposes an overly simple mechanistic conception of moral agency. This defective conception of moral agency, I conclude, contributes not only to errors in fixing responsibility, but also to poor medical practice.

[1]This is a revised version of a paper entitled "Medical Practice and the Theory of Action," which was presented at the Conference in Philosophy, Law and Medicine sponsored by Kalamazoo College and Western Michigan University, October 15–17, 1976, in Kalamazoo, Michigan. I am grateful to Gerald C. MacCallum, who commented on the earlier draft, for many helpful criticisms and suggestions.

I. ACTING NEGATIVELY VS. SIMPLY NOT ACTING

The conception of agency I have in mind is revealed most dramatically in disputes over active euthanasia. Many people, including many physicians,[2] believe that active euthanasia is morally worse than passive euthanasia and that the difference lies primarily in the fact that in the former, the physician kills the patient while in the latter he or she merely lets the patient die. Active euthanasia is believed wrong, then, because it involves a proscribed *act*—killing. But passive euthanasia, it is believed, involves *no act* at all. The doctor does nothing; he or she merely lets the patient die. This difference is sometimes characterized as one between "man acting" and "nature acting."[3] Implicit is the view that to act, to be a moral agent, is necessarily to make directed bodily movements of a certain kind that are mechanistically related to certain foreseeable (and usually intended) consequences.

James Rachels[4] has given an intuitive argument to show that such an account of the difference between active and passive euthanasia is untenable. The argument is effective, given its immediate purpose. But, Rachels does not unpack what underlies his appeal to our intuitions. Had he done so, he would have exposed a simple-minded notion of moral agency which pervades medical practice in many contexts other than those raising questions of euthanasia.

Rachels sets out to show that insofar as the distinction between active and passive euthanasia is based on a distinction between killing and letting die, it is not well grounded. For, as he argues, the difference between cases of impermissible killing and permissible allowing to die is a function of factors other than the former's involving an agent's mechanistic participation in the event and the latter's not. In other words, killing is not *in itself* morally worse than letting die, even though many fully described cases of killing are worse (morally) than many fully described cases of letting die. To demonstrate this, Rachels presents a pair of cases in which all of the variables are the same except that one involves killing and the other allowing to die. (Refer to the Smith-Jones cases in Section III of Rachels' essay in the present volume.)

In considering these cases, we are not inclined to say that what one agent (Smith) did is morally worse than what the other (Jones)

[2]D. Crane, in J. A. Behnke and S. Bok, eds., *The Dilemmas of Euthanasia*, Garden City, New York, Anchor/Doubleday, 1975, pp. 107–119 and *Hastings Center Report*, 6, p. 2, 1976.

[3]V. J. Collins, *J. A. M. A.* 206, pp. 389–392, 1968.

[4]James Rachels, *N. E. J. M.*, vol. 292, pp. 78–80, 1975.

did, even though one is a case of killing and the other a case of letting die; for each acted deliberately, each had the same reprehensible end in view, and each acted from the same base motive (personal gain). It is the identity of the latter (deliberateness, end in view, and motive) rather than the difference between the former (killing as opposed to letting die) that provides the basis for our moral appraisal.

More generally, this pair of examples shows that moral responsibility—and hence moral agency—can be ascribed to a person for certain states of affairs even though that person's bodily movements are not causally related *in any straightforward mechanical fashion* to them. But, the question now arises, how are we to distinguish those persons who are morally responsible for, though in no way mechanistically related to, someone's death from those who are not? For, certainly in Rachels' example, there were others besides Jones who did not save the drowning child. The answer to this question requires us to recognize the distinction between *simply not saving a life* and *allowing someone to die.* At any given moment, of course, there are an infinite number of things we are not doing (including not saving a number of lives). All of these fall under the heading of what I will call *simply not acting;* and, for them, questions of moral agency and ascriptions of moral responsibility do not arise. But, *negative acts* are to be sharply distinguished from simply not acting. For, unlike simply not acting, which may be ascribed to rocks and tables as well as to persons, negative acts may be performed only by persons who are moral agents; moral responsibility may then be ascribed for their consequences. Thus, Jones, unlike anyone else we may care to imagine in Rachels' example, performed a negative act which resulted in the cousin's death; hence, Jones alone is morally responsible and to blame for the death.

II. LETTING DIE VS. SIMPLY NOT SAVING

How, in general, do we distinguish those people who perform a negative act by allowing someone to die from the much larger class of people who perform no act by not saving the dying person? I suggest that if the following four conditions have been satisfied, we say that an agent, *A,* has refrained from saving someone or allowed someone to die, rather than saying that *A* simply did not save the person.

(a) A either has assumed an obligation or has a natural duty to save or prolong the life of the dying person.

(b) A knows or can reasonably be expected to know of the dying person's plight.

(c) A has the means and competence necessary to save or prolong the life of the dying person.

(d) Conditions are normal (that is, there are no unusual defeating conditions, such as being restrained by force from attending the dying person, and so on).

Let me now provide a brief explanation of each of these conditions.

(a) A either has assumed an obligation or has a natural duty to save or prolong the life of the dying person. Following J. Rawls,[5] I use "obligation" and "natural duty" to mark a distinction between those things we owe others in virtue of our voluntary acts—obligations—and those things we owe others without regard to our voluntary acts—natural duties. Obligations are owed to particular persons and are assumed (for example, by the voluntary act of making a promise or having a child). Natural duties, on the other hand, obtain between all as equal moral persons regardless of their voluntary acts. They are owed to persons generally and not only to those with whom we have voluntarily entered into explicit relationships which generate rights and correlative obligations. An example of a natural duty is what Rawls terms the duty of mutual aid; that is, "the duty of helping another when he is in need or jeopardy, provided that one can do so without excessive risk or loss to oneself."[6] A physician who decides to go to a party rather than respond to the known medical needs of a patient who will otherwise die does not fulfill an *obligation* to the patient. A passerby who fails to rescue a child who is face down in a shallow pool has not fulfilled the *natural duty* of mutual aid.

We must also distinguish a prima facie duty or obligation from a duty or obligation *all things considered.*[7] The complexity of our lives often confronts us with multiple duties and obligations. These are, however, initially only prima facie duties and obligations. When two or more conflict, or it is otherwise impossible to satisfy all of one's prima facie duties and obligations, one must decide which of them, all things considered, is (are) of overriding importance. The one(s) selected will usually be thought to be the more stringent or, if the conflicting duties or obligations seem equally stringent, the most consistent with the full system of one's moral principles and precepts.[8] The duties and obliga-

---

[5] J. Rawls, *A Theory of Justice,* Cambridge, Mass., Harvard University Press, 1971.

[6] *Ibid.,* pp. 114. See also pp. 338 f.f.

[7] *Ibid.,* pp. 339–342.

[8] *Ibid.,* pp. 340 f.f.

tions spoken of in condition *(a)* are to be construed as prima facie. For, even if a prima facie duty or obligation to save or prolong life is, all things considered, justifiably overridden, it is still the case that if the remaining conditions are met, one *acts* negatively with regard to the dying person. Note, too, that it follows from this that, all things considered, allowing someone to die may be justifiable in some circumstances and excusable in others, even though one may have a prima facie obligation to prolong or save life. For example, in some circumstances, the obligation to acknowledge a conscious, competent, adult patient's right to refuse life-saving medical treatment may justify a physician's overriding his or her prima facie obligation to preserve the patient's life.

(b) A knows or can reasonably be expected to know of the dying person's plight. Suppose that, as I sit here over my typewriter, someone alone in an office across the hall has an attack of some kind. After three hours, the person dies. If someone had known of the attack and had summoned medical aid at anytime within two-and-a-half hours after the onset, the victim's life would very likely have been saved. Assuming that I had no reason to believe that the victim ran any greater risk of such attacks than anyone else, we may say that although I did not save the person, I did *not allow the victim to die* or refrain from saving the person. The reason for this is that I neither knew nor could reasonably be expected to have known of his or her plight.

But, suppose that I am babysitting for a two-year-old. Although I know that two-year-olds need fairly constant watching and that this one in particular is especially active and accident-prone, instead of remaining with the child while the child is in the bath, I go to another room to watch my favorite television program. As it happens, while I am deeply absorbed in what is happening on the screen, the child slips in the tub and falls face down into the water. With some thrashing about, which I do not hear, the child then drowns. Now, even though I did not know of the drowning child's plight, I can *reasonably be expected to have known of it* in virtue of the obligations I assumed in agreeing to be the babysitter. It follows, then, that as a corollary of some of our obligations or natural duties, we may reasonably be expected to know or find out about certain things. And, therefore, the deontic condition, *(a),* and the epistemic one, *(b),* are not unrelated.

(c) A has the means and competence necessary to save or prolong the life of the dying person. Suppose that the only three people in a stalled elevator are *P,* a physician, *M,* a musician, and *L,* a well-known lawyer specializing in representing the plaintiff in medical malpractice suits. While they are waiting to be rescued, *L* has a heart attack. Now, both *P* and *M* satisfy conditions *(a)* and *(b)*. Each has a natural duty

to save or prolong L's life and each knows of L's plight. (Note that if P were already L's personal physician, P would have not merely a duty, but an obligation to help L). But, since only P satisfies *(c)*, only P is in a position to allow L to die or refrain from saving L. For, assuming that M hasn't the competence to save L, M can hardly be said to let L die or refrain from saving L, though it is true that M does not save L. Thus, *(c)* is an important condition for a person's allowing someone to die rather than simply not saving the person. Note, too, that *(c)* is not independent of *(a)*, in that in virtue of *(a)*, in certain circumstances, a person may reasonably be expected to fulfill *(c);* for example, a physician, in virtue of an obligation to his or her patients, may be expected to upgrade his or her knowledge and skills in accord with certain advances in medicine.

(d) *Conditions are normal.* This is included simply to anticipate unusual, but imaginable, circumstances which would rule out a charge of one's allowing someone to die even though *(a), (b),* and *(c)* had been satisfied. Condition *(d)* is not unique to the sort of situation we are considering. It is a defeasibility condition which, the world being as complex and unpredictable as it is, must be presumed to accompany any manageable characterization of moral agency. An example of a situation where *(d)* would do its work is a case where a doctor who satisfied *(a), (b),* and *(c)* is prevented at gunpoint from attending the dying person.

It is important, at this point, to explicitly recognize the extent to which this way of identifying the negative act of allowing to die presupposes a conception of moral agency which necessarily involves normative considerations. Such a conception is to be distinguished from those which are essentially mechanistic, focusing as they do on the causal relationship between bodily movements and other physical changes. The latter emphasize those respects in which human conduct can be explained in terms applicable to other elements of the natural world, while the former stresses the network of concepts used to characterize and regulate what we do *as persons* capable of moral choice. It is, I think, a shortcoming of mechanistic, nonnormative conceptions of human agency that they are unable to provide satisfactory criteria for identifying and tracing the causal consequences of negative acts. I turn now, then, to showing how it is that an agent, A, who satisfies these conditions, figures in the causal explanation of death.

Suppose that the stalled elevator mentioned in the previous discussion of condition *(c)* contains only M, the musician, and L, the lawyer, and that L has a heart attack. If L dies before L can receive medical attention, we would conclude that *the* cause of death was the heart attack.[9] But, make the following change in the scenario: *M* is replaced by *P,* the physician. Suppose, too, that if certain medical procedures are initiated shortly after the onset of a heart attack, the chances of dying are greatly reduced. Now, assuming that *P* knows these procedures, if *P* does no more for *L* than *M* did (in the previous case) and if *L* then dies, we must include *P's* refraining from initiating these procedures as causally contributing to *L's* death. Indeed, if there is strong reason to believe that these procedures definitely would have prevented *L* from dying, we may go so far as to say that it was *P's* omission, and not the heart attack, that is *the* cause of death. Under the circumstances, it is the failure to employ these procedures, and not simply the heart failure, that made the difference.[10]

Such shifts are not unusual in practical contexts where the causes we look for are characterized as "levers"[11] and the causal explanations that result are characterized as "recipes."[12] For example, advances in knowledge and technical skills may bring with them a shift in what we deem causally responsible for a famine. Whereas in an earlier era, people may have attributed famine to a drought, advances in knowledge and technical skill may induce us to attribute it to people's failure to have taken preventive measures which would have avoided or diminished the famine in spite of the drought. As Hart and Honoré put it:

> When we do learn to establish techniques for controlling these things [for example, famine-causing drought], we may cease to look upon them as the cause and shift to speaking of the failure to use the established technique (in the case of famine and drought, food reserves and catchment areas) as the causes."[13]

Moreover, as John Harris has recently argued, the technique's being an "established" one is sufficient, but *not* necessary for the failure

---

[9]The discretionary, contextually relative selection of *the* cause of an event from among a large number of causal factors making some contribution to it is examined by J. Feinberg, *Doing and Deserving,* Princeton, Princeton University Press, 1970, pp. 143–147, 162–168, 202–207.

[10]M. Benjamin, *Hastings Center Report,* 6, pp. 15–16, 1976.

[11]R. G. Collingwood, *An Essay on Metaphysics,* Oxford, Clarndon, 1940, Part 3-c.

[12]"The notion of cause here elucidated is the fundamental or primitive one. It is not the property of scientists; except for those whose work most directly bears on such things as engineering, agriculture or medicine, and who are naturally interested in helping their practical colleagues, scientists hardly ever make use of the notion. A statement about causes in the sense here outlined comes very near to being a recipe for producing or preventing certain effects." (D. Gasking, *Mind* 64, p. 486, 1955.)

[13]H. L. A. Hart and A. M. Honoré, *Causation in the Law,* Oxford, Clarendon, 1959, p. 34.

to use it being a significant causal factor.[14] All that is required is that the technique be known, capable of being implemented, and very likely to prevent significant harm. Thus, for example, the failure to employ a newly discovered, reasonably safe and effective cure for a fatal disease may *become* the cause of ensuing deaths even though its use is not yet established or customary. Indeed, as Harris forcefully maintains, it is because not using the remedy in these circumstances becomes a causal factor in the deaths that we can argue that its routine administration ought (morally) to be established.

The upshot of all this, then, is that allowing someone to die involves moral agency; and, unlike simply not saving someone, it is a negative act for which one can be held morally responsible. Those who perform negative acts by allowing someone to die may be distinguished from the much larger class of people who do not perform such an act by appealing to conditions *(a–d)* set out previously. Moreover, if, in certain circumstances, the only intrinsic difference between performing active and passive euthanasia is that one involves killing and the other allowing to die, then from this point of view they are morally on a par. Both involve full-blooded intentional acts with the same motive and purpose. Hence, if it is permissible to allow a newborn with Downs Syndrome and easily correctable duodenal atresia to die, it is permissible to kill a newborn with Downs Syndrome; if it is not permissible to kill a newborn with Downs Syndrome, neither is it permissible to allow one to die when a routine operation would save its life. In some cases, however, an appeal to extrinsic factors may indicate that *if euthanasia is permissible at all,* active euthanasia is preferable to passive euthanasia; for, in these cases, other things being equal, the consequences of the former will include less pain and suffering than the latter. Thus, active euthanasia may be morally preferable to passive euthanasia if requested by a competent adult dying of incurable cancer of the throat and suffering from pain which can no longer be satisfactorily alleviated.[15] Killing an anencephalic infant may be better than withholding various forms of life-prolonging treatment.

III. NEGATIVE ACTS IN GENERAL

The foregoing account centered on allowing to die which is often, though not always, a *culpable* negative act. But, if, as was suggested,

---

[14]John Harris, *Phil. and Public Affairs* 3, pp. 192–220, 1974.
[15]Rachels, *op. cit.*

some cases of allowing to die may not be culpable because the prima facie duty or obligation to save life is, all things considered, overridden by a more stringent duty or obligation, it is also the case that many negative acts are unquestionably virtuous. For, although a parent should be blamed for not attending to a child's obvious nutritional needs, a parent should also be praised for resisting the temptation to help all of the child's attempts to overcome obstacles, thereby allowing the child to develop certain skills and later enjoy the satisfaction of having exercised them well. Thus, the conditions set out above for allowing to die have to be generalized and loosened up a bit to allow for other sorts of negative acts, including those that are prima facie nonculpable.

This can be accomplished by expanding and generalizing the first condition so that it reads as follows:

(a') A has some desire, duty, or obligation to do X.

The main change, apart from generalization, is the addition of a *bare* desire to the deontic reasons an agent may have for performing a certain action. The remaining conditions would then be:

(b') A knows or can reasonably be expected to know of the possibility of doing X.

(c') A has the means and competence to do X.

(d') Conditions are normal (that is, there are no unusual defeating conditions which would otherwise prevent A from doing X.

If these conditions have been satisfied, we say that a person who does not do X has performed a negative act, has refrained from doing X. Whether the negative act is praiseworthy, blameworthy, or morally neutral will then depend upon the manner in which condition *(a')* is satisfied. If, for example, A's not doing X violates a prima facie duty or obligation which is also A's duty or obligation *all things considered,* the negative act will be blameworthy. If, on the other hand, A's not doing X runs counter to a strong desire to do it and is in accord with a duty or obligation not to do it, the negative act will be praiseworthy (for example, resisting a strong impulse to strike a screaming infant). And, finally, if X's occurring or not is of no moral consequence, refraining from doing X will be morally neutral (for example, not scratching an area of skin infected by poison ivy in the presence of a very strong desire to do so).

IV. NEGATIVE ACTS IN THERAPY

Philosophers have recently demonstrated how a failure to recognize the nature and status of negative acts obscures the moral issues involved in controversies over euthanasia and abortion.[16] What has not been generally noticed, however, is the extent to which reliance on a simple mechanistic conception of moral agency which does not acknowledge the nature and status of negative acts pervades the practice of medicine. We have, for example, heard a great deal lately about an epidemic of unnecessary treatments, drugs, and operations which result, at best, in needless risk and expense, and, at worst, in death and iatrogenic disorders.[17] Although numerous factors have been identified as contributing to this state of affairs, one which has gone generally unnoticed is the failure, on the part of both physicians and patients, to appreciate the significance of negative acts in the medical context.

I have often heard physicians explain, and sometimes try to justify, unwarranted and occasionally harmful medical intervention by stating that all of their medical training was aimed at "acting." Since, for them, *acting means some form of (physical) intervention,* to have stood by in such-and-such circumstances and "done nothing" would have run up against all their training and seemed a dereliction of duty. Medical sociologist Eliot Freidson makes a similar observation in an examination of professional values: "The aim of the practitioner is not knowledge but action, and while successful action is the aim, the tendency is to assume that any action at all is better than none."[18] If "action" is taken to include negative acts, this assumption may well be true. But, if, as more likely, it is interpreted, within a mechanistic conception of moral agency, to mean directed bodily movements of an intervening sort, it is certainly false that "any action at all is better than none." As one of my medical colleagues has expressed it: "Sometimes the best treatment is no treatment at all." If "no treatment at all" is not simply not acting, but rather performing a negative act, it is not negligence, but rather a responsible exercise of moral agency for which the physician may be credited.

Perhaps the clearest example of how a simple mechanistic conception of moral agency infects medical practice is the indiscriminate use of placebos in therapy. It is well known that a large proportion of

---

[16] J. Bennett, *Analysis* 26, pp. 83–102, 1966, and Rachels, *op. cit.*
[17] I. Illich, *Medical Nemesis,* New York, Pantheon, 1976.
[18] Eliot Freidson, *Professional Dominance,* New York, Atherton, 1970, p. 98.

medical prescriptions are for placebos. But, why are placebos prescribed so extensively? According to medical economist Victor Fuchs:

> Some physicians defend their practice of prescribing placebos by arguing that it "cements the physician-patient relationship:" the patient who expects to be given a prescription may feel that the physician who fails to write one hasn't *really done anything for him or doesn't really care to* (author's emphasis).[19]

But in view of the direct and indirect harmful consequences of such extensive reliance on placebos, surely there must be better ways to "cement the physician-patient relationship."

Sissela Bok has observed that:

> ... the number of patients receiving placebos increases as more and more people seek and receive medical care and as their desire for instant push-button alleviation of symptoms is stimulated by drug advertising and expectations of what "science" can do. Reliance on placebic therapy in turn strengthens the belief that there really is a pill or some other kind of remedy for every ailment. As long ago as 1909 Richard C. Cabot wrote, in a perceptive paper on the subject of truth and deception in medicine: "The majority of placebos are given because we believe the patient... has learned to expect medicine for every symptom and without it he simply won't get well. True, but who taught him to expect a medicine for every symptom? He was not born with this expectation. ... It is we physicians who are responsible for perpetuating false ideas about disease and its cure. .... With every placebo that we give we do our part in perpetuating error, and harmful error at that."[20]

Thus, in certain circumstances, physicians might better "cement" their relationships with their patients by placing more stress on their role as educator and less on their role as dispenser of nostrums. Such education would include information about the inevitability of certain aches and discomforts, the limitations of medical understanding and techniques, the healing power of time, the importance to health of certain patterns of living, and so on.[21] But, empirical information of this sort, important though it is, may not be enough; for, the patient may still feel that the physician "hasn't really done anything for me or doesn't really care to." In this event, the physician may have to remind him- or herself and the patient about the nature of moral agency and negative acts.

---

[19]Victor Fuchs, *Who Shall Live?* New York, Basic Books, 1974, p. 24.
[20]Sissela Bok, *Sci. Amer.* 231, pp. 17–23, 1974.
[21]L. Thomas, *The Lives of a Cell,* New York, Viking, 1974, pp. 81–86.

V. CONCLUSION

Although many problems remain in working out a comprehensive understanding of moral agency and negative acts, I think the claim and argument I have presented here can, apart from matters of detail, be endorsed by most philosophers and understood by nonphilosophers. If I am correct in this, we have here another instance of the way in which the interests of physicians and their patients may be served by a more philosophically informed view of medical practice.[22]

---

[22]S. Gorovitz and A. MacIntyre, *Hastings Center Report,* 5, pp. 13–23, 1975.

12

A Reply to Rachels on Active and Passive Euthanasia[1]

Tom L. Beauchamp

*Department of Philosophy and Kennedy Institute,
Georgetown University, Washington D.C.*

James Rachels has recently argued that the distinction between active and passive euthanasia is neither appropriately used by the American Medical Association nor generally useful for the resolution of moral problems of euthanasia.[2] Indeed, he believes this distinction—which he equates with the killing/letting die distinction—does not in itself have any moral importance. The chief object of his attack is the statement, adopted by the House of Delegates of the American Medical Association in 1973, which appears in Section I of Rachels' essay in this present volume.

Rachels constructs a powerful and interesting set of arguments against this statement. In this essay, I attempt the following: *(1)* to challenge his views on the grounds that he does not appreciate the moral reasons which give weight to the active/passive distinction; *(2)* to provide a constructive account of the moral relevance of the active/ passive distinction; and *(3)* to offer reasons showing that Rachels may

---

[1]This paper is a heavily revised version of an article by the same title first published in T. Mappes and J. Zembaty, eds., *Social Ethics,* N.Y., McGraw-Hill, 1976.
[2]James Rachels, "Euthanasia, Killing, and Letting Die," this volume, p. 153.

nonetheless be correct in urging that we *ought* to abandon the active/passive distinction for purposes of moral reasoning.

I. THE BASICS OF RACHELS' ARGUMENT

I would concede that the active/passive distinction is *sometimes* morally irrelevant. Of this, Rachels convinces me. But, it does not follow that the distinction is *always* morally irrelevant. What we need, then, is a case in which the distinction is a morally relevant one and an explanation why it is so. Rachels himself uses the method of examining two cases which are exactly alike except that "one involves killing whereas the other involves letting someone die"[2a]. We may profitably begin by comparing the kinds of cases governed by the AMA's doctrine with the kinds of cases adduced by Rachels in order to assess the adequacy and fairness of his cases.

The second paragraph of the AMA statement is confined to a narrowly restricted range of passive euthanasia cases, namely, those *(a)* where the patients are on extraordinary means, *(b)* where irrefutable evidence of imminent death is available, and *(c)* where patient or family consent is available. Rachels' two cases involve conditions notably different from these. (Refer to the Smith/Jones cases in Section III of Rachels' essay in this volume.)

You will recall that Rachels says there is no moral difference between the cases in terms of our moral assessments of Smith and Jones' behavior. This assessment seems fair enough, but what can Rachels' cases be said to prove, as they are so markedly disanalogous to the sorts of cases envisioned by the AMA proposal? Rachels concedes important disanalogies, but thinks them irrelevant:

> [T]he point is the same in these cases: the difference between killing and letting die does not, *in itself,* make a difference from the point of view of morality. If a doctor lets a patient die, for humane reasons, that doctor is in the same moral position as if he or she had given the patient a lethal injection for humane reasons.[2b]

Three observations are immediately in order. First, Rachels seems to infer that from such cases we can conclude that the distinction between killing and letting die is *always* morally irrelevant. This conclusion is fallaciously derived. What the argument in fact shows, being

---

[2a]James Rachels, "Euthanasia, Killing, and Letting Die" this volume, p. 160.
[2b]*Ibid.*, p. 162.

an analogical argument, is only that in all *relevantly similar* cases the distinction does not in itself make a moral difference. Since Rachels concedes that other cases are disanalogous, he seems thereby to concede that his argument is as weak as the analogy itself. Second, Rachels' cases involve two *unjustified* actions, one of killing and the other of letting die. The AMA statement distinguishes one set of cases of unjustified killing and another of *justified* cases of allowing to die. Nowhere is it claimed by the AMA that what makes the difference in these cases is the active/passive distinction itself. It is only implied that one set of cases, the justified set, *involves* (passive) letting die, while the unjustified set *involves* (active) killing. While it is said that justified euthanasia cases are passive ones and unjustified ones active, it is not said either that what makes some acts justified is the fact of their being passive or that what makes others unjustified is the fact of their being active. This will prove to be of vital importance.

The third point is that in both of Rachels' cases, the respective moral agents—Smith and Jones—are morally responsible for the death of the child and are morally blameworthy—even though Jones is presumably not causally responsible. In the first case, death is caused by the agent, while in the second it is not; yet, the second agent is no less morally responsible. While the law might find only the first homicidal, morality condemns the motives in each case as equally wrong, and it holds that the duty to save life in such cases is as compelling as the duty not to take life. I suggest that it is largely because of this equal degree of moral responsibility that there is no morally relevant difference in Rachels' cases. In the cases envisioned by the AMA, however, an agent is held to be responsible for taking life by actively killing, but is not held to be morally required to preserve life, and so not responsible for death, when removing the patient from extraordinary means (under conditions *a-c* above). I shall elaborate this latter point momentarily. My only conclusion thus far is the negative one that Rachels' arguments rest on weak foundations. His cases are not relevantly similar to euthanasia cases and do not support his apparent conclusion that the active/passive distinction is *always* morally irrelevant.

II. MEDICAL FALLIBILITY AND MORAL RESPONSIBILITY

I wish first to consider an argument that I believe has powerful intuitive appeal and probably is widely accepted as stating the main reason for rejecting Rachels' views. I will maintain that this argument fails, and so leaves Rachels' contentions untouched.

I begin with an actual case, the celebrated Quinlan case.[3] Karen Quinlan was in a coma, and was on a mechanical respirator which artificially sustained her vital processes and which her parents wished to cease. At least some physicians believed there was irrefutable evidence that biological death was imminent and the coma irreversible. This case, under this description, closely conforms to the passive cases envisioned by the AMA. During an interview, the father, Mr. Quinlan, asserted that he did not wish to kill his daughter, but only to remove her from the machines in order to see whether she would live or would die a natural death.[4] Suppose he had said—to envision now a second and hypothetical, but parallel case—that he wished only to see her die painlessly and, therefore, wished that the doctor could induce death by an overdose of morphine. Most of us would think the second act, which involves active killing, morally unjustified in these circumstances, while many of us would think the first act morally justified. (This is not the place to consider whether in fact it is justified, and if so under what conditions.) What accounts for the apparent morally relevant difference?

I have considered these two cases together in order to follow Rachels' method of entertaining parallel cases in which the only difference is that the one case involves killing and the other letting die. However, there is a further difference, which crops up in the euthanasia context. The difference rests in our judgments of medical fallibility and moral responsibility. Mr. Quinlan seems to think that, after all, the doctors might be wrong. There is a remote possibility that she might live without the aid of a machine. But, whether or not the medical prediction of death turns out to be accurate, if she dies then no one is morally responsible for directly bringing about or causing her death, as they would be if they caused her death by killing her. Rachels finds explanations which appeal to causal conditions unsatisfactory; but perhaps this is only because he fails to see the nature of the causal link. To bring about her death is by that act to preempt the possibility of life. To "allow her to die" by removing artificial equipment is to allow for the possibility of wrong diagnosis or incorrect prediction and hence to

---

[3]As recorded in the Opinion of Judge Robert Muir, Jr., Docket No. C-201-75 of the Superior Court of New Jersey, Chancery Division, Morris County, November 10, 1975. The relevant sections of this document are reprinted in *Ethical Issues in Death and Dying,* Tom L. Beauchamp and Seymour Perlin, eds.

[4]See Judge Muir's Opinion, p. 18—a slightly different statement, but on the subject.

absolve oneself of moral responsibility for the taking of life under false assumptions. There may, of course, be utterly no empirical possibility of recovery in some cases since recovery would violate a law of nature. However, judgments of empirical impossibility in medicine are notoriously problematic—the reason for emphasizing medical fallibility. And, in all the hard cases, we do not *know* that recovery is empirically impossible, even if good *evidence* is available.

The above reason for invoking the active/passive distinction can now be generalized: Active termination of life removes all possibility of life for the patient, while passively ceasing extraordinary means may not. This is not trivial, since patients have survived in several celebrated cases where, in knowledgeable physician's judgments, there was "irrefutable" evidence that death was imminent.[5]

One may, of course, be entirely responsible and culpable for another's death either by killing the person or by letting the person die. In such cases, of which Rachels' are examples, there is no morally significant difference between killing and letting die precisely because whatever one does, omits, or refrains from doing does not absolve one of responsibility. Either active or passive involvement renders one responsible for the death of another, and both involvements are equally wrong for the same principled moral reason: it is (prima facie) morally wrong to bring about the death of an innocent person capable of living whenever the causal intervention or negligence is intentional. (I use causal terms here because causal involvement need not be active, as when, by one's negligence, one is nonetheless causally responsible.) But, not all cases of killing and letting die fall under this same moral principle. One is sometimes culpable for killing, because morally responsible as the agent for death, as when one pulls the plug on a respirator sustaining a recovering patient (a murder). But, one is sometimes not culpable for letting die, because not morally responsible as agent, as when one pulls the plug on a respirator sustaining an irreversibly comatose and unrecoverable patient (a routine procedure, where one is *merely* causally responsible).[6] Different degrees and means of involve-

---

[5]This problem of the strength of evidence also emerged in the Quinlan trial, as physicians disagreed whether the evidence was "irrefutable." Such disagreement, when added to the problems of medical fallibility and causal responsibility just outlined, provides in the eyes of some one important argument against the *legalization* of active euthanasia, as perhaps the AMA would agree.

[6]Among the moral reasons why one is held to be responsible in the first sort of case and not responsible in the second sort are, I believe, the moral grounds for the active/passive distinction under discussion here.

ment assess different degrees of responsibility, and assessments of culpability can become intricately complex. The only point which now concerns us, however, is that because different moral principles may govern very similar circumstances, we are sometimes morally culpable for killing, but not for letting die. To many people, it will seem that in passive cases we are not morally responsible for causing death, though we are responsible in active cases.

This argument is powerfully attractive. Although I was once inclined to accept it in virtually the identical form just developed,[7] I now think that, despite its intuitive appeal, it cannot be correct. It is true that different degrees and means of involvement entail different degrees of responsibility, but it does not follow that we are *not* responsible and therefore are absolved of possible culpability in *any* case of intentionally allowing to die. We are responsible and *perhaps* culpable in either active or passive cases. Here Rachels' argument is entirely to the point: It is not primarily a question of greater or lesser responsibility by an active or a passive means that should determine culpability. Rather, the question of culpability should be decided by the moral *justification* for choosing either a passive or an active means. What the argument in the previous paragraph overlooks is that one might be unjustified in using an active means or unjustified in using a passive means, and hence be culpable in the use of either; yet, one might be justified in using an active means or justified in using a passive means, and hence not be culpable in using either. Fallibility might just as well be present in a judgment to use one means as in a judgment to use another. (A judgment to allow to die is just as subject to being based on *knowledge which is fallible as a judgment to kill.*) Moreover, in either case, it is a matter of what one knows and believes, and not a matter of a particular kind of causal connection or causal chain. If we kill the patient, then we are certainly causally responsible for that person's death. But, similarly, if we cease treatment, and the patient dies, the patient might have recovered if treatment had been continued. The patient might have been saved in either case, and hence there is no morally relevant difference between the two cases. It is, therefore, simply beside the point that "one is sometimes culpable for killing . . . but one is sometimes not culpable for letting die"—as the above argument concludes.

Accordingly, despite its great intuitive appeal and frequent mention, this argument from responsibility fails.

---

[7]Mappes and Zembaty, *op. cit.*

III. WEDGE AND RULE-UTILITARIAN ARGUMENTS

There may, however, be more compelling arguments against Rachels, and I wish now to provide what I believe is the most significant argument that can be adduced in defense of the active/passive distinction. I shall develop this argument by combining *(1)* so-called wedge or slippery slope arguments with *(2)* recent arguments in defense of rule utilitarianism. I shall explain each in turn and show how in combination they may be used to defend the active/passive distinction.

(1) Wedge arguments proceed as follows: if killing were allowed, even under the guise of a merciful extinction of life, a dangerous wedge would be introduced which places all "undesirable" or "unworthy" human life in a precarious condition. Proponents of wedge arguments believe the initial wedge places us on a slippery slope for at least one of two reasons: *(i)* Our justifying principles leave us with no principled way to avoid the slide into saying that all sorts of killings would be justified under similar conditions. Here, it is thought that once killing is allowed, a firm line between justified and unjustified killings cannot be securely drawn. It is thought best not to redraw the line in the first place, for redrawing it will inevitably lead to a downhill slide. It is then often pointed out that as a matter of historical record, this is precisely what has occurred in the darker regions of human history, including the Nazi era, where euthanasia began with the best intentions for horribly ill, non-Jewish Germans and gradually spread to anyone deemed an enemy of the people. *(ii)* Second, our basic principles against killing will be gradually eroded once some form of killing is legitimated. For example, permitting voluntary euthanasia might lead to permitting involuntary euthanasia, which will in turn lead to permitting euthanasia for those who are a nuisance to society (idiots, recidivist criminals, defective newborns, and the insane, for example). Gradually, other principles which instill respect for human life will be eroded or abandoned in the process.

I am not inclined to accept the first reason *(i)*.[8] If our justifying principles are themselves justified, then any action they warrant would be justified. Accordingly, I shall only be concerned with the second approach *(ii)*.

---

[8] An argument of this form, which I find unacceptable for reasons given below, is Arthur Dyck, "Beneficent Euthanasia and Benemortasia: Alternative Views of Mercy," in M. Kohl, ed., *Beneficent Euthanasia,* Buffalo, Prometheus Books, 1975, pp. 120ff.

(2) Rule utilitarianism is the position that a society ought to adopt a rule if its acceptance would have better consequences for the common good (greater social utility) than any comparable rule could have in that society. Any action is right if it conforms to a valid rule and wrong if it violates the rule. Sometimes, alternative rules should be measured against one another, while it has also been suggested that whole moral *codes* (complete sets of rules) rather than individual rules should be compared. While I prefer the latter formulation (Brandt's), this internal dispute need not detain us here. The important point is that a particular rule or a particular code of rules is morally justified if and only if there is no other competing rule or moral code whose acceptance would have a higher utility value for society, and when a rule's acceptability is contingent upon the consequences which would result if the rule were made current.

Wedge arguments, when conjoined with rule utilitarian arguments, may be applied to euthanasia issues in the following way. We presently subscribe to a no-active-euthanasia rule (which the AMA suggests we retain). Imagine that in our society we make current a restricted-active-euthanasia rule (as Rachels seems to urge). Which of these two moral rules would, if enacted, have the consequence of maximizing social utility? Clearly a restricted-active-euthanasia rule would have *some* utility value, as Rachels notes, since some intense and uncontrollable suffering would be eliminated. However, it may not have the highest utility value in the structure of our present code or in any imaginable code which could be made current, and therefore may not be a component in the ideal code for our society. If wedge arguments raise any serious questions at all, as I think they do, they rest in this area of whether a code would be weakened or strengthened by the addition of active euthanasia principles. For, the disutility of introducing legitimate killing into one's moral code (in the form of active euthanasia rules) may, in the long run, outweigh the utility of doing so, as a result of the eroding effect such a relaxation would have on rules in the code which demand respect for human life. If, for example, rules permitting active killing were introduced, it is not implausible to suppose that destroying defective newborns (a form of involuntary euthanasia) would become an accepted and common practice; that, as population increases occur, the aged will be even more neglectable and neglected than they now are; that capital punishment for a wide variety of crimes would be increasingly tempting; that some doctors would have appreciably reduced fears of actively injecting fatal doses whenever it seemed to them propitious to do so; and that laws of war against killing would erode in efficacy even beyond their already abysmal level.

A hundred such possible consequences might easily be imagined. But, these few are sufficient to make the larger point that such rules permitting killing could lead to a general reduction of respect for human life. Rules against killing in a moral code are not *isolated* moral principles; they are pieces of a web of rules against killing which forms the code. The more threads one removes, the weaker the fabric becomes. And if, as I believe, moral principles against active killing have the deep and continuously civilizing effect of promoting respect for life, and if principles which allow passively letting die (as envisioned in the AMA statement) do not themselves cut against this effect, then this seems an important reason for the maintenance of the active/passive distinction. (By the logic of the above argument, passively letting die would also have to be prohibited if a rule permitting it had the serious adverse consequence of eroding acceptance of rules protective of respect for life. While this prospect seems to me improbable, I can hardly claim to have refuted those conservatives who would claim that even rules which sanction letting die place us on a precarious slippery slope.)

A troublesome problem, however, confronts my use of utilitarian and wedge arguments. Most of us would agree that both killing and letting die are justified under some conditions. Killings in self-defense and in "just" wars are widely accepted as justified because the conditions excuse the killing. If society can withstand these exceptions to moral rules prohibiting killing, then why is it not plausible to suppose society can accept another excusing exception in the form of justified active euthanasia? This is an important and worthy objection, but not a decisive one. The defenseless and the dying are significantly different classes of persons from aggressors who attack individuals and/or nations. In the case of aggressors, one does not confront the question whether their lives are no longer worth living. Rather, we reach the judgment that the aggressors' morally blameworthy actions justify counteractions. But, in the case of the dying and the otherwise ill, there is no morally blameworthy action to justify our own. Here, we are required to accept the judgment that their lives are no longer *worth living* in order to believe that the termination of their lives is justified. It is the latter sort of judgment which is feared by those who take the wedge argument seriously. We do not now permit and never have permitted the taking of morally blameless lives. I think this is the key to understanding why recent cases of intentionally allowing the death of defective newborns (as in the now famous case at the Johns Hopkins Hospital) have generated such protracted controversy. Even if such newborns could not have led meaningful lives (a matter of some controversy), it is the wedged foot in the door which creates the most intense worries. For, once we decide to allow a restricted infanticide justification or any justification at all on grounds that a life is not meaningful or not worth living, we have qualified our moral rules against killing. That this qualification is a matter of the utmost seriousness needs no argument. I mention it here only to show why the wedge argument may have moral force even though we *already* allow some very different conditions to justify intentional killing.

There is one final utilitarian reason favoring the preservation of the active/passive distinction.[9] Suppose we distinguish the following two types of cases of wrongly diagnosed patients:

(1) Patients wrongly diagnosed as hopeless, and who will survive even if a treatment *is* ceased (in order to allow a natural death);

(2) Patients wrongly diagnosed as hopeless, and who will survive only if the treatment is *not ceased* (in order to allow a natural death).

If a social rule permitting only passive euthanasia were in effect, then doctors and families who "allowed death" would lose only patients in class *2,* not those in class *1;* whereas, if active euthanasia were permitted, at least some patients in class 1 would be needlessly lost. Thus, the consequence of a no-active-euthanasia rule would be to save some lives which could not be saved if both forms of euthanasia were allowed. This reason is not a *decisive* reason for favoring a policy of passive euthanasia, since classes *(1)* and *(2)* are likely to be very small and since there might be counterbalancing reasons (extreme pain, autonomous expression of the patient, and so on) in favor of active euthanasia. But, certainly it is *a* reason favoring only passive euthanasia and one which is morally relevant and ought to be considered along with other moral reasons.

IV. THE BARE DIFFERENCE BETWEEN KILLING AND LETTING DIE

It may still be insisted that my case has not touched Rachels' leading claim, for I have not shown, as Rachels puts it, that it is "the bare difference between killing and letting die that makes the difference in these cases."[10] True, I have not shown this, and in my judgment, it

---

[9] I owe most of this argument to James Rachels, whose comments on an earlier draft of this essay led to several significant alterations.

[10] Rachels, *op. cit.*, p. 163.

cannot be shown. But, this concession does not require capitulation to Rachels' argument. I adduced a case which is at the center of our moral intuition that killing is morally different (in at least some cases) from letting die; and I then attempted to account for at least part of the grounds for this belief. The grounds turn out to be other than the *bare* difference, but nevertheless *make* the distinction morally relevant. The identical point can be made regarding the voluntary/involuntary distinction, as it is commonly applied to euthanasia. It is not the bare difference between voluntary euthanasia (for example, euthanasia with patient consent) and involuntary euthanasia (that is, without patient consent) that makes one justifiable and one not. Independent moral grounds based on, for example, respect for autonomy or beneficence, or perhaps justice will alone make the moral difference.

In order to illustrate this general claim, let us presume that it is sometimes justified to kill another person and sometimes justified to allow another to die. Suppose, for example, that one may kill in self-defense and may allow to die when a promise has been made to someone that that person would be allowed to die. Here, conditions of self-defense and promising justify actions. But, now suppose that *A* promises in exactly similar circumstances to kill *B* at *B*'s request, and also that *C* allows *D* to die in an act of self-defense. Surely *A* is obliged equally to kill or to let die if *A* promised; and surely *C* is permitted to let *D* die if it is a matter of defending *C's* life. If this analysis is correct, then it follows that killing is sometimes right, sometimes wrong, depending on the circumstances, and the same is true of letting die. It is the justifying reasons which make the difference whether an action is right, not merely the kind of action it is.

Now, *if* letting die led to disastrous conclusions, but killing did not, then letting die but not killing would be wrong. Consider, for example, a possible world in which dying would be indefinitely prolongable even if all extraordinary therapy were removed and the patient were allowed to die. Suppose that it costs over one million dollars to let each patient die, that nurses consistently commit suicide from caring for those being "allowed to die," that physicians are constantly being successfully sued for malpractice for allowing death by cruel and wrongful means, and that hospitals are uncontrollably overcrowded and their wards filled with communicable diseases which afflict only the dying. Now, suppose further that killing in this possible world is quick, painless, and easily monitored. I submit that in this world we would believe that *killing is morally acceptable but that allowing to die is morally unacceptable.* The point of this example is, again, that it is the circumstances that make the difference, not the bare difference between killing and letting die.

It is, however, worth noticing that there is nothing in the AMA statement which says that the bare difference between killing and letting die itself and alone makes the difference in our differing moral assessments of rightness and wrongness. Rachels forces this interpretation on the statement. Some philosophers may have thought bare difference makes the difference, but there is scant evidence that the AMA or any thoughtful ethicist *must* believe it in order to defend the relevance and importance of the active/passive distinction. When this conclusion is coupled with my earlier argument that from Rachels' paradigm cases it follows only that the active/passive distinction is sometimes, but not always, morally irrelevant, it would seem that his case against the AMA is rendered highly questionable.

V. CONSEQUENTIALIST ARGUMENTS FOR ACTIVE/PASSIVE EUTHANASIA

There remains, however, the important question whether we *ought* to accept the distinction between active and passive euthanasia, now that we are clear about (at least one way of drawing) the moral grounds for its invocation. That is, should we employ the distinction in order to judge some acts of euthanasia justified and others not justified? Here, as the hesitant previous paragraph indicates, I am uncertain. This problem is a substantive moral issue—not merely a conceptual one—and would require at least a lengthy assessment of wedge arguments and related utilitarian considerations. In important respects, empirical questions are involved in this assessment. We should like to know, and yet have hardly any evidence to indicate, what the consequences would be for our society if we were to allow the use of active means to produce death. The best hope for making such an assessment has seemed to some to rest in analogies to suicide and capital punishment statutes. Here, it may reasonably be asked whether recent liberalizations of laws limiting these forms of killing have served as the thin end of a wedge leading to a breakdown of principles protecting life or to widespread violations of moral principles. Nonetheless, such analogies do not seem to me promising, since they are still fairly remote from the pertinent issue of the consequences of allowing active humanitarian killing of one person by another.

It is interesting to notice the outcome of the Kamisar-Williams debate on euthanasia—which is almost exclusively cast by both writers in a consequential, utilitarian framework.[10] At one crucial point in the debate, where possible consequences of laws permitting euthanasia are under discussion, they exchange "perhaps" judgments:

> I [Williams] will return Kamisar the compliment and say: "Perhaps." We are certainly in an area where no solution is going to make things quite easy and happy for everybody, and all sorts of embarrassments may be conjectured. But these embarrassments are not avoided by keeping to the present law: we suffer from them already.[11]

Because of the grave difficulties which stand in the way of making accurate predictions about the impact of liberalized euthanasia laws—especially those that would permit active killing—it is not surprising that those who debate the subject would reach a point of exchanging such "perhaps" judgments. And that is why, it seems to me, we are uncertain whether to perpetuate or to abandon the active-passive distinction in our moral thinking about euthanasia. I think we *do* perpetuate it in medicine, law, and ethics, because we are still somewhat uncertain about the conditions under which *passive* euthanasia should be permitted by law (which is one form of social *rule*). We are unsure about what the consequences will be of the California "Natural Death Act" and all those similar acts passed by other states which have followed in its path. If no untoward results occur, and the balance of the results seems favorable, then we will perhaps be less concerned about further liberalizations of euthanasia laws. If untoward results do occur (on a widespread scale), then we would be most reluctant to accept further liberalizations and might even abolish natural death acts.

In short, I have argued in this section that euthanasia in its active and its passive forms presents us with a dilemma which can be developed by using powerful consequentialist arguments on each side, yet there is little clarity concerning the proper resolution of the dilemma precisely because of our uncertainty regarding proclaimed consequences.

---

[10]Williams bases his pro-euthanasia argument on the prevention of two consequences: *(1)* loss of liberty and *(2)* cruelty. Kamisar bases his anti-euthanasia position on three projected consequences of euthanasia laws: *(1)* mistaken diagnosis, *(2)* pressured decisions by seriously ill patients, and *(3)* the wedge of the laws will lead to legalized involuntary euthanasia. Kamisar admits that individual acts of euthanasia are sometimes justified. It is the rule that he opposes. He is, thus, clearly a rule-utilitarian, and I believe Williams is as well (compare his views on children and the senile). Their assessments of wedge arguments are, however, radically different.

[11]Glanville Williams, "Mercy-Killing Legislation—A Rejoinder," *Minnesota Law Review,* 43, no. 1, p. 5, 1958.

VI. CONCLUSIONS

I reach two conclusions at the end of these several arguments. First, I think Rachels is incorrect in arguing that the distinction between active and passive is (always) morally irrelevant. It may well be relevant, and for moral reasons—the reasons cited in section III above. Second, I think, nonetheless, that Rachels may ultimately be shown to be correct in his contention that we ought to dispense with the active-passive distinction—for reasons adduced in sections IV–V. But, if he is ultimately judged correct, it will be because we have come to see that some forms of active killing have generally acceptable social consequences, and not primarily because of the arguments he adduces in his essay—even though *something* may be said for each of these arguments. Of course, in one respect I have conceded a great deal to Rachels. The bare difference argument is vital to his position, and I have fully agreed to it. On the other hand, I do not see that the bare difference argument does play or need play a major role in our moral thinking—or in that of the AMA.

13

Euthanasia and the Transition From Life to Death

David Mayo

*Department of Philosophy, University of
Minnesota, Duluth, Minnesota*

and

Daniel I. Wikler

*Department of Philosophy, University of
Wisconsin, Madison, Wisconsin*

In discussions of medical ethics, euthanasia is sometimes referred to as
if it involved a single issue. But the problems involved are numerous:
Must any attempt to justify euthanasia refer exclusively to the interests
of the patient? Must death be requested by the patient? Who has the
right to make the decision? Is there a moral difference between killing
and letting die?[1] The list goes on. One difficulty facing anyone who is

---

[1]The killing/letting die distinction is a very difficult issue, one which we wish to
avoid here. In order to keep our language neutral with respect to this issue, we will
speak about the moral desirability of "acquiescing" to certain transitions from one state
to another, and thereby leave open for further discussion the question of whether the
moral acceptability of "acquiescing" might depend on whether, in a particular case, it
was a matter of accelerating the transition, or of merely not acting to decelerate it.

discussing euthanasia generally is that of finding a way to relate all of these questions, particularly since their answers may be interdependent.

The advent of modern life-saving technology has made the situation even more complex. Previously, the issue concerned the propriety of acquiescing to a clear and unmistakable transition from life to death. That transition is no longer so clear, and we must now consider transitions from and to various states. The moral acceptability of any position on euthanasia may vary, depending on whether the transition under consideration involves full consciousness, coma independent of life support systems, coma dependent on life-support systems, or functional decomposition. Since medicine now has the ability to sustain patients in many cases in any of these states, it must develop moral policies which are appropriate to each. Extant views of euthanasia which were conceived with only the transition from the first to the last of these states in mind may fail for lack of specificity. The problem must be addressed anew.

In Part I of this essay, we will give brief descriptions of the four states just mentioned, and we will proceed to examine some aspects of the euthanasia question as they apply to transitions from each of the first three to the fourth. Part II is concerned with the matter of the definition of death itself. The definition of death has been regarded as having significant logical and moral relationships to the question we are considering. By labeling these states neutrally in Part I, we postpone any discussion on this matter until Part II. Since the disposition of a body after death is not considered to be as serious a moral issue in medical ethics as that of euthanasia, the claim that any one of the states we define is death would imply that any transitions to subsequent states were not really matters of major moral importance. We will argue, however, that death is properly construed as the last of these states only, and hence that it is appropriate to regard the acquiescence to any transition to the final state as euthanasia. And we find fault with recent "redefinitions" of death, in part because they seem to be motivated by the mistaken notion that substantive moral issues can be side-stepped by simply clarifying or reinterpreting our concept of "death."

I. TRANSITIONS

This section highlights some of the moral considerations which are relevant to assessing the moral desirability of transitions between various states occurring near the end of human life. We begin with rough and ready descriptions of four possible states of a human organism, which are described in terms which do not presuppose an answer to the question, to be explored in Part II, of how death is to be defined.

State 4: Most or all principle life systems—cardiovascular, central-nervous, and pulmonary—have irreversibly ceased functioning.

State 3: The cortex and brain stem have ceased functioning irrevers-ibly; the patient is irreversibly comatose. Metabolic processes in the patient's body continue only because cardiovascular and pulmonary functions are sustained by artificial life-support systems.

State 2: The cortex has permanently ceased functioning, and the patient is irreversibly comatose; but principle life functions continue without artificial support due to brain stem activity.

State 1: The patient is moving quickly and inexorably to subsequent states; however, the patient is conscious and suffering pain, and wishes to be in state 4, rather than in pain.

For patients in any of the first three states, the transition to state 4 is usually more or less imminent, with no significant chance of transi-tion in the direction of regained health. There are three fundamental moral principles which usually bear on the question of whether the inevitable transition to state 4 should always be resisted as long as possible, at whatever cost, or whether there may be circumstances under which one should acquiesce to such a transition:

The Primacy of Life Principle: The preservation of human life is not only valuable, but something the value of which so exceeds any other values we may have that it must never be subordinated to them.

The Principle of Beneficence: A doctor ought to do what is in the best interests of the patient's well-being.

The Principle of Autonomy: Whenever possible, individuals should themselves be the ones to make decisions in matters which involve pri-marily their own welfare (unless of course their proposed courses of action might infringe on the rights of others).

The fact that each of these principles has an air of plausibility to it, combined with the fact that any two of them may come into conflict, accounts in large measure for the moral difficulty of decisions which confront modern medicine in the treatment of persons in states 1, 2 or 3, and it is to specific consideration of these cases that we now turn.

Patients in State 1

The conflict of principles is straightforward enough in the case of patients in state 1: the Principle of Autonomy supports the view that patients' wishes to acquiesce to the transition to state 4 should be respected. Similarly, the Principle of Beneficence would dictate that patients should be spared unnecessary suffering, and the terminal nature of their condition suggests their suffering may be useless and hence unnecessary. However, the Primacy of Life Principle would dictate that patients' lives must be preserved as long as possible, since the value of life overrides competing values, including the values we place on beneficence and autonomy.

Since the Primacy of Life Principle figures prominently in much popular thinking about these issues, it is worth taking time here to scrutinize this principle carefully. Specifically, we argue against this principle by pointing out that anyone who consistently acted on it would lead an outrageously eccentric and unattractive life. We then deal with the question of what might have seduced anyone in the first place into thinking they should accept a principle, the implications of which are so obviously objectionable.

The Primacy of Life Principle claims that the value of preserving human life is so great that it should never be subordinated to competing values. Reflection suggests that this is a very strong principle, for the force of the word "never" precludes the possibility of compromise, or of weighing life-sustaining considerations against other pressing concerns we may have. In this it differs, for instance, from the much weaker but ultimately more defensible principle that human life has *some* value. Adherence to the Primacy of Life Principle would require that people never do anything which involved risking their lives in any way if they could avoid doing so, however valuable the risk-taking activity might be in other respects. But everyone takes avoidable risks with their lives. Nearly all of us ride in cars and planes and cross streets when we could avoid doing so, and pursue careers in fields in spite of actuarial evidence indicating other vocations would be safer from the point of view of longevity. Many of us live in polluted metropolitan areas, smoke, keep ourselves in less than peak physical shape, and indulge in cuisine proscribed by considerations of taste as well as by considerations of diet. Some people even seek out risks by mountain climbing, sky diving, motorcycling or space exploration. Nor is such behavior universally regarded as irrational; while different people draw the line between courage and foolhardiness at different points, most of us tend to admire certain persons precisely because they do take such risks. Conversely, people who consistently opted only for behavior which involved no avoidable risk to life would be viewed as terribly odd, and rightly so, for they would lead very dull and eccentric lives. Such persons would have to forgo not only aspiration to high public office, but even passionate, emotional involvements with other human beings, since both increase the risk of being murdered. And any woman who accepted the principle with respect to her own life or even all existing lives would have to forgo childbearing.

We believe these considerations show the Primacy of Life Principle is unacceptable. But if this is so, the question arises of how sensible people could ever have come to espouse it? The most obvious answer is that usually we place a very high value on preserving lives, and in the absence of critical scrutiny this *high* value might mistakenly be thought to be an *absolute* one. Some, doubtless, have accepted it on religious grounds. Religious dispute is well beyond the scope of this essay, but it is perhaps relevant to note that many contemporary Western religious authorities in fact endorse acquiescence to death under certain circumstances, and hence do not accept the Primacy of Life Principle. Anyone who did endorse the Primacy of Life Principle on religious grounds, it seems, would also be obliged to lead the very bizarre risk-free life we have sketched previously in our critique of the principle.

A somewhat subtler argument is sometimes given for the Primacy of Life Principle: people value many things, including being alive. But since people must be alive before they can pursue any of their other values, and before they can experience any of the experiences they value, the value on life assumes a special significance. Pursuing the value one places on being alive is a prerequisite for pursuing any other values one may hold. This tempting argument seems to yield the Primacy of Life Principle, which in effect holds that preserving life is to be valued above all other things. But this argument embodies two confusions: the first identifies valuing something with valuing the experience of that something. This mistaken identification may go undetected because *many* of the things we value *are* experiences. But this is not always the case. People may have values which can be satisfied without their experiencing these values being satisfied, and, indeed, which can be satisfied only without their lives being preserved; the most obvious case of this sort may be the value terminally ill patients in state 1 place on the end of their suffering. (Others would be the value people place on having their estates distributed as they wished after their death, or of being fondly remembered, or of being buried in such–and–such a place.)

The second confusion identifies the requirement that one be alive at one time in order to experience something one values experiencing, with a requirement that one be alive as long as possible afterwards. Even though one may value some kind of experience, it does not follow that that value could not lead the person to act in a way which would ultimately speed death. There would be no logical blunder, nor indeed even any irrationality, in people placing such a high value on the cultural advantages of a big city that they opt to live in cities, even though they realized that they would probably die a few years earlier because of the accompanying tensions and pollution.

The Primacy of Life Principle must be rejected as too strong, and it is clear that some weaker principle must be substituted. Even though we do not place an *uncompromisable* value on preserving human life, we still place a *very high* value on doing so as a rule. A reasonable alternative to the Primacy of Life Principle is this weaker, but more realistic one:

> *The Preservation of Life Principle:* Unless there are overriding considerations to the contrary, human life should be preserved whenever possible.

We suggest there are such considerations in the medical context. The first has to do with the fact that while human life is generally of value, some lives are of greater value than others, and just how valuable a particular life may be depends on a number of things. That different lives are of different values *to others,* or to society at large, is evidenced by some of the considerations that go into triage policies. That different lives are of different value to the persons whose lives they are, is evidenced by the fact that some persons wish their lives would end as soon as possible. Thus lives of unmitigated suffering which are the lot of persons in state 1 are reasonably held to be of less value than healthy lives. That some such persons wish to die because of the pain and hopelessness of their situation certainly shows that their lives are held *by them* to have negative value *for them,* all things considered.

We feel this consideration significantly strengthens the case in favor of acquiescing to the transition from state 1 to state 4, particularly in light of the relatively high value we place on treating others beneficently and on respecting personal autonomy. In our view, these considerations add up to a strong *prima facie* case in favor of respecting the wishes of an individual to acquiesce to the transition from state 1 to state 4, in many cases.

However, this is only a *prima facie* case, for in certain situations, the relevance of beneficence and respect for autonomy may not be so straightforward. For instance, imagine persons whose conditions are terminal and who are suffering greatly at the moment, but for whom the best prognosis is that they will have some relatively pain-free months ahead before they finally succumb. Here, one may feel the Principle of Beneficence requires that such persons be kept alive through the passing period of pain, and even in spite of their present pleas for the release death would bring. A more general doubt may be raised about the relevance of the Principle of Autonomy. All but the most ardent libertarians, for instance, concede that a person's autonomy should not be absolute, and that if people are "not in control of themselves"—whether from fear, anger, depression, pain or some other form of stress—it may be right to intervene to prevent them from doing significant and irreparable harm to themselves. Of course, persons who are in pain and who are told their condition is terminal may very well "lose control" in this sense—or else be so drugged as to be unable to appraise their situation realistically or reasonably. In such cases, the Principle of Autonomy hardly requires that we respect their stated wishes. Indeed, their stated wishes may even fluctuate wildly from one moment to the next.

The seriousness of this problem should not be underestimated; virtually all serious euthanasia legislation has been sensitive to it. Legislation considered in Great Britain involved a provision whereby persons in state 1 who requested active euthanasia would be given a "cooling off" period during which they could reconsider their request before being killed. The Euthanasia Educational Council's "Living Will" is a document which they urge people to consider and discuss with those who will be involved in decision-making, *prior* to finding themselves in the grips of a terminal illness.

On the basis of such considerations, some have argued that the wishes of a person in state 1 should *never* be respected. It is the feeling of the present authors, however, that no such simplistic conclusion is legitimate. Rather, we believe the conclusion to be drawn is that these matters must be considered on a case-by-case basis, in light of the three principles that we have been discussing, along with any others which may apply in particular cases—for instance, those which may involve rights or special interests of other parties. It is our suspicion that in many cases the difficulties cited above are not sufficient to warrant paternalistic intervention, and that to some extent wholesale resistance to respecting the wishes of patients in such situations stems more from an uncritical commitment to the Primacy of Life Principle than it does from any legitimate appeal to considerations which would justify overriding beneficence and the autonomy of the individual.[2]

---

[2]The medical context generates some curious paradoxes with respect to our usual thinking about autonomy. Many of our decisions in life—whom to marry, whether to go mountain climbing—are made on impulse, even in confusion. They may have irreversible consequences. But no one makes us prove that we are in a rational frame

The conclusion which emerges regarding persons in state 1 is that there is no general reason why all should be denied the transition they wish for to state 4, and that in cases where their wishes are denied, the burden of proof should be on those who feel such paternalistic intervention is warranted. Viewed in this light, the problem of persons in state 1 comes to be seen as a special case of the problem of determining the conditions under which it is proper to intervene paternalistically at the expense of someone else's autonomy. A more general point also emerges, however, and that is that any simple principle which would stipulate a standard handling of all cases is highly suspect, for the considerations which are relevant to such cases are moral considerations, the proper weighing of which depends upon the specifics of individual cases.

Patients in State 2

State 2 is the state in which the cessation of cortex function results in irreversible coma, but life functions continue without the aid of artificial support due to brain stem activity. What considerations are relevant in this case to the morality of acquiescing to a transition to state 4?

It seems clear enough that here the Principle of Beneficence is irrelevant. The comatose experience no pleasure or pain, and hence the question of what is conducive to their well-being is moot; in an important sense, such individuals really have no "well-being."

The relevance of the Principle of Autonomy may at first seem likewise negated. In a very straightforward sense, persons in state 2 have and will continue to have no decision-making capacity, and to that extent they lack autonomy. (This is surely one consideration behind the frequently made claim that such individuals are no longer "persons.") Thus on first blush it seems that neither acquiescing nor refusing to

---

of mind before we are allowed to act in these matters. Similarly, sick persons may decide not to see doctors, and that, too, is their privilege. Once the patient is in the doctor's care, however, the requirements for free action are made more stringent. Patients must show that they are rational before their wish to die is respected—and it may not be respected even then. The patient, who may be suffering from cancer or other physical disease, is treated as a psychiatric patient. We do not want to claim that obviously confused or irrationally depressed patients should be allowed to order their own deaths. The issue is much subtler, and our own intuitions are mixed. Yet, we wish to point out the inconsistency: perhaps physicians' fealty to the principle that they must do all they can for their patients should not lead them to forget that this principle merely sets the limit on what may be asked of them by their patients. If the patients' autonomy is strictly respected, perhaps they must be free to ask for less.

acquiesce to the death of such patients could constitute a violation of their autonomy.

By the same token, irreversible coma may well be the most straightforward case of a special circumstance which absolves us from the general obligation imposed by the Preservation of Life Principle, since the factors which normally prompt us to attribute value to human life are completely absent. Surely, it would be wrong to claim that a person's continued existence in state 2 has value from *that person's* point of view; in fact, it seems difficult to make sense of the claim that that person even continues to embody a "point of view." At the very least, the obligation imposed by the Preservation of Life Principle seems drastically weakened.

Within the Hippocratic tradition, it is generally held that peoples' medical care should be dictated by considerations having to do with their well-being, the value their life has for them, their wishes and their autonomy. If, however, all of these considerations become moot at the onset of irreversible coma, medicine then seems justified in departing from the traditional Hippocratic orientation which focuses on these patient-oriented considerations, and in turning instead to considerations having to do with the welfare or well-being of others. While one can imagine circumstances in which the continued maintenance of a person in state 2 is most desirable from the point of view of the welfare of others, this surely is not the standard case. Normally there are various stiff costs involved in maintaining individuals in state 2, as well as important benefits which are lost. The most obvious are the actual costs of the medical care. Next may be the "emotional costs" to relatives. Then come the indirect "costs" or loss of benefits which others might have received if scarce medical resources had been used on them instead of being tied up in the maintenance of "hopelessly" comatose patients. The final indirect cost—and surely an underlying consideration behind certain proposed redefinitions of death—is the cost in lives which could have been saved if organs of individuals in state 2 had been available for transplant. With the advent of transplant technology, parts of the comatose individuals themselves come to be regarded as "scarce medical resources" just as legitimately as the hospital beds and medical attention which are required to sustain them in state 2.

In our view, these considerations add up to an impressive case in favor of acquiescing to a transition from state 2 to state 4, unless there are special considerations to the contrary. Unfortunately, however, the matter is not quite this simple. Considerable philosophical complexity is injected into the above analysis, by the fact noted previously, that a person's interests may post-date that person's being interested in them, and even that person's death. Persons may have interests in events, and indeed are routinely granted decision-making autonomy over matters, which they themselves will never experience, because these events occur after their deaths. The most obvious example of this is found in the institution of wills. It is generally recognized that people are entitled to stipulate what is to be done with their property following their death, and that these stipulations will be respected. Similarly, organs to be used for transplant purposes must be donated, not just in the trivial sense that they were previously part of some other body, but in the stronger sense that someone—ideally the person they previously belonged to—must agree to their use by another.

This difficulty is compounded by the fact that survivors frequently invoke not only the expressed wishes of deceased persons in these matters, but also hypothetical wishes. Thus the claim that someone would have wanted his or her organs made available for transplant (had he or she gotten around to considering the matter) might well figure in the proxy decision by a relative to authorize the harvesting of organs and transplant.

There are a number of philosophical complexities surrounding the issue of posthumous interests. Is our respect for wills to be justified in terms of autonomy and posthumous interests, as we suggest above, or is it rather to be justified in terms of the comfort and security the living find in the belief that their wills will in turn be respected? Does the Principle of Autonomy really have any bearing on what becomes of one's kidneys, once one is dead? It is obviously not an issue which bears on the *life* of the deceased person. At what point do appeals to what a dead person wanted, or would have wanted, rely on sentimentality rather than on legitimate respect for the dead person's autonomy? These are all difficult issues, which have received little attention in the literature, and they will not be resolved here. Suffice to say at this point that in any event, unless we are particularly wealthy or particularly sentimental, most of us place some limits on the extent to which we feel the lives of the living are determined by the wishes of the dead, and we do so for the very sound reason that what we do is of no consequence to the dead, in the sense that it does not alter their experience in any way. Because the irreversibly comatose (even if they are alive) at least resemble the dead in this respect, it seems appropriate, in determining whether to acquiesce to the transition to state 4 of a patient in state 2, to at least weigh alongside any actual or hypothetical interest of the comatose patient those considerations having to do with the interests and welfare of others which were mentioned earlier.

As this is done in individual cases, the outcome may be far from clear. At one extreme, it would seem completely unreasonable to sustain a patient in state 2 who had never considered the possibility of being in that condition, if by doing so severe financial hardship were imposed on the family, and scarce medical resources were tied up which otherwise might make an important difference for other patients. At the other extreme, it might seem quite reasonable to sustain in state 2 a patient who had expressed a clear desire to be maintained in the event of having become irreversibly comatose, if the family had sufficient funds, and if doing so did not require scarce medical resources which would be readily available for others if they were not being used in maintaining the comatose patient. Although the vast majority of actual cases doubtless lie closer to the former of these cases than to the latter, difficult intermediate cases exist, and that is in part responsible for the fact that present medical practice is by no means consistent in handling cases of this type. Perhaps philosophical analysis might clear away some of the present confusion, with the result that increasing numbers of persons will clearly assert their own wishes in the matter—hopefully in the direction of acquiescing, in light of the stiff social costs which others must bear if a person is to be maintained in state 2.

Patients in State 3

The state of these patients differs from state 2 in that these patients have suffered irreversible loss of function of the entire brain, with the result that they are not only irreversibly comatose, but in addition they require artificial life-support systems to be maintained. Virtually all of the considerations relevant to the previous case derived from the fact that the patients were in irreversible coma, and hence apply to patients in state 3 as well. The only additional consideration which is relevant to patients in state 3 is that such persons require more in the way of scarce medical resources—the artificial life-support systems and the supervision required for their operation—and this, of course, becomes an additional reason for acquiescing to the transition to state 4. Even here, however, this does not strike us as absolutely decisive; there still remains the possibility that the various social costs might be small or could be easily met, and also that the patient might have expressed vigorous interest in being sustained in the event of irreversible coma. We feel that such cases would be rare, however, and that in the absence of such special circumstances, it would be morally desirable to acquiesce to the transition to state 4.

Mention should be given to a final consideration in favor of maintaining patients in either stages 2 or 3, which is quite different from any of the previous ones. When organs are transplanted, there is frequently some lapse of time between the time a person is selected as a suitable donor, and the time the donated organ is harvested for transplant. During this time, the individual is maintained in state 2 or 3, not for any of the reasons mentioned above, but simply in order to maintain the organ so it will be suitable when it is time to transplant. Of course, the need to preserve an organ for transplant would justify maintaining a patient for the brief period of time in question. However, it is important to note that in this case, the decision to "maintain" a patient in state 2 or 3 until the organ is needed for transplant already presupposes a decision to acquiesce to the transition to state 4 at the moment when the organ finally is needed, so this is a case of a "decision to maintain" only in the most trivial sense.

II. THE REDEFINITION OF DEATH

Throughout the previous discussion we have spoken in the clumsy idiom of "transitions between states" in order to avoid prejudging the question of which state(s) constitute death. It is to this question which we now must turn. To begin, it should be noted that the above discussion would not have strained common sense if it had been conducted in the language of euthanasia. Bearing in mind the literal meaning of the term "euthanasia"—"good death"—the discussion would then have been presented as dealing with the circumstances under which the transition from life to death would be a good thing rather than a bad one, and hence of the circumstances under which moral agents might acquiesce to death.

That issue, of course, is not an academic one. At this moment, there are in this country alone literally thousands of persons in state 3, as well as some in state 2, and thousands more—friends, relatives, and medical staff—who are presently agonizing over the questions of when these patients will undergo the transition to state 4, and what role, if any, they should play in speeding or delaying that transition. Some of these people (the medical staff) will continue to charge substantial fees for their services until that transition is complete, while others (the friends, relatives, and insurance companies) will doubtless pay those bills, firm in the belief that they are making payment for services rendered to someone who was dying. This belief is obviously shared by the medical staff, who do not as a rule knowingly minister and devote their closest attentions to the dead.

Dying is a process engaged in by the living. Death marks the end of the dying process, not the beginning or middle of it. Just as it is clear to all that someone in state 4 is dead, so it is clear to the vast majority of us that persons who are in states 2 and 3 are dying, and hence not yet dead. The transitions to state 4 from 2 and 3 constitute dying just as clearly as the transition to state 4 from state 1. Although different moral considerations are relevant to acquiescing to death depending on whether the patient is in state 1, or 2 or 3, it seems indisputable that the considerations which are relevant are moral ones in the latter cases just as clearly as in the first. In fact, while in practice it may be psychologically less trying to opt for death in the case of the irreversibly comatose than in the case of the terminal patient who is suffering and wants to die, the case of the comatose is perhaps the more difficult in theory, precisely because it involves the extremely subtle and difficult issues of the limits of a person's autonomy, as well as the shift from the Hippocratic mode of decision-making focusing on patient-related considerations, to a perspective which includes appeals to the welfare of others as well.

Nevertheless, there are those who insist that we are simply wasting our moral energy if we construe the problem of continued treatment of comatose patients as a moral issue. Their view is that it is not really a moral issue at all, but rather a conceptual or scientific one, having to do with the definition of death. If this view is sound, it is certainly of central significance, for it promises a way out of moral choices which are difficult by almost anyone's reckoning. It is to an examination of this strategy, then, that we must now turn our attention.

Several different definitions of death have recently been proposed, calculated to pluck us from the grips of a difficult moral decision to acquiesce to death, by the easy mechanism of redefinition of death. Although the so-called "Harvard definition" of death is only one such definition, it is the one which has presently received the widest attention and acceptance. Accordingly, it will be our central focus here, although one other redefinition of death which has similar objectives will be mentioned in passing.

The substance of the Harvard proposal is well known.[3] The report spells out tests designed to tell whether the patient's cortex and brain stem have irreversibly ceased to function; the tests range from reflex-tests to examination by EEG. It is an empirical claim that a patient who

---

[3]Ad Hoc Committee of the Harvard Medical School to Examine the Definition of Brain Death, "A Definition of Irreversible Coma," *J.A.M.A.* 205, No. 6, pp. 337–340, 1968.

meets these criteria is in fact in state 3 and irreversibly comatose, and medical scientists are obviously qualified to make such a claim if anyone is.

The crux of the Harvard proposal is that persons who meet these conditions should be considered (and pronounced) dead.[4] Thus, for those who accept the proposal, the question of acquiescing to the death of a comatose patient in state 3 is not *answered,* but rather *dismissed* as a logically mistaken question, with no need for any moral deliberation at all. According to the proposal, there really is no question here of "acquiescing to the death" of such patients, for one can only acquiesce to the death of someone who is living, and to accept the Harvard proposal is to accept the claim that patients in state 3 are already dead —and hence, presumably, that they are *not* dying. What has previously struck doctors, concerned relatives, and moral philosophers as a grim and weighty moral issue is in effect made to vanish.

We believe, however, that this is only conceptual sleight of hand, which obscures the inevitable moral component of the problem of the continued maintenance of the irreversibly comatose. The most that can be claimed in the name of cold, hard science is that certain conditions inevitably indicate irreversible coma and loss of brain function. The additional step of claiming that patients in state 3 are dead (and hence of course can be treated as dead people) is surely not cold, hard fact at all. It seems, rather, to be a claim which grows out of conceptual confusion, and which appears plausible only because it seduces with a promise of deliverance from the clutches of difficult moral decisions.

The conceptual confusion implicit in the Harvard proposal grows out of confusing value judgments with biological ones. It is enormously plausible to suggest that one of the conditions for a human life *having value* is the possibility of consciousness. But, while the possibility of consciousness seems quite clearly to be a condition of human life *having value,* that is not to say that it is a condition of a human being *having life.*

This might be illustrated by a somewhat facetious analogy. Imagine oil shortages reaching the point where neither heating oil nor synthetics for clothing are available, as a result of which we turn again to animal furs for clothing. Suppose further that rabbits come to be especially valued both because of their warm fur and because of their legendary breeding habits. If, for some reason, a rabbit should have the

---

[4]It is not entirely clear whether the Ad Hoc Committee proposed its tests as new tests for the same condition tested for by previous criteria, or whether a new condition was being defined; we will assume the latter here.

misfortune of being both bald and sterile, he would *not* be a valuable rabbit. But that is of course not to say that he would be a dead rabbit. In the case of both rabbits and persons, a creature having life is one matter, and that life having value is quite another. "Death" is not a value notion, but a biological notion, to be made sense of in terms of the absence of life, not in terms of the absence of value.

A similar confusion has prompted even more radical proposals for redefining death. While the Harvard proposal focuses on state 3, Robert Veatch[5] notes that state 2 is also an identifiable state: a person may suffer irreversible coma (through the death of the neo-cortex of the brain) even though lower brain stem activity makes spontaneous breathing and heartbeat possible. Such people are not in state 3 and do not meet the Harvard criteria for death, but Veatch argues that this is a defect of the Harvard proposal. The rationale Veatch provides for this is as follows: first, that death is the "irreversible loss of that which is essentially significant to the nature of man," and second, that what is essentially significant to the nature of man is the capacity for experience and social interaction. When these are lost, Veatch argues the person should be regarded as dead. An integral part of Veatch's position is the identification of what is essential to being human, with what is essential to a human being being alive. But of course this too is a confusion, for those are two very different things. Humans are only one kind of living thing: what is essential to being human is something that *differentiates* us from other living things, something which we *do not* share with dogs or trees or mosquitoes. Being alive, on the other hand, is something we *do* share with other living things. To extend our rabbit analogy, suppose we singled out as particularly valuable those rabbits which were especially fertile and whose offspring were particularly furry, and labeled them "schmabbits." Then, a rabbit who first made the status of schmabbit and then became sterile would no longer manifest what was "essentially significant to the nature of schmabbits"—that is, it would no longer be a schmabbit. But that, again, does not mean that it would properly be considered a dead schmabbit, much less that it would be dead *simpliciter.*

More generally, the death of a rabbit, a schmabbit, or of a human being has nothing to do with the loss of those characteristics which differentiate each of them from other kinds of living things, but rather with the loss of what they have in common with other living things. Biologists have a concept of life, or of when an organism is alive, that

---

[5]Robert M. Veatch, "The Whole-Brain-Oriented Concept of Death: An Outmoded Philosophical Formulation," *J. Thanat.* 3, pp. 13–30, No. 1 for 1975.

does not appeal to what is unique to some particular living species, but which appeals instead to features common to all living things. It is only because biology has some notion of what life is, apart from the specifics of any species, that it was possible to ask meaningfully "Is there life on Mars, and if so, what is it like?" Being alive is something we have in common with our pets and the lawns and trees in front of our houses; we are all living things. The proper place to turn for a definition of death is not to the kinds of considerations which make this or that life valuable, or which make it different from other forms of life, but rather to the kinds of general biological considerations which justify saying that something is alive.

An adequate definition of life is beyond the scope of this essay, but a few preliminary remarks may be in order. Since life is a process, or rather a structured group of processes, an adequate definition of life will presumably be in terms of the occurrence of life processes, and the definition of death will then be in terms of the cessation of these processes. The matter is not simple, for these processes go on at different levels, and, of course, do not stop all at once. Specifically, being alive cannot mean that all parts are functioning normally (they don't in a deaf, sterile or blind person), or that no parts are machine- or drug-dependent (the diabetic and pacemaker patients are alive). When a biologist says an organism is dead, he or she surely means something like "principle life systems have irreversibly ceased to function." Of course, this raises a series of difficult issues, including the questions of which life systems are the principal ones, how many of them have shut down, and how completely. No biological sophistication is required to realize that they may shut down by degrees—this strikes us as obvious in the case of large plants such as trees, because the processes shut down over long periods of time. Unfortunately, for many purposes we need —or at least presently feel we need—to be able to speak of the "moment of death," and if modern medicine continues to refine its techniques for prolonging the process of dying, it is possible that our present notion of death will prove to be inadequate. Our thesis is not that a redefinition of death will never be needed. Our only concern is to argue that when and if such a time arrives, two very different questions must be kept distinct. The question of when the life of an organism has ended is a conceptual question—one focusing on the central concept in biology— and it obviously must be answered in terms of our biological concepts and theory, for that theory embodies our understanding of what life *is*.

The question of when an organism's life *ought* to be terminated, on the other hand, is not a scientific question, nor a conceptual one, but a moral one. Unless these are seen to be very different questions, decisions about whether or not to acquiesce to a person's death—tough and important moral decisions which deserve all the honesty and precision our moral thinking can give them—will come to be regarded as "purely medical judgments," or "purely scientific" judgments, and moral debate and argument will be dismissed as irrelevant to them.

In the course of the Harvard proposal, it is urged that once it has been established that the patient is in an irreversible coma, the patient should be pronounced dead, and then the respirator turned off. It goes on to say:

> The decision to do this and the responsibility for it are to be taken by the physician-in-charge, in consultation with one or more physicians who have been directly involved in the case. It is unsound and undesirable to force the family to make the decision.[6]

While this eagerness to exclude non-professionals spares relatives from having to make a morally difficult decision, it also denies them their rightful role in such decision-making. But even more troubling is the fact that the Harvard Proposal would spare even the doctors the realization that they are in fact deciding that someone should die. Some such decisions are correct ones we believe, but all ought to be faced honestly for what they are—decisions to end someone's life.

[6]Ad Hoc Committee, *op. cit.* p. 338.

Subject Index

A

Abortion, 98, 140, 142–44, 150, 178; of minors, 89
Abrams, Natalie, xi
Absolutist ethic, 154
Accountability, 90
Acting at someone's behest, 18, 24; impartially, 6; on someone's behalf, 18, 20, 24, 30; rationally, 119
Active euthanasia, see Euthanasia, active
Act of charity, 52, 119; of supererogation, 119
Acts, negative, 171, 173–174, 176–180
Adults, normal, 76
Agape, principle of, 18
Agency, moral, vii, 169, 171, 174, 176, 178–180
Age of competence, 90
Age-of-seven rule, 81–83, 87, 89, 91, 97–99
Alfrieda/Bertha argument, 162f10
Allocating resources, 158
Allowing to die, see Letting the patient die
Altruism, 71
Amish, 89, 90
American Cancer Society, 158
American Medical Association, 156, 163, 166, 168, 181–184, 188, 189, 192, 194
Animal experimentation, see Experimentation
Approaches to anthologies, vi–vii

F

G

H

K

L

M

Paternalistic behavior, see Paternalism
Paternalistic intervention, see Paternalism
Payment of prisoners, 68
Personhood, 125, 140, 147
Physical harm, 36, 96
Physician–patient relationship, viii, ix, 76, 179
Piaget, 82
PKU, 32, 37, 38
Placebo, 17, 178, 179
Planned Parenthood v. Danforth, 89f22, 97, 98
Pope Pius XII, 102
Pornography, 86
Posthumous interests, 204
Preferential treatment, 110, 111
Preservation of Life Principle, 200, 203
Preservative principle of paternalism, 30, 31
Primacy of Life Principle, 197–201
Prima facie duty, 172, 173, 177
Primary rights, 116, 119, 120
Prince v. Massachusetts, 85
Principle, vii, viii, xi; of agape, 18; of autonomy, xii, 197, 201, 202, 204; of beneficence, xii, 197, 198, 200–202; of preservation of life, 200, 203; of primacy of life, xii, 197–201; of respect for developing autonomy, 89
Prior consent, see Consent
Prisoners, viii, x, 57, 67, 68
Prison experimentation, see Experimentation
Privacy, 37, 97; right to, 142, 143, 150
Private harm, 29, 30, 41
Procedures, nontherapeutic, 113, 116–121, 123, 127, 129, 132, 134; therapeutic, 116, 117; for consent, see Consent
"Protection of Human Subjects," 141
"Proxy Consent in the Experimental Situation," 121
Psychological aspects of pregnancy, 123, 133
Public advocation of violation of rules, 3–5, 7, 9, 10, 12, 13; for relation to "kind of violation," see 5, 6
Public good, 30, 37, 42

Q

Quinlan, Karen, 184

R

Rachels, James, xi, xii, 2f4, 170, 171, 181–183, 185–188, 190, 192, 194
Ramsey, Paul, 116–120, 122, 127, 128, 130, 142, 149, 150, 158, 159
Ratification theory of consent, 26
Rational nature of fetus, 120
Rawls, John, 26, 90, 172
Reasonable persons, 31
Relevant difference, morally, xi, 108, 144, 150, 151
Report and Recommendations on Research Involving Children, 81, 86, 99
Research Involving Prisoners, 58f1
Respect for humanity, 70; for life, xii, 189
Responsibility, ascribing, 169; for consequences, x, 79, 80; moral, 171; of physician, 160; social, 92
Right to be left alone, 21; to change one's mind, 142; to life, 141; to privacy, 142, 143, 150
Rights, viii, 18; human, 140; primary, 116, 119, 120
Risk, 54, 55, 123, 124, 149, 151f33; and no-risk interventions, 92; budget, 21, 22
Roe v. Wade, 97, 98, 139
Roman Catholic Church, 102
Rothman, David, 19
Rule-oriented dogmatism, 115
Rule utilitarianism, 8, 9, 187, 188

S

Sanctity of human life, 118
Scarce medical resources, 203, 205
Self-esteem, 73
Self-interest, 19
Sentience of fetuses, 122, 130, 131
Shaw, Dr. Anthony, 166
Sherwood, S. L., 106
Shuman, Samuel, xi
Sickle cell anemia, 32, 37
Siegel, Seymour, 116–118, 130
Slippery slope arguments, see Wedge arguments
Smith/Jones case, 161, 170, 171, 182, 183
Social costs, 205; harm, 36, 37, 96; obligations, 92; responsibility, 92; utility, 188